GUIDE TO
CHEESES
OF FRANCE
WILLIAM STOBBS

BY PHILIPPE OLIVIER

the apple press

This book was designed and
produced by The Oregon
Press Limited, Faraday
House, 8-10 Charing Cross
Road, London WC2H 0HG

First published in 1984 by The
Apple Press Limited, 293
Gray's Inn Road, London
WC1X 8QF

ISBN 1 85076 022 5

Design: Laurence Bradbury

Printed in Finland 1984, by
The OTAVA Publishing Co.
Member of Finland Printers Ltd.

Illustration acknowledgments
Mary Evans Picture Library,
London: back of jacket, title-
page, 20, 22, 27, 31, 56, 91, 93,
103
Food & Wine from France,
London: half-title
David Haslam: 5
Philippe Olivier: 38, 66
William Stobbs: opp. 16, opp.
17, opp. 32, opp. 33, opp. 48,
opp. 80, opp. 81, opp. 96, opp.
97, opp. 112, opp. 113, 123
Derrick Witty: opp. 49, opp. 64

*HALF-TITLE: Classic methods
of cutting cheese.
FRONTISPIECE: Milk churns
in the Haute Savoie.
TITLE-PAGE: Camembert-
making: the drying-room.*

CONTENTS

FOREWORD

The art of good eating and drinking must be safeguarded.

We must also make a stand against the loss of quality in gastronomy in all countries. We are fast heading towards the abuse of farm products, and cheese in particular, by remorseless industrialization.

In fact, several large industrial groups, thanks to their enormous financial means, launch new cheeses on to the market every week in the same way as washing powders. One day the product is round, the next oval, the next rectangular – the name, the packing and the design are also changed . . . but the product remains identical, pasteurized, homogenized, trivialized, and made banal. Millions of francs are spent on publicity, on television and the media in general. It has all been set up; and it works.

It is more and more difficult to uncover the 'real' cheeses, but they exist still, and what unforgettable joy it is to savour them.

Surely men and women of taste will not let themselves be ensnared by this so-called modern way of life.

Recognition for the tireless work of splendid farmers, cheesemakers and *affineurs* sometimes rarely extends beyond their own villages, but they still carry on and believe in it all.

For more than 15 years, with the help of my family, my teachers and my friends, while travelling through the provinces of France, I have endeavoured to get to know better or to rediscover these traditional cheeses and my hope remains great for the future.

Philippe Olivier

Philippe Olivier, Maître Fromager de France.

INTRODUCTION

In order to write a book about French cheeses you have to travel around and taste them, find the right wines to drink with them, and watch the farmers and cheesemakers when they are at work producing the cheeses. It involves going to cheese and cattle markets, and regional festivals where old customs, music, regional cooking, religious rites, cows, bulls, goats, *joie de vivre*, cheese and wine are all there, with the noise, smells and gusto that the French provinces can produce, each with its particular flavour. It means visiting mountain farms, valley farms and cottages among the vineyards where the custodians of the goats live.

I had been travelling in France for years, the pendulum swinging between various interests, mainly connected with the arts, together with a daily delight in regional wines and cooking, when my interest began to focus on wine and cheese. First, it was just a quiet astonishment at the seemingly endless variety of cheeses; second came a growing conviction that wine and cheese are brothers, in the Francis of Assisi sense, like Brother Fire and Brother Water; third and last came the realization that changing ephemeral milk into such a variety of more stable magic fruits was a phenomenon of some consequence. The concept of cheese as a fruit is not new. 'Fruit of the mountains' was a name given to sheep and goat's milk in medieval times when one of the kings, rabid with fiscal ideas, thought of taxing them. Henry II, after all, had taxed church bells, of all things, in order to finance Diane de Poitier's life style at the château of Chenonceaux.

Cheeses really are a kind of fruit; Androuët in his book *Fromage de France* calls them 'souls of the soil', which is a bit more spiritual. Some of them ripen from the inside out and some from the outside in. They can suffer, like fruit, and have bruises to prove that they have been maltreated. Black spots and swollen rind are bad signs. They can be ill and weep, and they can suddenly become over-age and be good enough only for the crock; elderly, hard, dried-up cheeses being grated into earthenware vessels, macerated with *marc*, mixed with oil, butter, pepper, herbs and spices, and sealed up for months, after which they come out as screaming old *fromages forts*, with a taste which is simply *frénétique*. Grand cheeses like Roquefort and Brie rarely seem to get into this predicament.

All cheeses need wine; they are inseparable. They both contain about fifty per cent of water for a start, and they both depend on the right geological structure, subsoil, inclination of land towards the sun and proximity to water – wines because of their vineyards, and cheese because of the grazers. Finally, both cheese and wine mature in caves or cellars. This being the case, why is wine so high and mighty about it, when cheesemaking is equally venerable and even more mysterious? The answer lies in the irrefutable well-being which wine can give; that wide spectrum of feeling. Cheese, however subtle the flavour, is what the Greeks gave towards the end of feasts, 'to revive thirst and enhance the flavour of the wine'. So much for feasts, but what about everyday life? Cheese is almost a complete everyday food in itself.

Medieval pilgrims going to the holy places on foot in their thousands were advised to carry cheese in their pouches by the two pilgrims' guide-books, which described the climate and customs of France together with advice on food, drink, general health and moral welfare. The first medieval guide-book, the *Codex Calixtinus* or Book of St James, was written expressly for pilgrims en route to the tomb of St James of Compostela in Spain; the second, by Almeri Picaud, slightly wider in scope, included

Map showing the 15 regions adopted by the author for this book.

architecture as well as cheese, wine and morality. There is something basically French and practical in the way the itinerant kings of France, travelling annually to their châteaux on the Loire, their Persian rugs, Flemish tapestries and best mirrors and portraits with them in the wagons, invariably stopped at Pithiviers to rest and collect Pithiviers au Foin and other cheeses, and on the return journey to Paris they took wagonloads of Loire valley wines and cheeses.

This book is the result of thirty years or more of travelling around in France and delighting in its food, its wine, its people and above all the way in which art of one kind or another is never far from everyday life. In addition to the catalogue of three hundred cheeses, there are facts about the regions of France that may help you decide on the direction of your next holiday, together with suggestions on what to eat and drink. Wherever you go there will be farms, and whichever region you visit, the types of cheese made there will be listed in this book. Usually, there is a notice outside the farm, saying 'Reblochon for sale' or whatever they make. And so long as you are courteous and friendly, and interested, you may be allowed to get near the heart of it all, with the warm smell of animals and the strong hands of the artisans.

Almost all fermented cheeses, like Brie, Camembert, Maroilles and Livarot, are the fruit of a rapid microbial evolution requiring an attentive and continual surveillance. In previous times, this delicate role devolved on the farmer's wife, who had to turn them, assess their maturity daily (that is, decide whether they were maturing too fast or too slowly); control the degree of humidity, or dryness, and look out for red spots, which declare the start of the important phenomena of fermentation. All this represented an activity, a patience and assiduity which the accelerating rhythm of life today has made impossible. The farmers' wives of yesterday were consecrated like nurses to safeguarding the fragile health of their charges. The whole process was handed down from mother to daughter, with a sharp critical tongue from grandmother as well. This is how all the farmhouse cheeses evolved.

Most of this work is now carried out by the *affineurs* and their artisans. Philippe Olivier, who has been kind enough to write the foreword to this book, is not only an *affineur*, he is also a *maître-fromager* and an idealist. He has done much more than write the introduction; he inspired the book, helped to plan it, and has always given his time generously.

CHAPTER I
THE HISTORY OF CHEESE AND GASTRONOMY

The extraordinary richness of French cheese-making, rooted in the diversity of the geography and geology of the country, is maintained by that vivid interest in food and wine which is at the heart of France. There are more than three hundred different cheeses made in France, but some are so rare that they never leave the village where they were made. France makes more than 900,000 tons of cheese a year, of which it exports only 165,000 tons, because the French, next to the Greeks, have the biggest annual consumption of cheese per head in the world: Greece 15 kg (33 lb), France 14.8 kg (32.6 lb), the United States 5.8 kg (12.8 lb), Britain 5.75 kg (12.7 lb).

Cheese has kept daily bread company as a basic food from the beginning: David was taking ten sheep's milk cheeses to Saul when he met Goliath (1 Samuel xvii). The archaeologists have discovered cheesemaking pots with holes to let out the whey from much earlier than that – the sixth millenium BC in fact, at Lake Neuchâtel in Switzerland – and numerous reliefs show cheesemaking in Mesopotamia and Egypt from around 2000 BC.

The Greeks have been enjoying cheeses since the 6th century BC, serving them at the end of feasts 'to revive thirst and enhance the flavour of the wine'. Homer frequently praised goats' milk cheese, even recommending it to cure wounds, and Hippocrates himself enjoyed it, but gave a warning that it was bad for rheumatics. The Romans not only made cheese, but took a keen interest in those they found abroad, sending Cantal, Roquefort and Chester back to Rome, together with most of the Alpine cheeses from the Haute Rhône to the Dalmatian Alps. Pliny the Elder (AD 23-79) had a chapter in his *Historia Naturalis*, 'Diversitae Casedrum', describing both Italian and French cheeses. The cheese-making descriptions in the *Georgics* of Virgil (70-19

BC) are comprehensive, and Columella (1st century AD) in his writings on agriculture gives a description of smoking cheese while evaporating wine simultaneously, thus making the wine stronger and the cheese not merely smoked, but suffused with a wine aroma. It is surprising that nothing of this sort is available at that mecca of cheeses, Androuët's shop in Paris.

Fortunately the cheese recipes of Marcus Apicius have been preserved; one, which was Cicero's favourite, makes Brondade, one of my favourites, seem kid's stuff. 'Take some salt fish and cook it in oil; remove the bones; mix the fish with cooked brains, bird's liver, hard-boiled eggs and fresh cheese. Mix and perfume it in a sauce of origan, rue, honey, wine and oil, and cook again gently. Serve it with cooked yellow eggs and garnish it with cumin seeds.'

Eginard or Einhard (*c.* 770-840), secretary and historian of Charlemagne, records anecdotes about cheese: the Emperor's liking for Roquefort for example, and his eating of Brie to the point of gluttony on numerous occasions; finally his command that both of these cheeses should be sent to Aachen (Aix-la-Chapelle) annually. The Anglo-Saxon King Ine of Wessex (d.726) also demanded in his famous laws a tithe including 'Five salmon, one hundred eels, ten geese, twenty hens, ten sheep, three hundred round breads, twenty honey combs, and ten cheeses' (George Puhy, *Rural Economy and Country Life in the Medieval West*).

Cheese was one of the staple foods carried by the medieval pilgrims in their pouches as they walked across Europe. Sadly, apart from the two 'guides' mentioned in the Introduction, the pilgrims themselves enjoyed a steady flow of miracles, magnificent architecture and sculpture, escorts by Knights Templar, courtesy by all the villagers of France along the routes, entertainments by troubadours and wandering minstrels galore, and yet did nothing in return, it would seem, except to pray fervently and continually for their own salvation.

During the Middle Ages, only large cheeses, hard and durable like Cantal and Gruyère, were transportable; perishable and fragile cheeses were sold in their immediate neighbourhoods. When European colonization and the spread of world trade reached massive proportions in the 16th and 17th centuries, however, it became necessary to consider transport and storage as an important issue. Dutch Edam, in demand all over the world, improved its cheesecloth to form a well-closed rind, primitive presses were replaced by ones similar to those that had recently been invented for printing, and the protective coloured rind was added. Side by side the early Dutch printing and cheese presses are almost identical; and Dutch Edam, designed for storage and transport, became one of the first world products. Meanwhile the settling of experienced cheesemakers in overseas colonies meant a diversity of varieties.

Cheesemaking remained an art rather than a scientific process until the 20th century. Although steam engines were introduced into European dairies in the 1880s to drive butterchurns and skim milk, the cheese was still made in the same old medieval way.

Modernization came suddenly and, in some ways, drastically. The German chemist Justus von Liebig stated the fermentation of cheese in scientific terms in 1836. Then Louis Pasteur's findings, published in 1876, together with those of his partner the Russian biologist Ilya Mechnikov (or Metchnikoff), brought about radical changes. It was recommended that milk should be 'pasteurized': treated with heat to destroy harmful bacteria. Pasteurized milk, robbed of the bacteria needed to make certain cheeses, is used almost exclusively in the factories and is the main reason why cheeses produced there lack the taste and bouquet of farm versions. Scientists in the field of biochemistry, however, have also prepared pure starter cultures and standardized rennets in the laboratories, which *are* an advantage. They are used on the farms as well as in the large dairies.

The first cheese factories were those established in the 19th century in New York State by Jesse Williams, where milk from many farms was processed. When European countries were in stalling their first cheese factories, in 1870-5, America already had over two thousand units (compared with thirteen in Britain). By 1890, however, the Americans were skimming the milk for other uses and reconstituting the content by adding fat from other and cheaper sources. It did not take a gourmet to detect the difference. The American cheese export market collapsed and was taken over by Canada, which has remained the larger cheese exporter. American cheese production recovered, of course, and now makes 1,410,000 tons of cheese a year but only exports 3200 tons, whereas France makes 900,000 tons and exports 165,000.

The industrialization of cheese has grown to unforeseen proportions and will no doubt continue to do so. At the modern Hutin-Stenne dairy in France, concentrated milk is put into one end of a machine and it is programmed to produce this or that cheese, which then appears at the other end, ready to be put into its labelled plastic box. This is an exceptionally modern dairy, using high technology. In most cases, the *laitiers* use pasteurized milk as a base.

Pasteurized processed cheese is produced by mixing and heating several varieties of cheese with emulsifying agents into a homogeneous mass. Depending on the processed cheese to be made, a combination of cheeses is selected and heated to 21°C, to remove the rind covers. The mixture is then subjected to a grinding process and a predetermined mixture of whey powder, water and butter is added. Next, the meats, fruits, nuts, vegetables, herbs or spices are added to give some spark of flavour to the smooth bland paste which eventually is extruded, because it has little taste of its own.

The mixture is then heated and stirred in a jacketed vat, into which steam is directed under pressure. A layer of clear fat appears, which is dissolved by adding salts and raising the temperature. A granular curd then appears, which is changed by more heat into a smooth glossy paste. Checks on the chemical composition of this lake of white paste follow, after which it is fed to packing machines, labelled, passed along cooling tunnels, and finally stored in warehouses. An enormously popular processed cheese has dispensed with the various additives and simply uses a thin black plastic rind which is covered with grape pips – processed cheese to look like farmhouse.

The United States legally controls pasteurized process cheese. The moisture and fat content should correspond with those of the natural cheese from which it is made, and 51% of the total weight must be cheese. Moisture content should be 44% maximum and fat content 23%. It is estimated that probably one third of United States production consists of processed cheese. 'Flexible plants' in the United States can produce a wide variety of cheeses, to adjust to changes in demand and fluctuations of taste.

American cheese, the product eaten with apple pie as part of the American way of life, is still consumed in enormous quantities. It is interesting to see how innovatory the Americans have been with English Cheddar, the basis of American cheese. They have variegated the shapes to include wheels, discs, cubes, bricks and barrels. They have flavoured it with pimento, port, sage and cumin, washed the curd, smoked it, and enlarged the size to 300 kg (660 lb) – the barrel shape of cheese that travels in a metal vat, like beer, en route to the fast food bars. Basically it is the same old English Cheddar, following precisely the same centuries-old cheddaring process.

Research into eating habits in America has shown, not surprisingly, that foreign-born Americans have the highest purchase ratio of natural to processed cheese, but within one generation they are won over either by the latter's smooth bland flavour, or more probably by its convenience and longevity.

The qualities of 'farmhouse' cheeses are obtained from a long sequence of events and methods which have been in practice for thousands of years in many cases. There seemed to be no way in which the old process could be speeded up, until the affineurs took over the work of curing. The word affinage in relation to cheese corresponds to élevage in winemaking. In the same way that wines recently pressed and placed in barrels require attention in the cellars, so do cheeses that have been taken out of their moulds. Each type of cheese requires the particular care demanded by its nature. The ferments, yeasts and moulds with which they are sprinkled or impregnated and which set up biophysical and biochemical changes,

depending upon the particular type of cheese and its development, are part of the affineur's work, together with temperature and humidity control to exacting standards. The caves of the affineurs consist of areas with different temperatures and humidity, separated by sealed doors. The more cheeses an affineur controls, the greater the size and complexity of his caves. Some affineurs, of course, specialize in only one cheese, and this is especially so with the larger sizes such as Gruyère de Comté and Emmental.

The length of time taken to cure cheeses varies with each type. A Camembert is cured in three weeks, whereas a Livarot or a Maroilles takes three to four months at least, after it has thickened, and hard cheeses are cured for three months to a year or more. Washed-rind cheeses require the liquids particular to their nature, such as salt water, white wine, cider, beer, brandy, marc, or olive oil. Other cheeses may require hay, or ashes made from a particular wood such as acacia, oak, ash or vine prunings. Marc, vine or chestnut leaves are required as surface embellishments for some cheeses. Originally most of this work was carried out by the farmer's wife on the farms where the cheeses were made. In some areas this is still done, but there is an increasing tendency for farms to send their cheese blancs to the affineurs.

In the past, 'arrivage des fromages' was an urgent matter, because when cheeses were brought on horse-drawn wagons to the cities they had been getting riper all the way, so boys were sent out in the streets shouting this phrase, warning buyers to hurry before the cheeses were sold out or gone off. This is no longer necessary because not only do the affineurs practise their skill, but the cheeses are stored in the shops better now than in the past, each type of cheese receiving special attention.

The importance of cheese in relation to gastronomy was emphasized by Anthelm Brillat-Savarin in his Physiologie du Goût (1825): 'A meal without cheese is a beautiful woman with only one eye.' It was this remark that made him world famous, because it has a touch of Rimbaud in it, and a lot of humanity.

The fact that cheese was invariably a part of haute cuisine can be proved by reading the old menus printed in books on gastronomy. Brillat-Savarin also expressed the opinion that gastronomy has been a stronger cultural force than linguistic or other influences: not an easy view to maintain as it is difficult to isolate gastronomy. The Atheneans believed in nourishing body and spirit simultaneously, and their feasts were accompanied by music, poetry and dancing. There is documentary proof that aristocratic Greek feasts were accompanied by Anthotiri and Anari, and we know that the daily food of peasants invariably included Feta, sometimes exclusively.

The Romans enjoyed cheese at all levels from foot soldiers to emperors. Hadrian's daily rations for a legionary, in modern measures, were:

    832 g corn
    117 g mutton (or 969 g lard)
     27 g cheese
     21 g salt
    ½ litre wine

and the amount of cheese given to Roman sailors on long voyages was considerably more (40 g) to help maintain a balance in their diet. Roman emperors ate Roquefort and Cantal at their banquets, but 'with sixty kinds of fish, together with wild boar, venison, beef, pork, veal, lamb, ostrich, peacock and all manner of waterfowl and birds of the air', and it is not recorded when during the course of the meal they ate the cheese. Ice was brought from the Alps, for Lucullus, together with truffles, mushrooms and Cantal cheese from Gaul, wild boars from Corsica, and mullet and lampreys from Sicily. The French were given imaginative leads by the Romans. Petronius in the *Satyricon* in the 1st century AD describes a feast, in which: 'A donkey is brought in on a tray, encircled with silver dishes bearing dormice dipped in honey. Live thrushes fly up from a pie and a roast pig is opened to reveal black puddings.' Cheese gets no mention at this feast, but an ancestor of 'Sing a song of sixpence' is revealed.

The Gallic leader Vercingetorix had banquets before the Roman conquest of Gaul that included crane, heron, peacock, roebuck, hedgehog and wild boar. The spits and cauldrons were placed 'conveniently near to the diners' and there is no mention of furniture, whereas Charlemagne some eight centuries later had tables strewn with flowers, ivy on the walls, silver and gold utensils,

and there were ladies at the table: a gigantic step forward, as they had been forbidden during the Vercingetorix period. Charlemagne enjoyed Roquefort, having tasted it in the Rouergue. He not only had cartloads sent annually to Aachen, but there were *formes* of Roquefort in the food wagons that accompanied him to Spain.

Probably the first French cook book, *La Viander* of 1375, was written by Guillaume Tirel, called Taillevent, chef to Charles VI. His menus show heavy seasoning with the known spices – cinnamon, cloves, ginger and nutmeg, for the usual medieval reason that some of the meats were often 'high' and needed spices to disguise the smell. Sauces were made by mixing bread with gravy, as with the Romans; coarse elementary cooking. Yet they also went to cruel and bizarre lengths. At the court at Avignon, for example, geese were not only plucked and roasted alive, but *kept* alive as long as possible. While the birds were surrounded by fire, their necks and heads were kept out of the flames, sponged with cold water and given maize to eat. Ideally, the denouement of the goose should coincide with its being done to a turn, and served while still vibrant with its last spark. Lesser mortals – for these were the sophisticated aristocrats – had tables of blackbird and thrush pâtés together with a variety of cheeses, including Roquefort and Cantal.

When the Renaissance started in Italy, gastronomy was part of it. In the quattrocento, Vincenzo I, Duke of Mantua, celebrated a wedding feast in which there were 'salads with fantastic animals made of citron and candied flowers, unicorns or marzipan, dragons made from tunny fish, and a Venus, very real, almost come to life, made of salmon, caviare, flaky pastry, sweet almond twists, pistachio nuts, pine kernels and Milanese biscuits. Inside, she was filled with fresh grapes, strawberries, wild cherries and asparagus cooked in butter.' Quite a girl. This is art and decoration, however, not cuisine. It goes on: 'Indian turkey hens stuffed with nuts, roasted on the spit, and marinated pullets, followed by bowls of myrtle berries.' This *is* gastronomy. Italian craftsmen provided elegant dishes for this imaginative cuisine. Lorenzo the Magnificent was a patron who inspired artists, sculptors and craftsmen to produce original art forms. While the tumult of new vision and form produced architecture and all the other arts and crafts associated with it, menus to match these triumphs were being served, on silver dishes by Benvenuto Cellini, and eaten from Venetian glass plates: quenelles of fish, truffles, liver crépinettes, artichoke hearts, sweetbreads, larks, and zabagliones. The mountain cheese, Taleggio, and Fontina from the Valle d'Aosta in Piedmont were served, as well as being eaten continually by the boys who served the meals. There was trouble if they ate too much Fontina, as it was in the same category as Roquefort – exclusive and expensive, especially as it had to be transported over long distances by horse wagons.

France was already aware of the new art forms of the Italian Renaissance, and its effect upon silver dishes as well as cuisine, when Lorenzo's great-granddaughter Catherine de Medici married Henry II of France. This accelerated the fusion of French and Italian art and cooking.

Besides long-forgotten estates, money and land, Catherine brought with her as part of her dowry a retinue of Florentine chefs, schooled in the subtleties of this cuisine. Her own favourite dish was cock's combs and kidneys, served with artichoke hearts. She also brought a grander fashion sense, including rich materials, costume designers, and dressers. It is sad that when Catherine brought such gifts with her, Henry II should not only spend so much of his time with Diane de Poitier, but that he should also give her Chenonceaux, the most beautiful of all the châteaux of the Loire. Catherine de Medici was well aware of this romance. She had an organized retinue of beautiful girls and young men who were her 'moles' in all the châteaux so that she received news not only of Diane and Henry, but countless other matters of interest. It is surprising that she did not dispatch Diane, because she had in fact a background steeped in intrigue and assassination. Her room at Blois was known when she was alive to have secret panels, but during reconstruction due to woodworm within the last fifty years, even more were discovered, revealing state papers on foreign policy, diaries of a personal nature, dried-up jars and phials of beauty lotions, lethal poisons, and drugs for a variety of purposes. Possibly Diane had reliable wine and food tasters. She also kept to a diet that included goats' milk and fresh goats' milk cheese, together with cold baths and early morning rides in the forests. Being twenty years older than Henry was one reason, but the other was that she was a natural athlete, and enjoyed it. Catherine, for psychological reasons no doubt, had a weight problem and was more than once carried, sitting in her chair, to her room moaning that she might burst. Her dinners at Blois were in marked contrast to those at Chenonceaux. The cuisine at Blois was as near totally Italianate as possible. Lutes were played and songs sung as a background to splendid eating and drinking. At Chenonceaux, Diane organized more athletic entertainments, with meals on decorated barges while young ladies of noble birth swam around disguised as mermaids, fêtes champêtres in the woods, with the same noble young ladies as nymphs, and young scions as satyrs. There were also very realistic tournaments for the knights, and it was in 1559 during one of these contests that Henry received a lance wound which killed him. So Catherine outlived Henry, and immediately bartered Chaumont for Chenonceaux. She then set about making it her own, with sculpture from Florence, caryatids, larger windows, more buildings and a park, treating it as a possession. Diane had used it as an integral part of her daily life of joie de vivre.

Marie de Medici, Catherine's cousin, later married Henry IV of France, so the Italianate influence in France continued. Marie's chef, La Varenne, however, was French and wrote a cook book, Le Cuisinier François (1652), which shows clearly that the basics of French cuisine were now established. La Varenne, for example, cooks fish in a fumet – fish stock made with fish trimmings. His roasts are served in their own juices, to retain the essential flavours. Roux has arrived, the sauce made with flour, butter and stock. Jonchées (cream cheeses) and caillebottes (curd cheeses) were now an essential part of the desserts of French pastries with fruit and cream, which were the finale to the banquets, served with fruit liqueurs.

The next chef to direct the path of French cuisine, about ten years later, was Henri Vatel, with a biography like a cruel fairy tale. The son of a labourer, Vatel nevertheless managed to study mathematics and literature as well as cooking, but it was for this last skill that he made a name for himself. Summoned by Nicolas Foucquet, the most corrupt, ambitious and powerful man in Europe, and Treasurer of France, to be his chef, he immediately showed his intelligence in other matters. Foucquet realized Vatel's potential and made him steward (*maître d'hôtel*) of his estate. Then he moved him to the French Treasury because he had 'the best organized head in the world'. Vatel bought not only the horses for the army, but much of the armaments as well. He also had presence, and personally repaid loans to cardinals and others who were involved in the enormous Foucquet embezzlement web. Next, Vatel was in charge of the building of Vaux-le-Vicomte, Foucquet's château, which cost over 300,000 livres.

People were now beginning to talk about Foucquet. When Louis XIV was depressed to find that work on the Louvre had to stop because of shortage of money, Foucquet made the ultimate mistake of inviting him to his own newly completed Château de Vaux-le-Vicomte. Vatel organized the reception. Fabulous meals continued for three days and nights, with food served from 6000 silver dishes on Sèvres porcelain plates. Molière provided the plays and Lully the music for dancing. Louis enjoyed it all thoroughly, but every moment of it made the fact that Foucquet was a crook more certain, so he was put in prison. Vatel visited him there and gave him all his savings, to make his life easier. Thirty, penniless and unemployed, Vatel then had ten years of misery. When the impoverished Prince de Condé at Chantilly, notorious for never paying anyone, offered him the position of chef, he accepted. The next month, Louis XIV, like a recurring nightmare, was to arrive at Chantilly. Vatel tried too hard. Undermined by years of misery and poverty he went without sleep for a week as he organized it. Just as the King arrived, he became confused in the head. Some tables had no chairs, others had no forks; the entire fish course had gone astray; the musicians had no music stands. Vatel killed himself. He was buried in a field; no one knows where.

Louis XIV, who was the centrepiece of so many of these gargantuan feasts, was genuinely interested in cuisine, and ate prodigiously. He was known to start with three different soups, followed by a stuffed pheasant and a brace of partridges. Then, please note, a plate of salad. Mutton cooked in its own juices and garlic would be followed by a plate of spiced ham. There were vestiges of priority but

quite a lot of chaos, especially with regard to cheese, which was piled up regardless on side tables together with fruit, cakes, preserves and liqueurs. The cooking was still fighting losing battles with a variety of enemies and obstacles. First of these were the kitchens themselves, which were further away from the banqueting tables than they had been in the Middle Ages. With an inferno of several whole beasts on spits, and sixty chefs or more together with their assistants all making different dishes and sauces on a variety of fires, the chaos was diabolical. Meanwhile, the retinue would be marshalled: archers, the Lord Steward, the tasters, servers with baskets of knives, forks and spoons, toothpicks and salt cellars, more baskets full of Sèvre porcelain plates; finally the food itself held high, with shouts of 'the King's meat'. Some of this meat came from the royal forests and the hunts; the vegetables and fruit were now grown in the gardens at Versailles, supervised by La Quintinie, a lawyer turned agronomist. The chefs of this period are generally remembered only if they wrote cook books. Examples are Menon with his *Nouveaux Traits de la Cuisine* and *Les Soupers de la Cour* (1755); and François Marin, who wrote *Les Dous de Comos*, in which sauce Béchamel appeared: a historic moment, named after Louis XIV's *maître d'hôtel*, the Marquis de Béchamel.

The reason why so many women today seem to have a Cordon Bleu for cooking is due directly to a feminist trick played by Madame du Barry on Louis XV. There were no women chefs at that time. Louis who often had supper with her offered to confer an honour on her chef because he so consistently produced imaginative menus. 'Right, France, I have you,' said Madame du Barry. 'My chef is a woman, so I will not accept less than a Cordon Bleu.' (This originally indicated the sky-blue sash of the great Ordre du Saint Esprit.)

The reigns of Louis XV and XVI saw more order and logic in the cuisine so that just before the Revolution, Brillat-Savarin could say:

The ranks of every profession concerned with the sale or preparation of food, including cooks, caterers, confectioners, pastry cooks, provision merchants and the like, have multiplied . . . New professions have arisen including the pastry cook – in his domain are biscuits, macaroons, cakes, meringues . . . The art of preserving has become a profession in itself, whereby we are enabled to enjoy, at all times of the year, things naturally peculiar to one season . . . French cuisine has also annexed dishes of foreign extraction.

One of the major effects of the Revolution on French cuisine was to bring it out into the open. It had previously been housed in the châteaux, palaces and other great residences. The chefs now had few grand houses in which to practise their art, so they opened restaurants, which became a new and better arena for French cuisine.

Probably the most important of post-Revolution chefs was Marie-Antoine Carême, who dominated 19th-century cuisine in France. At various times chef to Napoleon, Talleyrand, the Tsar of Russia, the British Prince Regent, and finally the Rothschilds in Paris, he preferred Talleyrand because he had said that cuisine was more important than battles and congresses. (He could never forgive Napoleon for the fact that fifty of France's best chefs died on the retreat from Moscow.) Carême was noted especially for his *pièces montées* (the precursors of wedding cakes), which were elaborate structures made up of various edible materials so that the meal looked like an architectural work of art. These were considered a mistake by Prosper Montagne (1864-1948), who not only created the *Larousse Gastronomique*, but began the movement towards simplicity and first essentials which is still with us and gathering momentum; it was the first step towards *nouvelle cuisine*.

Montagne's work was brought to the notice of Georges-Auguste Escoffier (1846-1935) who was delighted by it as it was in line with his own movement towards culinary reform; *faites simple* was his watchword. He shortened menus, accelerated service and reorganized kitchens to produce food more efficiently. His Poularde 'Derby' is well known, but not really as an example of *faites simple*: roast chicken with truffles and *foie gras* stuffing, and garnished with truffles and *foie gras*. He named many of his creations after friends and celebrities: Tournedos Rossini (also, incidentally, garnished with *foie gras* and truffles, like Lord Derby's chicken); the Australian soprano Nellie Melba got toast and Pèche Melba; and Adolphe Duglère, chef

at the Café Anglais and a rival, Sole Duglère, to confuse everyone.

Escoffier's influence was achieved partly by his books, but mainly by the fact that he extended the idea of *grand cuisine* beyond restaurants to hotels. In collaboration with César Ritz he established Ritz hotels in Paris, Rome, Madrid, London, Budapest, New York, Montreal, Philadelphia and Pittsburgh. His books are *Le Guide Culinaire* (1921); *Le Livre des Menus* (1924); and *Ma Cuisine* (1934). Escoffier was rather short, and wore built-up heels to avoid burning himself on the stoves. He banned smoking, drinking and shouting in his kitchens. He provided jugs of iced barley water, which he said was essential because the square metre of red-hot charcoal for grills, together with other fires and stoves, gave off a lot of heat, and windows could not be opened or everything would get too cold or covered with flies.

He removed, like a good Frenchman, the words *espagnole* and *allemande* from sauces, saying that they were simply derivatives of basic French sauces. He was a visionary. Like Soyer, who had transformed cooking in England, and also military cooking during the Crimean War, he worked out methods of improving cooking for the poor in institutions, and had ideas about a welfare state. He died in Monte Carlo, leaving £335. Too many geniuses have died in poverty.

In the 1850s service *à la française* was replaced by service *à la russe*, which is how we now dine, with food brought to the table in sequence, and hot. This was due to the influence of Félix Urbain-Dubois, who was chef to the Tsars of Russia for many years. One of the sad pragmatic facts about *haute cuisine* as an art form is that it disappears immediately after reaching its apogee: *au point* one minute and gone the next, particularly in the case of those tortured Avignon geese.

As art critics had now appeared to sort out and explain the visual arts, so gourmet writers arose to exert an influence on cuisine. Charles Monselet (1828-88) with *Le Triple Almanach Gourmand* was notable, but his last words are memorably hideous: 'I would like to be buried *aux truffes*.' Curnonsky (1872-1956) was dominant in his lifetime. Born Maurice-Edmond Sailland, he changed his name to Curnonsky to give himself a Russian flavour. He was probably the greatest writer on food in France

OPPOSITE Gruyère de Comté, one of the classic French cheeses being made in a fruitière *in the Jura (page 77).*

after Brillat-Savarin, especially with his major work *Le Trésor Gastonomique de France* (1933), which gives the regional cooking of France in detail.

Today, in the 1980s, Escoffier's *faites simple* has moved to the lean *nouvelle cuisine*, which mirrors the essential needs of our times as Carème did in his century. Purity of ingredients, simplicity but perfection of cooking, to be a gourmet without dewlaps, and with cheese after the main course, using the last of the wine, before the dessert.

So much for today's civilized eating, but what of the future? The engineered beef steak has arrived. It has been customary to make use of only 30% of a carcass, but now it is possible to use 72%, by shaving many parts not previously eaten, such as gristle and connective tissues, knuckles, heels, flanks. Blending and folding them together, salting, freezing, extruding and pressing at some 35 kg per square centimetre (500 lb per square inch), and then slicing them into cuts that look exactly like filet mignon.

The US Army Research and Development command has been active in this direction for five years, producing among other things veal cutlets structured from mixed flaked parts not normally eaten, which the soldiers thought very superior to genuine veal cutlets. The Massachusetts Institute of Technology has found new uses in foods for the pulpy residue left from squeezing fruits for juice, as well as the structural material in lobster and clam shells. Cornell University researchers have produced a canned minced-fish product which dupli-

cates tuna from Alaskan pollack. 'Pouch' foods, which need no refrigeration, only the addition of boiling water, originally developed for astronauts, will soon be on the market. Milk will not need refrigeration either, because by heating raw milk to far higher temperatures than Pasteur ever thought of, it will last almost for ever and be drunk after a chemical 'improvement' additive has been put in to rid it of its slightly weird flavour. So much for our talk of the 'bouquet' of some cheeses, using unpasteurized milk. The cows are also in for more research, especially at the Animal Research Center in Beltsville, Maryland, where the polyunsaturated cow is being designed.

Microbiological research has produced results that seem familiar and closely related to our subject of cheese. Single-celled microbes such as algae, bacteria, fungi, and yeast are already part of foods. Bacteria are consumed in trillions with cheese and yoghurts. Many meat substitutes are now dependent on microbes. Soaked, cooked, wheat-coated soya beans become overgrown with the mould *Aspergillus oryzae*, used in meat substitutes, in the same way that *Rhizopos oligosporus*, an edible mould from the traditional Indonesian meat analogue *tempeh*, knits itself into a nutritious compact cake, used in soups or fried. Researchers in America are certain that microbial cells grown in massive quantities could be consumed in some form directly by man as a major source of food. The transitional phase of making imitation filets of steak will probably soon be overtaken by no-camouflage foods by the turn of the century, with fried *Aspergillus oryzae* on the menu.

So it has come full circle: the advance researchers have rediscovered how invaluable moulds and microbial cells are, and how they can be accommodated into major diets in the future, while the makers of many cheeses – Roquefort, Cantal, Camembert, Brie, and so on – have been using them for, in some cases, thousands of years.

Tourism of the 21st century may take in our current *haute cuisine*, viewing it as being as peculiarly old and fascinating as the roasting of whole beasts in ancient château kitchens. It will be interesting to see how long it takes *nouvelle cuisine* to change into the new scientific cuisine, including the astronauts' pouch foods, but perhaps with a little more flair.

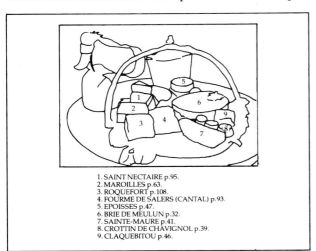

1. SAINT NECTAIRE p.95.
2. MAROILLES p.63.
3. ROQUEFORT p.108.
4. FOURME DE SALERS (CANTAL) p.93.
5. EPOISSES p.47.
6. BRIE DE MEULUN p.32.
7. SAINTE-MAURE p.41.
8. CROTTIN DE CHAVIGNOL p.39.
9. CLAQUEBITOU p.46.

OPPOSITE Some of the best cheeses of all France.

CHAPTER II

CHEESEMAKING

Cheese is found in enormous variety all over the world, and in every case the type of cheese is due not only to man's resource and inventiveness but to the environment: climate, geology, soil, vegetation, history, and the species of milk-producing animals that live there. Milk may be whole or skimmed, pasteurized or unpasteurized. The heating to pasteurize milk removes the bacteria which are necessary to produce most of the cheese mentioned in this book.

Cows' milk cheeses The ten-month lactation period of dairy cattle is followed by a two-month dry period, but staggered calf production produces an all-the-year-round milk supply. The first milk produced after calving, called beestings or colostrum, is rarely if ever used for cheesemaking. The 'new milk' that follows it is high in protein and fats, which decline until the end of the lactation period, when it increases in fats once more. Milk produced just at the end of a milking is also richer than at the beginning. (Reblochon was traditionally made from this.) Cows, milked morning and evening, can have their milk used as a mixture for some cheeses, or separately as for Morbier, which is fastened together in two halves.

Ewes' milk cheeses These are highly seasonal. In France the milk is available from January to mid-May, so the cheese, with takes three months to ripen, is available from April to mid-August.

Goats' milk cheese Available from February to October-November. Goats' milk, exceptionally high in fat content, is free from many of the pathogens found in cows' milk and it is rarely pasteurized.

Cheesemaking began as a domestic skill that became an art, then a science, and is now an industry. Almost all national cheese types have evolved from farmhouse originals. The milk-into-cheese formula depends primarily on the milk itself, followed by the process. Milk is dependent on grazing, and grazing is influenced by the geological substructure, the climate and the animal itself. Each cheese type encapsulates these elements into a unique combination before the cheesemaker begins his work.

The first essential in cheesemaking is the same for all cheeses: to remove the fluid that makes up the bulk of the milk (87%) but retain the remainder – vitamins, milk fat, proteins, milk sugar, albumen, globulin, mineral salts and so on. To simplify the stages of a very complicated process into its basic principles, this involves: coagulating the milk; treating the curds; moulding, pressing and finishing; ripening or curing.

Coagulating the milk

The milk used may be morning, evening, or a mixture; it may be skimmed or fortified; it may be dyed (annatto) or mould spores may be added to promote blue veins. To encourage the gases that make holes, propionic acid bacteria may be used.

The coagulation is begun by means of a starter, which is a culture of sour milk containing a concentration of lactic acid. Coagulation is achieved entirely by the starter for acid-curd cheeses, but most require rennet, an enzyme extracted from the stomach of a young lamb or calf. The cheesemaker tests the levels of acidity and temperature, which vary for each type of cheese, and then adds rennet, which produces the reaction of curds and whey.

Plant rennets are used for some cheeses in regions of Asia where the cow is sacred, and in some countries that actually prefer them. Plant rennets are fig leaves, melon seeds, sunflower seeds, thistle seeds, and *caille-lait*.

After renneting, by whatever method, the milk

forms into a mass of curds or junket.

Treating the curds

The softness or hardness of the cheese to be made depends on how the curds are cut and drained. Softer cheeses are cut sparingly, ladled into the moulds and allowed to drain by themselves. Harder cheeses have their curds cut both vertically and horizontally with special wire cutters and combs. When the curds have settled they are cut again. Then they may be 'pitched', or 'cheddared' to expel more of the whey. For very hard cheeses the vat is then heated and the curds are either scalded or cooked.

Moulding, pressing and finishing

This is the stage where diversity really begins. The curds are ladled into a wide variety of moulds, all perforated for drainage. The moulds vary from rush baskets to stainless-steel drums, and include wooden hoops of all sorts and sizes. Curds are left to firm up naturally, or they may be pressed lightly or heavily. Lightly usually means placing a circular disc of wood on top (Reblochon), and heavily means wrapping the curds in a cheesecloth, putting them into a mould, and squeezing in a hydraulic press (Gruyère de Comté).

There is a wide range of possible processes that may be introduced at this stage. The cheese may be sprayed with mould-forming spores, soaked in brine, waxed, washed with water, wine, beer or alcohol, buried in boxes of ashes, oiled, smoked, or left on a bed of hay or ferns to ripen. Hence the diversity of French cheeses.

Ripening or curing

Curd is a flavourless damp white mass, which eventually turns into the delicacy that no dinner can be without, the snack no ploughman can forgo. It starts the movement towards gastronomy with no further aid. Casein, the most important protein in cheese, contains twenty-one amino acids as well as other chemical elements, and as the casein decomposes, acids and elements, liberated and free to move in the curd, start producing an aroma and a taste. The milk fat is split by another enzyme and fatty acids begin to generate. Bacteria from the milk sugar produces gas in some cheeses and this makes holes. Following the natural ripening process, the longer a cheese is cured, the harder it becomes.

This is a critical stage in cheesemaking. The length of time in curing varies considerably from fresh cheeses, which are barely ripened, to possibly two years or more for a really hard cheese. Strangely, the ripening period may vary within the same cheese type. This is the arena of the *affineur*, who has cellars with separate areas, each with its own level of temperature and humidity, regulated for different kinds of cheese. The aroma and colour, texture and 'feel', shape and even sound, all contribute towards an understanding of the state of *affinage* or curing; whether the cheese is ready or not. For the larger cheeses like Cantal or Cheshire, a cheese iron is inserted which cuts out a long, thin cylinder of cheese for inspection. The texture and smell, colour and feel of this sample core of cheese are all keenly examined before it is replaced, and sometimes the *affineur* listens to it for little gurgling sounds, which indicate moisture excess.

If the cheese iron brings out a core which is really suspect the whole cheese is cut in half and the atmosphere in the curing room becomes very tense, especially when there are, say, five hundred cheeses on racks, and there may be others with this ghastly malady.

Special characteristics, like the blue veining in Roquefort, the holes in Gruyère de Comté and the mould on Camembert, are all promoted by various devices at this stage. Stainless-steel needles aerate the paste and help the blue veins along in Bleu d'Auvergne; the Comté is turned regularly to help an even distribution of holes; and Camemberts are injected to improve the bloomy rind. What used to be done by luck, rule of thumb, and more than a touch of mystery, is now scientifically administered by the *affineurs* with little or no element of chance.

Casein, the most important protein in cheese, contains twenty-one amino acids as well as many other elements, and as the protein decomposes, these are liberated in the cheese to produce its ultimate taste and aroma. The milk fat also undergoes a chemical change, one part being split by another enzyme, the resulting fatty acids contributing part of the final flavour.

It is the length of the ripening period that determines the cheese type; as we have seen, the longer it ripens, the harder it gets.

Cheese rinds

Fresh cheeses have no rind, but the remainder fall into four groups:

1. Dry natural rinds (Tomme de Savoie) and those that are sometimes brushed or oiled (Comté).
2. Bloomy rinds, with a white mould that is brushed off until the right thickness of rind is reached. The mould is assisted by spraying with *Penicillium candidum* (Camembert).
3. Washed rinds, which are washed with water, wine, beer or brine and also a culture of *Breyibacterium lunens*, which encourages a bacterial growth (Trappist, monastery cheeses).
4. Artificial rinds which may use herbs, leaves, ashes, paint, wax or plastic.

Quality control

Legal regulations control the making of cheese in almost all countries. Fat content must be stated on the cheese or the package. Starter cultures and rennets are examined regularly. Cleanliness and hygiene standards must be impeccable. In 1951 the Stresa Convention fixed international agreements between nine countries, protecting the names of particular cheeses and their area of origin. For Roquefort, the areas where it can be made are precisely laid down. Bleu du Haut-Jura and Cantal must be produced above 800m (2625ft). Comté must be made exclusively in the province of Franche Comté and only from the milk of cows from the breed Pie rouge de l'est or Montbéliard. In 1967 the Food and Agriculture Organization (FAD) and the World Health Organization (WHO) drew up a code of quality standards for the 6 million tons of cheese made annually by 33 countries (a sobering thought!).

TYPES OF FRENCH CHEESE

Cheeses can be separated into many categories, but the first and simplest classification is by the type of grazing animal that started it off with its milk.

Cows' milk cheeses show considerable variety due to different methods of curing as well as the breed of cow.

Abbey or monastery cheeses are made in many regions:

Belval in Picardy.
Bricquebec in Normandy was formerly made by Trappists, but is now produced under the name Providence by the cooperative dairy at Valognes, using pasteurized milk.
Campenéac in Brittany.
Chambarand in Dauphiné, formerly named Beaupré.
Cîteaux in Burgundy.
Enchournac in Périgord.
Entrammes in Maine. The abbey previously made this as Port-Salut but sold the name and the recipe to the SAFR dairy, which uses pasteurized milk. The abbey makes its Entrammes with unpasteurized milk.
Igny in Champagne.
La Meillerade in Brittany.
Laval in Maine.
Tamie in Savoie.
Thymadeuse in Brittany.

Most abbey cheeses are pressed and uncooked with washed rinds.

Seventeen cows' milk blues

Bleu d'Auvergne. Inspired by the older Roquefort, but made from cows' milk, this cheese has a blue

Cheesemaking in the Auvergne, c. 1870.

internal mould. It is neither pressed nor cooked, but salted, sprinkled with penicillium and pierced with needles, and fermented. Produced near the Puy-de-Dôme, it is made by the old traditional methods in stone *burons*, passing through several changes of humidity and temperature. It is then sprinkled with *Penicillium glaucum* and pierced with needles so that a passage of air can develop the blue veins from the heart of the cheese to the rind. After degreasing it is given a metal foil covering. It is used in regional dishes: in salads; fish sauce, especially eel; with poultry – chicken, pheasant and turkey; and in particular with cream as a dip for *crudités*. Other blue cheeses can be used for all these recipes, but Bleu d'Auvergne is better because it has a buttery taste – unlike Roquefort's much drier flavour.

Bleu de Bresse. Created in 1950 at Servas near Bourg-en-Bresse and an imitation of Saingorlon, which is an imitation of Gorgonzola. Like Saingorlon it is made from pasteurized milk and is best eaten before it has been too long in the refrigerated storerooms.

Bleu des Causses. Made in the same way as Bleu d'Auvergne but in *batardes*, which are caves in the mountains with *fleurines* or ventilation cracks just like those that keep the temperatures and humidity right for Roquefort.

Bleus du Haut-Jura, Gex and Bleu de Septmoncel. All these are protected by an *appellation d'origine*. They are made in wooden moulds, called *seilles*. The curds are worked, cut with a little of the whey, and sprinkled with *Penicillium glaucum*. After passing through the normal blue cheese processes, the cheeses are matured in old wine *caves*, which they say give them an unusually pleasant perfume. They go very well with Jura *vin jaune*.

Bleu de Laqueville. Made since 1850 and invented by a farmer in the Puy-de-Dôme area, it is always eaten 'warmed up'. Weighs 2.5 kg (5.5 lb). It has a red rind and is less salty, and more fragrant, than Bleu d'Auvergne. It is also more difficult to cure. The smallest deviation or mistake by the *affineur* and the taste loses its subtlety. It also goes off altogether quite rapidly.

Bleu du Pelvoux and Bleu du Queyras. Now only made as 'little bleus' in the Briançon district.

Fourme d'Ambert. Known since Roman times. A cylinder 20 cm (8 in) high and 12 cm (5 in) in diameter, usually cut in half horizontally and surrounded with a white serviette like a Stilton. Port, both white and red, sherry and Madeira are all agreeable with it. It is mixed with any of these to make canapés. Real amateurs of d'Ambert drink a vintage Port or an exceptional Sauterne with it.

Bleu du Quercy. Made in Aquitaine. Like Bleu d'Auvergne but more crumbling and savoury. It needs a strong, no-nonsense wine like Cahors (or one of the Spanish red wines like Marqués de Macares.)

Bleu de Sassenage. One of the 'Songs of Gastronomy' by Joseph Berchoux (1805) includes quite a bit about the qualities of this 13th-century cheese:

Les parfums de Paphos, dont l'amour fait usage,
Ne peuvent s'allier à ceux de Sassenage

Made in 6 kg (13 lb) moulds, it deserves a Chambertin.

Bleu de Thiézac. Made in the Causses. Salted when warm, tastes like Laqueille and is difficult to mature.

Bleu du Velay, Bleu de Loudes, Bleu du Costaros. Made in the Haut-Loire, Le Puy, and Saint-Etienne.

Olivet Bleu. A soft paste, with mild pale-blue veins, and a flowery rind which turns reddish after three weeks as a sign of maturity. Made like Brie or Camembert but with a more rustic smell. The taste is very like Brie de Melun; sometimes preserved in plane tree leaves (or *cendre*). This cheese of the Orléanais region is good enough to be included with classics like Brie.

Boules and Boulettes

La Bouille. Made by Monsieur Fromage with a soft paste, bloomy rind and double cream it can be eaten fresh, bloomy or fully cured. Rich and perfumed, it is an excellent stimulant when accompanied by a suitable wine, like a good Muscadet, Vouvray or Coteaux Champenois.

Boule de Lille, Vieux Lille. Other names for Mimolette.

Boulettes d'Avesnes, de Cambrai, de Thiérache. D'Avesnes contains whey and buttermilk when made on the farms. In the industrial dairies it is made with pieces of Maroilles, pounded up before curing. The curds are mixed with tarragon, parsley, clover, pepper and salt, shaped into a cone and cured for four months. Being a northern cheese it is usually eaten with gin or strong beer. Boulette de Cambrai has no parsley and is eaten fresh but is still tasty, and needs a lager or gin. Boulette de Thiérache is made in the industrial dairies like Maroilles and tastes like d'Avesnes.

Boulette de la Pierre Qui Vire, Boules des Moines. A fresh cheese savoured with herbs and made in Burgundian monasteries. Often eaten as a snack at rugby matches or picnics, with a bottle of the lesser regional wines.

Six versions of Brie

The section of this book concerned with the cheeses of the Île de France contains a few stories about Brie, but there are many more. Marie Leczinska, Louis XV's queen, said it was one of the most perfect *bouchées à la Reine*. Rabelais wrote that Gargantua and Gargamelle fed their son Pantagruel on Brie and herrings. Victor Hugo said that a small piece of Brie was worth a dozen good poems in alexandrine couplets. J. K. Huysmans said, 'Yes, Brie is ambrosia when *au point*, but when it is the colour of old teeth, it has the smell of a charnel house.' It is known that the particular Brie that won the 'King of Cheeses' gourmet competition at the

Congress of Vienna in 1814-15 was made on a farm named Estouville at Villeroy, near Meaux. The French remain silent about all Bries not made in France, or in the wrong regions. Some even say that if eaten in Paris, the taste will be memorable right round the world.

Brie de Meaux. More often made in industrial dairies near Paris than on farms, but with unpasteurized milk, and tended by *affineurs* who follow the ancient traditional methods like some sacred ritual.

Brie de Melun. Probably the ancestor of all the Bries, it is made from full milk. The curds are shaken up to activate the taste throughout its 4.5 cm (1.8 in) thickness. Bleu de Melun is covered with powdered charcoal. The taste is more ample and also more piquant than the other Bries.

Brie de Montereau, Ville-Saint-Jacques. Very rare, but mainly made on farms.

Brie de Coulommiers. The smallest of the Bries. It is made fresh, *mousse*, or matured. *Fougeru* is Coulommiers with a sprig of bracken.

Camembert and Brie

Brie was already being made in 774 (according to Eginhard, chronicler of Charlemagne) whereas

Making Brie, 1854.

Camembert was not produced until 1705 (according to Thomas Corneille's *Dictionnaire des Arts et Sciences*). The popular version that it was created by Marie Harel at the end of the 18th century in Vimoutiers is only part of the truth. Marie Fontaine, who later married a farmer named Harel, received the recipe from a priest as an enormous dowry – with a potential of millions of francs – and started making a kind of Camembert. They had a daughter, also named Marie Harel, who further improved the recipe and exploited it. At the beginning of the 20th century an American doctor found that eating Camembert provided a cure for various illnesses. He sought out the origins of the cheese and put up a statue to Marie Harel in 1928. This was damaged in 1944 during World War II and replaced with another statue by an industrial dairy making Camembert nearby.

These early Camemberts were not like those of today: lying on straw mats, they had a wild blue rind like a duvet. The white flowery and bloomy rind did not appear until 1912. It was in the 1920s that Alexander Fleming's work led to the discovery of penicillin in *Penicillium nautanum*. The French obviously think that they were aware of the curative powers of *Penicillium candidum* long before Fleming (and there were no doubt hundreds of medieval witches, boiling up herbs in black cauldrons, who produced an equally efficacious paste to cure dropsy, gout and gangrene, but were inhibited from advertising these near-magical cures by fear of the stake).

Camembert was never given an *appellation d'origine* and is consequently made in seventy-two French *départements* and in most of the industrial countries of the world, including Russia, America, Argentina, South Africa and Switzerland. There is, however, a label with the letters VCN (Véritable Camembert de Normandie) which guarantees that the cheese has been made in the traditional way in Normandy, and is not the standard pasteurized-milk variety, covered with a startlingly white bloomy rind low in savour but high in artifice.

Cantal

Cantal fermier is made in *burons*, or wooden *mazues*, which are long low chalets. The milk is carried in buckets on long wooden trays carried by two men and given the first pressing while still warm. The curds are cured in natural mountain caves. As the cows go up to the mountain pastures on 25 June and come down on 18 October, the cheeses may either be sold when the cattle descend, or the curing may be continued until they are fully matured at six months.

Cantal Laitier is made from pasteurized milk in the cooperative dairies and cured for six months.

Cantal-Salers or Salers or Fourme de Salers is made *only* from the milk of Salers cows whereas La guiole is made from Aubrac cows (more *café au lait* coloured than red).

Cendrés

Cheese ripened in wood ashes. Many soft-paste cheeses are cured in the ashes of various woods, such as oak, vine prunings, beech and elm. The vine-ash cheeses are kept in boxes, still surrounded by ash, for the time of the vine harvest and are guaranteed to produce an enormous thirst – together with a desire for strong sensations which is satisfied in an aggressive way.

Aisy Cendré or Cendré d'Aisy. Made in Montbard in Burgundy, and Aisy-sur-Armagon.

Cendré d'Argennes or Rocroi.

Cendré des Voves. Very rare.

Cendrés de Champagne or Cendré des Riceys. Used especially at France's Champagne Festival.

Fourmes

Fourme. The root from which the French word *fromage* derives.

Fourme d'Ambert. See page 21.

Fourme des Monts du Forez. Made in the Forez mountains; also called Fourme de Montbrison.

Fourme de Rochefort-Montagne or Cantalon. Small Cantals of 3 to 12 kg.

Fourme du Haut-Vivarais. Made from either goats' or cows' milk. Cured in cases in caves until the crust is dark brown.

Jonchées

Fresh cheeses named after the rush basket in which they were contained. *Jonchées* are generally made from cow's milk in Brittany, goat's milk in Poitou and ewe's milk in Oléron.

Fronjoncousse. A *jonchée* made in the Pyrenees with fresh cheese, honey and fine herbs.

Poustagnacq. A *jonchée* of Aquitaine made with

cow's, ewe's or goat's milk. The fresh curds are sparkled with pimento, fermented a little and baptized with Armagnac (Gascony and the Landes). *Jonchée d'Aunis/d'Oléron/Sabeau*. Very subtle.

Tommes or Tomes

Tomme, Savoyard patois for cheese, also used in the Dauphiné and Auvergne. In Provence the word is *tumo*. Some *tommes* are made with goat's milk.

Tomme des Bauges. Made near Ecolé, Savoie.

Tomme de Belleville. Made in Savoie on the Dranse.

Tomme Boudane. Made mainly for farm use.

Tomme du Chamsaur or de Laye. Authentic mountain cheese.

Tomme Fraîche. Name for curd kneaded and pressed as the preliminaries to making Cantal.

Tomme de Lomagne. Made in Gers.

Tomme au Marc. An outstanding cheese, cured (and macerated) in earthenware pots of *marc*; as a result the grape pips stick to the crust. The locals drink the gentian eau-de-vie of the mountains with it. Made in the Isère valley near Chambéry.

There is an industrial version consisting of a processed curd with a thin plastic rind on which grape pips have been stuck (for export only including, sadly, to Britain, which imports a large quantity).

Tomme du Pays Niçois. Similar to Tomme de Valberg. A large *tomme* from cow's milk, pressed but not cooked, in the mountain farms above Niçois, and also Vésubie, Valberg and Tende.

Tomme du Revard. A kind of Tomme au Marc.

Tomme de Romans. It takes its name from Romans-sur-Isère, where it is made. An industrial *tomme* with a soft paste and natural crust, made as a small disc of only 250 g.

Tomme de Savoie or Tomme Grise. One of the best *tommes*. Made from partially skimmed milk, and sometimes from goat's milk. After the curd has been cut it is mixed with the whey. It is cured for one month in fresh airy caves or cellars before being placed in the proper *tomme* caves, which are much colder and damper, for six weeks. The *tommes* vary between 1500 and 2500 kg or even 4000 kg. The paste changes from yellow to grey. The crust when fully cured is covered with grey marbling, pigmented with yellow and red.

Tomme de Vivarais. This is a goat's milk *tomme*. Good in the spring with a dandelion salad, and excellent mixed with wine vinegar, pimento, garlic and olive oil, and eaten with mashed potatoes. *Tommes* made with goat's milk: Allues, de Belley, Chevret de Bresse, de Combovin, de Corps, de Courchevel, de Crest, de Pelvoux, de Sospel, de Vercors, de Vésubie.

Goat's milk cheeses

In the previous century and earlier these were thought of as the cheese of the poor, with little grannies leading their goats, *biques*, along the narrow overhung tracks of Berry, Touraine, Poitou, Charentes and the Dauphiné. During the 20th century, however, the nanny goats have become proper little queens, capricious, turbulent and even impossible. They eat everything they can see, even research material, the refuse and chemicals from laboratory wastes. They climb trees and destroy them by chewing off the bark, and if tethered with a strong collar and chain, they make an instant desert right to the perimeter of their circuit. Goat's milk is dearer than cow's milk and has more protein and lipides, as well as casein. Unlike cows, which are able to give milk all year, thanks to the advantages of artificial insemination, female goats cannot avail themselves of this neat artifice: goat sperm cannot be preserved by refrigeration.

Goat's milk cheese can therefore be made only during the period of lactation, which is from the end of January to November. Before that the milk is used to raise female goats to replace any that are inadequate in some way or another. A young billy goat stands a poor chance of survival, unless he is a really good specimen capable of replacing the magnificent patriarch of the herd. The female can produce six litres of milk a day.

More and more goat's milk cheeses are appearing because of city dwellers taking up this pastoral industry, partly out of a distaste for urban life.

Before buying a goat's milk cheese you should consider the following points:

1. Eat between February and October.
2. Cheeses from the vineyard districts are the best.
3. Easter is the very best time of the year.
4. Look at the label: *Pur chèvre* is better than simply *Lait de chèvre*.
5. Crust should be bluish with a crisp firm contour.
6. Look after it. Keep it in a soup dish with a damp cloth wrapped around it.

Sheep's milk cheeses

Sheep's milk costs twice as much as cow's or goat's milk. Some 16,000 tons of Roquefort cheese are made every year, 10 per cent being exported. The French keep most, as they do with champagne. Made entirely of sheep's milk in the Rayon area, which comprises Aveyron, La Lozère, Le Tarn, Le Gard, L'Hérault, Alpes de Haute-Provence, Pyrenees and Corsica. In order to have the right to its *appellation d'origine*, the cheese must also be cured in the caves of Combalu, which provide an atmosphere at 7°C with a humidity of 95 per cent. *Penicillium roqueforti* on breadcrumbs is added, and the *affineurs* salt the curds for five days (every facet). Piercing by needles starts and develops the internal moulds. After 60 days, the cheese is covered with metal foil in which it attains its full maturity, in about 90 days. A Roquefort weighs 2.5 kg.

A red sheep, stamped on the label, guarantees a Roquefort's authenticity. This cheese is the uncontrovertible world classic; choosing what should go in second, third place, etc. can keep cheese gourmets contentious for years.

Wines also provide an argument: champagne; vintage port, like the British with their Stilton; Madeira, Côtes d'Agly, gentian eaux-de-vie, Monbazillac? In America they sell what is basically vinaigrette sauce named Roquefort dressing.

Amou. Not generally on sale in the marketplaces of France, just locally, in the Landes.

Ardi Gasna. Cheese from the Basque country.

Arneguy. From the same locality as the above.

Belloc (Abbaye de). Monastery near Urt in the Pyrénées-Atlantiques. A gentle cheese.

Bleu de Corse. Blancs or *gâteaux de caille* (whites, or cakes of curd) are sent from Corsica to Combalu for curing.

Brousses. These cheeses can be made from any of the three kinds of milk.

Camargue or Tomme Arlésienne. A long triangular section of cheese, smelling of thyme, savory and pepper.

Engordany. From the Andorran valley of that name.

Esbareich. From the Pays Basque: still made in the mountain *burons* in the valley of the Lourse. Sold in June especially: when older it has to be grated.

Larzac (Brebis de). A fresh paste, sold in pots, with a taste reminiscent of Roquefort.

Fromage du Pays Basco-Béarnais. There are two cheeses, Gabas and Laruns. Gabas is a Béarnais cheese, Laruns is the cheese collected from the shepherds on the mountains; both are good.

Oléron (Brebis de). A fresh cheese, mixed with sugar or salted and mixed with wild garlic.

Perrail. Small cheeses made in the Rouergue when there is insufficient ewe's milk cheese to send to Roquefort.

Rébarbe. A *fromage fort* of Rouergue.

Roquefort. Described on page 103.

Tomme Arlésienne. A marvellous cheese, with bouquet, *éclat* and a delectable flavour, but it is becoming rarer.

Tomme de Brach. A rustic cheese, made in a *boule* shape, in earthenware pots, cured for two to four months.

Venaco. This is made with goat's milk from February to October, but with ewe's milk in winter. The ewe's milk version is much sweeter.

Classification of cheese types

Types	Examples	Water	Protein	Lipids*	Calories
FRESH	Fontainebleau, Lune Rousse	70-80	10	10-20	100-200
SOFT (Bloomy rind)	Brie, Camembert	55-60	18	16-20	200-300
SOFT (Washed rind)	Epoisses, Livarot, Maroilles	40-50	26	20-33	300-340
SOFT (Goats' milk)	Valençay, Saint-Maure	40-60	33	16-27	280-380
INTERNAL MOULDS, BLUE	Roquefort	40-45	24	25-30	320-350
PRESSED (Uncooked)	Tomme de Savoie, Saint-Nectaire	35-45	27	20-26	300-350
PRESSED (Cooked)	Beaufort, Comté, Emmental	35-40	30	26-30	350-400

*Lipids: Fats or fat-like substances.

composition per 100g

CHAPTER III
STORING, SERVING AND CUTTING CHEESE

HOW TO STORE CHEESE

Cheese, like flowers, fruit or fish, is alive and eventually will be inedible. Parmesan will last for a hundred years, so they say, keeping its flavour, but this really is the exception. The French, in most provinces, grate old cheeses into earthenware crocks and macerate them into a new and different substance. To suspend a living cheese, to stop its movement towards the end, is virtually impossible. You can hurry cheeses along to an untimely and smelly demise by accidentally leaving them near the kitchen stove, or stop them in their tracks by putting them in the freezer, but the sensible course is as follows.

Buy sufficient cheese to last for a week. Let the cheesemonger worry about storing these living creatures. Having bought it, keep it in a cool humid atmosphere. Most cheeses can be kept, separately of course, in plastic bags in the refrigerator fruit tray.

The fresh cheeses, double and triple creams, need separate plastic bags. The blues should be wrapped in a damp cloth and put in a lidless plastic box. Soft, bloomy rinds should be kept in their packages *and* wrapped in damp cloths.

Goats' milk cheeses can be left without wraps, but semi-soft, fragile cheeses like Saint-Nectaire need to be kept away from the air with plastic wraps.

It is usual to wrap soft cheese types in paraffined paper or aluminium foil. Parchment paper may also be used to absorb moisture with cheeses like Munster.

Hard cheese that has been cut into pieces should be wrapped in translucent foil, which will serve for a few days.

Hard and semi-hard cheese varieties can be kept for weeks, so they may be bought in large quantities, which is cheaper than buying small pieces. Store them carefully and cut a piece large enough to be eaten within a few days.

Hard cheeses tend to 'sweat' their fat if the temperature is not right. Wipe off these drops with a dry cloth and change the temperature.

Soft cheeses such as Brie and Camembert have a tendency to become runny. Buy them *almost* ripe and eat them the next day, wrapping in aluminium foil at room temperature. Once a cheese runs, it will not solidify but only dry out.

Firmer cheeses like Reblochon and Pont l'Evèque can be kept for several days, but as they are always ripening, once they are past their peak the quality will deteriorate.

Strangely, triple-cream cheeses are less sensitive than they look and can be kept in the bottom compartment in the refrigerator for some weeks, suitably foil-wrapped.

A slate shelf in the cool part of a larder is the best place to store them all, covered with a fine-mesh metal sieve, to keep the air circulating and the cat out. Both humidity and temperature are crucial.

HOW TO SERVE CHEESE

Cheese should be served on a basket-type tray of wicker, with leaves or paper napkins under the cheese. Marble was once used, probably an Italian influence, but if you ask the *affineurs*, who live with cheese, they all say wicker trays.

Keep the cheeses separate; about four different kinds is quite enough for a dinner. A damp cloth to cover the cheese until serving is essential. The tray needs two knives, thin sharp ones, and forks, together with a cloth to dry them and a small bowl of hot water. Chives and shallots are good with fresh goats' milk cheeses; celery, radishes and tarragon are refreshing with many cows' milk cheeses. Walnuts are served with Roquefort in the Rouergue and Pyrenees. Pickled walnuts are good with many goats' milk cheeses.

Cheese should be served between the salad and the dessert, to finish the wine and complete the main meal before the change of direction to the dessert. Wine is the natural companion to cheese. Water is positively unhealthy as an accompaniment to cheese, and I think the Swiss should stop drinking tea with their fondue. Beer, cider and Calvados are all drunk with some cheeses in northern France, in Normandy and Alsace; being the regional drinks they naturally harmonize with the cheese.

HOW TO CUT CHEESE

Round or square soft cheeses	like a cake
Small goats' cheeses	in half
Pyramid or cone shapes	horizontal slices
Fourmes of Cantal or similar	horizontal discs and then like cake
Large blue cheeses	horizontal discs and then like cake and skew cut
Wheels, like Comté	best cut by a cheesemonger

Camembert being poured into moulds, c. 1870.

CHAPTER IV

THE REGIONS AND THEIR CHEESES

CHEESE FLAVOUR GUIDE

Cheeses have a wide range of flavours, difficult to tabulate. In the tables given in this chapter on the Regions and their Cheeses, flavours are indicated by letters, from *a* to *f*, with the additional *z* for macerated cheeses, which can reach the quality and strength known as *frénétique* by the French. A mathematical 'to the power of 2' sign (a^2) is used to indicate that the cheese also has a bouquet, or an extra quality of resonance beyond the normal taste. For the same flavour with a tang, if the taste is really vibrant, a 'to the power of 3' sign is used (f^3).

a	bland cooked cheeses made from pasteurized milk
a^2	all fresh cheeses
b	slightly cured, with a high butter fat: e.g. Boursault
c	cheeses not fully matured: young Camembert and Cantal, young Brie and Tommes de Montagne
d	fully matured Brie, Camembert, Cantal, Fourme de Rochefort
d^2	the same with bouquet and an extra quality
e	most monastery cheeses, fully matured Tommes and many goats' cheeses
e^2	fully cured Comté and dry goats' cheeses
f	Maroilles, Livarot, Epoisses
f^2	Cheeses cured long and slowly
g-z	all macerated cheeses.

Other abbreviations used in the tables

C   cows' milk
E   ewes' milk
G   goats' milk

Cheeses: Distribution throughout the regions of France

The same cheese can have many names as this list shows, hence the absurdity of being too definite about the total number.

District	No. of: Names	Cheeses
Île de France	36	27
Loire and Centre	37	26
Burgundy	39	28
Normandy	34	21
Brittany	13	7
Northern France	30	19
Champagne and the Ardennes	18	11
Alsace, Lorraine and the Vosges	23	14
Franche-Comté and the Jura	10	7
Rhône Valley and Haute-Savoie	59	35
Auvergne	30	17
Poitou, Charente and Limousin	42	26
Pyrenees, Aquitaine, Rouergue, Languedoc and Roussillon	56	38
Provençe, Alps & Côte d'Azur	24	14
Corsica	13	8

1. ÎLE DE FRANCE

At the centre of the Île de France is Paris, the most beautiful city in the world, which encapsulates more of the arts than most capitals. It is also the centre (with Lyon as a close second) of gastronomy, and almost all of the cheeses mentioned in this book can be found there. (On pages 120-3 there is a list of recommended cheese shops telling you precisely where.)

Town planners now provide cities with green belts. Paris has always had one, in the form of the Île de France, the land encircled by the Seine, the Marne and the Oise. Sixty dolmens prove that people were living there from around 2000 BC. Kings of France have always lived there and hunted in the forests. Evangelized from the third century AD, the area is rich in abbeys and churches. The aristocracy of seven centuries have built innumerable châteaux, with gardens, estates and forests. While the history of power and religion is reflected in these buildings, the villages and the farmhouses are in the main unspoiled, and show the history of the people and agriculture. The cows still eat buttercups and lilies of the valley, and the markets, as in medieval times, still sell the same butter and cheeses that have been made for hundreds of years.

In the forest of Rambouillet there is a château where French kings since François I have hunted deer, and the forest is still teeming with them. And so is the Château de Rambouillet itself. I have never seen so many disembodied stags' heads, witnesses to the pagan belief that there is some strange connection between killing stags and male fertility. Rambouillet is now the summer residence of the President of the Republic. In the gardens there is another of Marie-Antonette's dairies, close to our subject. In the state dining room, meals are served in the tradition of French *haute cuisine*, with cheese in its proper place; after the main course and before the dessert. The chef would eat his tongue rather than disregard this discipline.

There are two even greater forests in the Île de France, Fontainebleau and Compiègne. The Fontainebleau trees, awe-inspiring and taller than English trees, give evidence to the extraordinary fertility and depth of the soil.

It was in the village of Barbizon in the Fontainebleau district that Rousseau and Millet settled. Nearby, in the village of Milly-le-Forêt is a medieval timbered market place, which continues to house the farmers' wives every Saturday with their butter, cheese, flower and herb stalls. This is an area where herbs have always grown, and where Saint Blaise des Simples used them to cure the sick. Jean Cocteau was so impressed with the old chapel there that he decorated it with a mural of herbs, and was himself buried there in 1963. The *Route Ronde* passes near and gives an impression of modern planning, but it was actually constructed by Henri IV to make it easier for the court to follow his hunt. The château at Fontainebleau has known the influence of every French king since it was a hunting lodge in the 12th century. François I did the most, making it visually almost Italianate.

Melun, home of Brie de Melun, is a village on the edge of the forest of Fontainebleau. Like Paris, it covers an island and two banks of the Seine. The Clovis-Clotilde romance of early Frankish times started there, but we must stay with cheese; there *is* a cheese named Clovis. The Brie district is important for more than its special cheese, it is one of the most important agricultural regions in the Île de France, with rose nurseries and market gardens as well as cows. Corot lived there, in a white house at Crécy-en-Brie beside the river and near the Auberge du Pont Dom Gilles. Coulommiers, which was Julius Caesar's and Napoleon's favourite cheese, is made in the fruiteries outside that town, which have been selling farm produce since Roman times.

At Mormant is the château of Vaux-le-Vicomte, built by Nicolas Foucquet when he was Finance Minister to Louis XIV. It was a prototype for Versailles, and a work of art of some consequence. On being invited to the château where, as we have seen, music by Lully accompanied a dinner served from 6000 silver dishes, Louis realized that Treasury funds had been redirected, so put Foucquet in prison for embezzlement. He also admired his good taste, and gave the men responsible for Vaux-le-Vicomte the task of designing the enlargement of Versailles. These were Le Vau, architect, Le Brun, decorator, and Le Nôtre, garden designer.

Brie de Meaux, one of the best of the Bries, is made in a town resounding with history. Meux was originally a Roman town, Opidum Meldi, and the inhabitants are still called Meldois. The Cathedral of Saint-Etienne at Meux has a bishop's palace where Louis XVI and Marie Antoinette together with their children spent the night of 24 June 1789, on the eve of the Revolution – a royal-homely touch.

Pithiviers is noted not only for Pithiviers au Foin, that subtle cheese, but the fact that the Kings of France used to stay there at the castle of Ardoise, on their way between Fontainebleau to the Loire châteaux. Now an agricultural centre, it is full of gastronomic interest, which is a legacy from the ancient regal cuisines. *Pâtés d'alouettes* are sold, for example, as well as almond cakes and a gingerbread of some repute.

Dourdan, on the banks of the Orge, has celebrated its Foire Ventôse (the present name comes from the sixth month in the Republican calendar) on Passion Sunday since the Middle Ages, with a procession through the fields to bless the crops. The timbered marketplace sells most of the cheeses of the Île de France, as well as butter.

Chartres, 'Acropolis of France' as Rodin called it, looks just that when you drive across the plain of the Beauce. There are wells beneath the crypt, sacred to the prehistoric people who raised the standing stones. There are also remnants of a Roman temple to some goddess unknown. Her statue remained after the pillaging of the Dark Ages, so was kept in the basilica and renamed the Virgin. This particular statue survived the five major tragedies of the cathedral like the famous red chemise, but was finally destroyed at the Revolution.

Proust spent his boyhood at Illiers, 24 km (15 miles) away, and you can still buy his *Madeleines* in the village shop there. He never mentioned eating cheese.

Chevru, that fruity-flavoured, bloomy-rind cheese cured on beds of fern for a month, comes from the valley of Chevreuse (meaning goat country actually, but this is a cows' milk cheese). The town of Chevreuse is dominated by the Château Madeleine, where Racine once lived, as assistant controller.

Jean de la Fontaine was born in 1621 at the Château Thierry where his father was inspector of forests. At Compiègne is the palace, next in importance after Versailles and Fontainebleau. All the kings had visited and stayed at Compiègne because of the Forest and hunting, but Louis XV began a total reconstruction, designed by Jacques Gabriel and later, his son, Jacques-Ange Gabriel. His grand plan, begun in 1751, had hardly got started before it was stopped by the Seven Years War. Louis XVI then began again, and Marie-Antoinette personally supervised the design, furnishings and decoration of that part of the palace facing the park, replacing the old château of Charles V. Sadly, she never lived there; the events of 1789 were too near and too catastophic.

Some of the châteaux suffered more than others at the Revolution: Chantilly for example, was completely destroyed in 1793 (except for the Petit Château). Chantilly, visited by Racine, Boileau, Bossuet, La Bruyère, Molière, Madame de Sévigné and J. J. Rousseau, was also the scene of the three-day visit of Louis XIV when Vatel was chef to Condé.

The nomadic royal families and aristocrats who lived in the Île de France always moved to their châteaux in the Loire valley in the spring and then returned to Paris for the winter. They took many of their possessions with them, especially Persian rugs and Aubusson tapestries, so many of them are much travelled. In Angers, on the Loire, is the Musée des Tapisseries, the richest of its kind in the world. Housed in the tragically mutilated château of Angers, with its towers decapitated, the museum displays many classical tapestries showing the costumes of the people.

The most famous of them, woven in Paris by Nicolas Bataille, is the 'Tenture de L'Apocalypse', commissioned by Louis I of Anjou in 1373, which accompanied the dukes on their journeys to their other châteaux in Lorraine and Provence as late as the 15th century. The cathedral, which inherited it once, put it up for sale; it was almost lost at the Revolution; and over the years some of it has been cut away. It is still, however, one of the best in the world.

Festivals of the Île de France include nine concerned with horses, four regattas, three farm shows, and five musical concerts together with the international Organ Festival at Chartres on the third Sunday in September. There are two festivals to the lily of the valley, at Compiègne and Rambouillet; one for roses at Brie; and a large number concerned with individual châteaux, including *son et lumière*. There are two religious festivals – at Chartres and Saint-Augustin. All of the festivals include markets with stalls of food, wine and artifacts. It is on these market stalls that you will find all the cheeses of the region, all just as they should be.

Brie: general facts
First mentioned in the records of the Court of Champagne in 1217, Brie is known as the jewel of the Île de France and the *Roi de fromage*. First of the royal favourites, Brie was preferred by Philippe Auguste, Louis XII, Henri IV, Louis XV, Marie Leczinska and Louis XVI (just before the guillotine). At the Congress of Vienna of 1814-15, when statesmen from 30 nations were attempting to lay new diplomatic foundations after the Napoleonic period, Talleyrand organized a banquet to enliven the political monotony, with the object of deciding which was the best of the European cheeses. Brie was unanimously chosen from sixty famous cheeses, and crowned *'Roi de fromages'*. Until the mid-19th century, Brie was exclusively farmhouse made, with its famous red rind flora. The method of making it allows no deviations. Evening milk of the previous day is mixed with fresh morning milk. The curds are then spooned in six successive layers into a formerly wooden, but nowadays stainless-steel ring. The whey is remoulded with a perforated spoon and the cheese is turned regularly, clean reed mats being placed above and below. After six or seven days, the curds are sprinkled with powdered *Penicillium candidum*, and allowed to ripen for four weeks at a temperature of 11-12°C, and in a room with a current of air. Deviation of temperature is catastrophic, causing immediate changes in shape, colour and flavour. After ripening, the cheeses are packed in chipwood boxes, waxed paper-wrapped and given their label which guarantees quality and origin.

It is interesting that this soft-paste cheese, which is neither skimmed, heated, nor pressed, should have achieved the ultimate accolade of being regarded as perfection by controlled simplicity.

There are many varieties of Brie, varying in curing time, dimensions, weight, flavour, bouquet and taste.

'Brie was exclusively farmhouse made'.

Milk	Percentage fat	Weight	Type	Rind	Curing period	Form	Dimensions	Best season * = all year
BAGUETTE LAONNAISE/DEMI-BAGUETTE (half-disc)								
C	45%	460 g	soft	washed	3-4 months washing with brine	loaf	150 × 50 × 50 mm	2 3 4

Flavour: e and strong odour

Wine: Bouzy Rouge, Fitou

Milk	Percentage fat	Weight	Type	Rind	Curing period	Form	Dimensions	Best season * = all year
BOURSIN								
C	70%		triple cream					

Triple cream cheese made in commercial plants to patent, flavoured with garlic or herbs.

Milk	Percentage fat	Weight	Type	Rind	Curing period	Form	Dimensions	Best season * = all year
BRIE DE COULOMMIERS/BRIE PETIT MOULE/DEMI-COULOMMIERS (half-disc)								
C	45%	1.5 kg	soft	bloomy	1 month dry	disc	250 × 25 mm	1 3 4

Flavour: c^2 with bouquet

Wine: Pommard, Volnay, Krug even

Milk	Percentage fat	Weight	Type	Rind	Curing period	Form	Dimensions	Best season * = all year
BRIE DE MELUN AFFINÉ/BRIE DE NANGIS								
C	40-45%	1.5 kg	soft	natural	2½ months humid	disc	250 × 30 mm	2 3 4

The rind is red with white and golden spots

Flavour: d^2 with bouquet

Wine: The best available: Chassagne Montrachet, Côtes de Beaune-Villages

Milk	Percentage fat	Weight	Type	Rind	Curing period	Form	Dimensions	Best season * = all year
BRIE DE MELUN FRAIS								

This is fresh, unsalted, and with a subtle flavour.

Milk	Percentage fat	Weight	Type	Rind	Curing period	Form	Dimensions	Best season * = all year
BRIE DE MELUN BLEU								

This is the fresh cheese sprinkled with charcoal.

Milk	Percentage fat	Weight	Type	Rind	Curing period	Form	Dimensions	Best season * = all year
BRIE DE MONTEREAU/VILLE-SAINT-JACQUES								
C	45%	450 g	soft	natural	6 weeks humid	disc	180 × 25 mm	2 3 4

Flavour: c to d^2 with bouquet

Wine: Chassagne Montrachet, Savigny, Clos de Vougeot

OPPOSITE Reblochon waiting in the farm cellar. The cheeses will later be sent to market with thin circles of wood on each, and stacked in octagonal boxes (page 85).

Milk	Percentage fat	Weight	Type	Rind	Curing period	Form	Dimensions	Best season * = all year
CHEVRU								
C	50%	460 g	soft	bloomy	1 month on beds of fern	disc	160 × 40 mm	2 3 4

Flavour: c^2 with bouquet

Wine: Beaujolais Villages, Côtes de Beaune-Villages

Milk	Percentage fat	Weight	Type	Rind	Curing period	Form	Dimensions	Best season * = all year
CLOVIS								

Double cream cheese

Milk	Percentage fat	Weight	Type	Rind	Curing period	Form	Dimensions	Best season * = all year
COULOMMIERS/FOUGERU/DEMI-COULOMMIERS/BRIE A LA FOUGÈRE								
C	50%	460 g	soft	bloomy	1 month dry	disc	130 × 40 mm	2 3 4

Flavour: c^2 with bouquet and pleasant Brie smell

Wine: Côtes de Beaune or Champagne

Milk	Percentage fat	Weight	Type	Rind	Curing period	Form	Dimensions	Best season * = all year
DÉLICE DE SAINT-CYR/GRAND VATEL								
C	75%	460 g	soft triple cream	bloomy	3 weeks dry	disc	125 × 35 mm	*

Flavour: b to c and with more flavour than most triple creams

Wine: Non-vintage Champagne or Bouzy Rouge

Milk	Percentage fat	Weight	Type	Rind	Curing period	Form	Dimensions	Best season * = all year
EXPLORATEUR								
C	75%	300 g	triple cream	bloomy	3 weeks humid	cylinder	75 × 35 mm	*

Flavour: b

Wine: Blanc de Blanc or Coteaux Champenoise

Milk	Percentage fat	Weight	Type	Rind	Curing period	Form	Dimensions	Best season * = all year
FONTAINEBLEU								
C	60%		fresh					

Fresh, unsalted, mixed with whipped cream and sold in cardboard boxes with cheesecloth

Flavour: a

Wines not necessary

GOURMANDISE

Gourmandise, made by Establissements Siclet in the Île de France from pasteurized milk, is not cured, but processed. It is decorated with walnuts or flavoured with Kirsch, or smoked, or herb flavoured.

ÎLE DE FRANCE

Made by Establissements Henri Hutin from pasteurized milk, this is a soft bloomy-rind double cream cheese with a mild, slightly nutty flavour.

OPPOSITE Reblochon being made on a mountain farm in the Haute-Savoie (page 85).

Milk	Percentage fat	Weight	Type	Rind	Curing period	Form	Dimensions	Best season * = all year

LUCULLUS

Milk	Percentage fat	Weight	Type	Rind	Curing period	Form	Dimensions	Best season * = all year
C	75%	250 g	soft	bloomy	1 month humid	cylinder	75 × 50 mm	3 4

Flavour: b

Wine: Vins Mousseux or Bouzy Rouge

LUNE ROUSSE

Lune Rousse is a 250 g fresh cheese, flavoured with paprika sometimes, made in the Seine-et-Marne area.

MANICAMP

Milk	Percentage fat	Weight	Type	Rind	Curing period	Form	Dimensions	Best season * = all year
C	45%	250 g	soft	natural	2 months	cylinder	75 × 50 mm	2 3 4

Flavour: d and tang

Wine: Beaujolais

MOIX PRINCIÈRE

Moix Princière, a cows' milk cheese made in the Seine-et-Marne, weighs 200 g (7 oz), and has a flavour like Délice de Saint-Gyr.

PIPOCREM

Made by the Grièges cooperative dairy from pasteurized milk, this blue cheese is cured for 2 to 3 weeks depending on the size, which varies considerably. The taste is c and rather like Bleu de Bresse or Saingorlon.

POIVRIDOUX AU COGNAC

Poivridoux au Cognac, a Seine-et-Marne cheese, made from cows' milk with a flavour c^2.

RAMBOL

Rambol, made by Establissements Rambol in the Île de France, is a processed cheese similar to Gourmandise.

SAMOS 99

Samos 99, made in the Bel dairies from pasteurized milk, is a double-cream fresh cheese, sold in rectangular foil-wrapped pieces 100 × 60 × 25 mm seasoned with herbs, pepper or paprika.

SAINT-ANDRÉ

Saint-André is made by various Establissements Saint-Ollie from pasteurized milk; this is a mild, buttery cheese with a bloomy rind, cured dry for one week. Boxed, size 125 × 30 mm.

TARTARE

Tartare, made by Bongrain-Gérard from pasteurized milk, is a fresh cheese flavoured with herbs and garlic, in discs 60 × 25 mm, boxed and trademarked.

Milk	Percentage fat	Weight	Type	Rind	Curing period	Form	Dimensions	Best season * = all year
VACHEROL								

Vacherol is made from pasteurized milk. A pressed, uncooked, washed-rind cheese, the size is 175 × 30 mm and the taste b and lactic.

Milk	Percentage fat	Weight	Type	Rind	Curing period	Form	Dimensions	Best season * = all year
VOVES CENDRÉ								
C	40%	460 g	soft	ashes, natural	1 month humid 2-3 months ashes	disc	140 × 25 mm	2 3

Flavour: d

Wine: Coteaux de Touraine, Bouzy Rouge

2. PAYS DE LA LOIRE AND CENTRE

Most of the names of cheeses in the Loire valley can be seen on the map, because like the wines, they are also the names of villages.

The Loire valley has changes of aspect and soil, which are reflected in the different food, wine and cheese from one section to the next. So far as civilization is concerned, however, there is not another region in Europe where art has imprinted itself so deeply. It is more than the Royal châteaux, it is in the flint walls and tiled roofs of every village, and the capacity of the people of the Loire valley to develop this area, already so extraordinarily well provided with natural resources, into something unique.

Six hundred miles long, the river flows through an area with little geographical unity. There are three clearly differentiated zones: the Loire of the mountains, running through narrow gorges with the ruins of feudal châteaux; the Loire of the abbeys and the châteaux, which is the one that concerns us here; and the Loire of the sea, which has become a constantly expanding industrial zone. The diversity of the region accounts for the surprisingly wide range of the cheeses, which are made very often on small farms. Ten are made from goats' milk, including Sancerre, the generic name for three classical varieties of goats' cheese: Chavignol, Crézancy and Santranges. The remaining fourteen are all *small* cheeses made from cows' milk. These can be made from a small herd of ten or fewer – unlike the huge *fourmes* such as Cantal, which require enormous quantities of milk from large herds.

However badly the fish of the Loire have fared, and pollution used to turn many of them belly up, the climate and the soil of the valley in Anjou, the Touraine, Orléanais and Berry are so good that medlars, hydrangeas and magnolias all grow wild. It is therefore possible to cultivate almost everything. The garden of France, it grows trees, rose-bushes, orchards and all manner of flowers and vegetables, together with the vines which produce the Loire wines, and a remarkable collection of twenty-four cheeses. Of these, no fewer than eight are in the classical or special category, having a flavour and a bouquet that puts them in a class apart, like Grand Cru wines. These are Bondaroy au foin, also called Pithiviers au foin, Ligueil, Montoire, Pouligny-Saint-Pierre, Tournon-Saint-Pierre, Vendôme Bleu and Villebarou.

Probably the most famous of the wines are the Pinots, but many of the others – Sancerre, Reuilly, Sauvignon and the château wines of Amboise and Azay-le-Rideau – are superb. The cellars are often in former quarries, emptied of stone by the royal zeal in building châteaux, and now filled with barrels of wine, and also stored cheeses: a typically sensible piece of French opportunism. The quarries open into the white chalk of the hillsides so that the ox carts of the past and the Renault vans of today can go in and out easily. The same has been done near farms, where huge cool cellars are used for curing and storing cheese.

The quarries go deep into the hillside and open out into 'halls'. The wine brotherhoods, the

Sacavins of Angers, and the Chantepleures of Vouvray, who preserve the traditions of Loire valley viticulture, meet in these halls. Also the wine tasters on some occasions anxiously gather together to check the new vintage: aromatic Sancerre, Chinon with its taste of violets, Bourgueil with a suggestion of raspberries, Anjou and Saumur, whites and rosés.

The châteaux of the Loire are a species of architectural blossoming which could only have occurred in that complex of power, society, culture, civilization, climate and *joie de vivre* that existed in France, and in the Loire valley in particular. At the heart of any important building of that time was the master mason – men like Trinqueau, Sourdeau and Versigny, who made drawings and models, and set up a lodge together with a house to live in on the site. The lodge was at once a dormitory, refectory, workshop, school and guild headquarters. Young men who showed talent in drawing, mathematics or sculpture were sent off at the master mason's expense to see other buildings and sculptures which were rumoured to have new and interesting features. They came back with drawings, ideas and occasionally other young masons or sculptors. A living architecture in fact.

Châteaux began as fortified castles and centres of administration. Amboise, Loches and Angers, for example, were all constructed on hill tops, with military and seigneurial buildings, bailiff's court, provost marshal's building and barracks all grouped around it, until a fortified city evolved. These are sombre castles. In the 13th century, due to the influence of the Crusades, circular towers became general, with wooden galleries along the walls from which to pour the bubbling pitch and boiling oil. The 14th century saw these wooden tops replaced by stone machicolations. By the 15th century the towers had additional storeys, still for defence. In the 16th century all thoughts of defence disappeared and the windows were wide; there were also decorative effects such as lozenge-shaped panels in pink brick, blue slate roofs with gilded lead ornaments, and white stonework with smooth dressed surfaces showing a remarkable standard of mason's work. The châteaux also came down from the heights, to become completely romantic with river settings to mirror their beauty. Military features, some of which had been retained

for romantic or pseudo-regal conceits, disappeared completely in the 17th century and gardens were designed as an extension of the architectural plan. At Versailles they even encompassed large vegetable gardens and Marie-Antoinette's dairy.

The châteaux were not the only buildings to merit a good master mason, and one of the pleasures of visiting or living in Blois, Amboise, Tours or Chinon is to wander about in the narrow openings between old buildings and find courtyards with pillars, archways, galleries and arcadings; parts of buildings not recorded and now part-demolished, leaving fascinating pieces still standing and incorporated in new buildings.

The vivid life style in the châteaux existed in one form or another at all levels of society and was reflected and described in the work of Rabelais, Ronsard, Molière and Charles Pégny, all of whom lived in the region.

The court resided regularly in the Loire valley from the time of Charles VII (1422-61) to the last of the Valois, Henri III (1574-89). Chinon in fact was Charles VII's favourite but he left it for Loches, where Agnès Sorel was the intelligent beauty who helped him at all times. Rich in her own right, she owned a château of her own, Beauté at Nogent-sur-Marne. Agnès was generous, and gave a great deal to the Church, but when she died the canons decided that the presence of such a notorious sinner could not be permitted in the sacred precincts; her body must be buried elsewhere. Charles agreed, but insisted that her last gift to the church, which had been very large indeed, should accompany her, at which the scruples vanished.

Louis XI (1461-83) preferred Amboise and his queen, Charlotte of Savoy, lived there frequently. But her court was quiet compared with that of other queens. It was with the accession of Charles VIII (1483-98), 'King of Amboise', that the splendour really began. Amboise was begun by Louis XI, and it was here that Charles VIII was born. At 22 he decided that Amboise should be enlarged, and quickly. Work went on by torchlight and in winter, previously unthinkable, with fires to heat the stones as well as the masons. Later, after an expedition to Italy in 1495, he brought back not only furniture and works of art, but artists, craftsmen, tailors and dress designers. Pacello began the terrace garden at Amboise, and Il Boccador the architect worked on Blois, Chambord and the Hôtel de Ville in Paris. In Amboise at that time an inventory showed that there were two hundred Persian and Syrian carpets. There were Flemish and Parisian tapestries in every room, and much silverware. Charles was interested in many things. His armoury for example contained the nucleus of his personal collection – weapons of every kind, the battle axe of Clovis, sword and helmet of St Louis, the dagger of Charlemagne, swords of Charles VI and Louis XI and the armour of Joan of Arc. One wonders whether the antique dealers were not like those who found that amazingly untouched, perfect and expensive true crown of thorns for Louis IX, who gladly paid a million 'old' francs for it. He also collected rare birds and had a splendid aviary made for them. He bred huge mastiffs, and lions were bought to fight with them when available, as well as wild boars more or less every day.

For hundreds of years France achieved cultural standards that permeated the whole fabric of society, not least the sphere of wine and cuisine. While Charles VIII absorbed the influence of the Italian Renaissance by importing works of art and the artists themselves, the standards of viticulture and cuisine were already high due to the perennial French interest in their first essentials of living.

The frugal Louis XII, who lived mainly at Blois, was not spectacular but with François I (1515-47) the French court became a European centre for culture, art and elegance. Poets, artists, sculptors, scientists, architects and philosophers replaced the knights by whom Louis XII had been surrounded, and what is more important there was a radical change in the attitude to women in society. They were now to play a new and outstandingly brilliant role in the court. François bought expensive fabrics and the dress designers were encouraged to the peak of their imagination, so that the ladies of the court would be a decorative and emotive part of it. Anyone who was cynical about this had to be silent. The festivals at Amboise were magnificent and continued for weeks, comprising balls, dinners, tournaments, masquerades and, to compete with Rome, wild beast fights.

François I not only invited Leonardo da Vinci to Amboise, but gave him the manor house Le Clos Luce to live and work in for the last few years of his life. It was a house for which François had much

affection, as he had played there as a child, with his mother Louise de Savoie.

In François I's day 15,000 people lived around the king. When the court moved, it needed a minimum of 12,000 horses, and 5000 coaches and wagons. So much for transport – but think of the passions and psychological turmoils, the conflict of interests and ambitions, the subterfuge, conceits, prides and jealousies in this brilliant but dissolute small world! Meanwhile the Queen, Reine Claude, daughter of the previous King Louis XII, lived at Blois and died of anaemia at 25, having given the king seven children in eight years. It was François who added the most beautiful part to Blois: the staircase and what is called the François I Wing.

Blois was the habitual seat of the court for Henri II (1547-59) when he was not at the Louvre or Chenonceaux. When he was crowned, he gave the charismatic Chenonceaux to Diane de Poiter. There are a variety of stories by her contempories about how she retained her beauty; among them is her conviction that goats' milk and goats' milk cheeses have positive effects especially upon feminine beauty and stamina. Every morning she rose at six, drank fresh goats' milk, had a cold bath, and then rode in the forest for two hours. Also 'she had a wonderfully white skin and did not paint it'; and 'she took some sort of broth and various drugs every morning'. Diane was a widow twenty years older than François, and always wore black. The enlargements to Chenonceaux and her millionaire life style were paid for by a simple and inescapable tax levied by Henry. Every church bell had a levy of twenty livres, and it all found its way to Diane. Rabelais, who was alive and kicking at the time, wrote: 'The King has hung all the bells in the kingdom round the neck of his mare.'

Chenonceaux is called the 'château of six women' in the Loire valley. The first was Catherine Brigonnet, the wife of Bohier, the original owner. Working with a master mason she advised on how it should be organized with thoughts of service and function; thus rooms were placed on either side of a vestibule and a straight staircase was built instead of a spiral, being more practical. The second was Diane de Poitier whose château it really was, the other ladies mostly being interlopers of one sort or another. The third was Catherine de Medici, who had the two-storeyed gallery added to the bridge, and laid out a park. Louise de Lorraine was the fourth, called the 'White Queen' because she was in mourning for the death of King Henri III. Curtains, carpets, furniture and her bed were all black and crowns of thorns were painted in white on black ceilings. Madame Dupin, the fifth, was the wife of General Dupin who lived there in the 18th century. She had Jean-Jacques Rousseau as a tutor for her son. What is more important, she was much liked by the villagers, which saved the château from being ransacked and burned at the Revolution, like so many of the others. In 1864 Madame Pelouze bought Chenonceaux and restored it to the same condition as in the period of Diane, removing Catherine de Médicis' windows by walling them up and putting her caryatids in the park. She retained the sculptures which Catherine had brought from Florence. The château is now the property of the Menier family.

Six women spent much of their time and spirit polishing Chenonceaux to bring out the magic, but a much greater number were concerned with Fontevraud L'Abbaye, 20 km (21½ miles) west of Chinon. The Order of Fontevraud, founded by Robert d'Arbrissel, was different from all other abbeys. In five separate buildings there were monks, nuns, lepers and the sick, together with noblewomen who wished to withdraw from the world. Each convent was complete in itself. A woman who took the rank of abbess was the head of the community.

This order soon took on an aristocratic character. The abbesses, all members of noble families, procured gifts and protection for it. The Plantagenets poured wealth into it and made the abbey church their royal tomb. It became a refuge for old queen mothers, young repudiated queens, and daughters of royal birth who wished to take leave of the world. Louis XV sent his four youngest daughters to be educated there. Between 1115 and 1789 there were thirty-six abbesses including five who were of the house of Bourbon, the daughter of Henri IV, and Gabrielle de Rochechouart-Mortemart, sister of Madame de Montespan. The last-named made the abbey a cultural centre, as well as a spiritual refuge. The cellars of Fontevraud Abbey are a complex governed by an understanding of the needs of such a large community in storing all manner of foods, and in particular wine and cheese.

The kitchen of the abbey is extraordinary and original in design, with five wood-burning fireplaces and twenty chimneys designed to coordinate with them. Le Corbusier was fascinated by it, as well he might be, for here was a machine not so much for living in, but for feeding 5000 monks, nuns and lepers. It also gave ladies of high birth with positive ideas the opportunity to exercise to their hearts' content their authority and will to power.

The sense of form that produced high architectural qualities in the châteaux was manifest in a less exaggerated way in the farmhouses of the Loire, which are solid and dignified.

Milk	Percentage fat	Weight	Type	Rind	Curing period	Form	Dimensions	Best season * = all year

BONDAROY AU FOIN/PITHIVIERS AU FOIN

Milk	Percentage fat	Weight	Type	Rind	Curing period	Form	Dimensions	Best season
C	45%	300 g	soft	natural	5 weeks in hay-filled boxes	disc	125 × 25 mm	2 3

Flavour: d^2 with bouquet: an exceptional cheese

Wine: Touraine, Savennières, or Rosé d'Anjou

CHABRIS/VALENÇAY/LEVROUX/CHÂTEAUROUX

Milk	Percentage fat	Weight	Type	Rind	Curing period	Form	Dimensions	Best season
G	45%	250 g	soft	natural + charcoal dusting	5 weeks dry	truncated pyramid	75 × 75 × 75 mm	1 2 3

Flavour: c^2 and subtle, nutty

Also made in Poitou and Charentes.

Wine: Wines of Berry and Tours

CHAVIGNOL-SANCERRE

Milk	Percentage fat	Weight	Type	Rind	Curing period	Form	Dimensions	Best season
G	45%	75-100 g	soft	natural and blue	2 weeks dry	flattened ball	50 × 25 mm	2 3

Flavour: b

Wine: Sauvignon de Sancerre, Pinot Blanc and Pinot Gris

Sancerre is the generic name of 3 varieties: Chavignol, Crézancy, Santranges

CRÉZANCY-SANCERRE

Milk	Percentage fat	Weight	Type	Rind	Curing period	Form	Dimensions	Best season
G	45%	125 g	soft	natural and blue	2-3 weeks dry	flattened ball	65 × 35 mm	1 2 3

Flavour: b to c

Wine: Sauvignon and Pinot Gris

CROTTIN DE CHAVIGNOL

Crottin means horse droppings, which are brown, and the blue rind of goats' cheeses turns brown with age.
(Not marketed: obtainable from farmers)

Milk	Percentage fat	Weight	Type	Rind	Curing period	Form	Dimensions	Best season
G	45%	56 g	soft	natural	2-3 months dry	small ball		4

Flavour: anything from e to g and sharp with it

Calls to mind the 19th-century habit of chewing hard tobacco.

Drink: Immaterial – rum, perhaps

Milk	Percentage fat	Weight	Type	Rind	Curing period	Form	Dimensions	Best season * = all year

ENTRAMMES

Made in the monastery that originally produced Port-Salut. The name was sold to a dairy firm; the monastery then made Entrammes, a variant of Port-Salut.

Milk	Percentage fat	Weight	Type	Rind	Curing period	Form	Dimensions	Best season
C	40%	400 g	pressed uncooked	washed	5 weeks humid	disc	100 × 35 mm	*

Flavour: c

Wine: Muscadet or Quincy

FRINAULT

Milk	Percentage fat	Weight	Type	Rind	Curing period	Form	Dimensions	Best season
C	50%	150 g	soft	natural	3 weeks dry	disc	90 × 15 mm	2 3

Flavour: d^2 with bouquet

Wine: St Nicholas de Bourgueil, Savennières, Chenin Blanc

FRINAULT CENDRÉ

Milk	Percentage fat	Weight	Type	Rind	Curing period	Form	Dimensions	Best season
C	50%	150 g	soft	natural and ash	4 weeks in ash	disc	90 × 15 mm	2 3

Flavour: d

Wine: Chinon, Bourgueil

GIEN

Milk	Percentage fat	Weight	Type	Rind	Curing period	Form	Dimensions	Best season
G, C or CG	40-50%	200 g	soft	natural	3 weeks in ash or leaves	cylinder or cone	75 × 50 mm	1 2 3

Flavour: d or c depending on milk

Wine: Vins Gris

GRAÇAY

Milk	Percentage fat	Weight	Type	Rind	Curing period	Form	Dimensions	Best season
G	45%	450 g	soft	natural and powdered charcoal	6 weeks dry	truncated cone	100 × 60 mm	1 2 3

Flavour: c

Wine: Sauvignon, Quincy

LAVAL/TRAPPISTE DE LAVAL

Milk	Percentage fat	Weight	Type	Rind	Curing period	Form	Dimensions	Best season
C	42%	2 kg	pressed uncooked	washed	2 months humid	disc	250 × 40 mm	1 2 3

Flavour: c with a washed-rind tang

Wine: Muscadet, Beaujolais

Milk	Percentage fat	Weight	Type	Rind	Curing period	Form	Dimensions	Best season * = all year

LIGUEIL/SAINT-MAURE (also made in Poitou)/LOCHE/VERNEUIL

Milk	Percentage fat	Weight	Type	Rind	Curing period	Form	Dimensions	Best season * = all year
G	45%	300 g	soft	natural blue; pink dots	1 month dry	cylinder	150 × 35 mm	1 2 3

Flavour: c^2 with bouquet, deserving a good white wine

Wine: Clos de Papillon and Château de Chamboureau

MONTOIRE/TRÔO/VILLIERS-SUR-LOIR

Milk	Percentage fat	Weight	Type	Rind	Curing period	Form	Dimensions	Best season * = all year
G	45%	100 g	soft	natural blue rind; yellow dots	3 weeks dry	cone	75 × 50 mm	1 2 3

Flavour: x^2 with bouquet and faint goat smell

Wine: Rosé d'Anjou

OLIVET/BLEU/CHECY

Milk	Percentage fat	Weight	Type	Rind	Curing period	Form	Dimensions	Best season * = all year
C	45%	300 g	soft	natural with blue bloom	1 month in chalk caves	disc in plane tree leaves	125 × 25 mm	1 2 3

Flavour: c^2 with fruity taste

Wine: Saumur or Sancerre

OLIVET CENDRÉ

Milk	Percentage fat	Weight	Type	Rind	Curing period	Form	Dimensions	Best season * = all year
C	45%	300 g	soft	natural ash-coated	3 months dry in wood ash	disc	125 × 25 mm	2 3 4

Flavour: e deep savoury taste

Wine: Bourgueil and Cabernet d'Anjou

Balzac's favourite cheese, with nuts and wine.

PANNES CENDRÉ

Milk	Percentage fat	Weight	Type	Rind	Curing period	Form	Dimensions	Best season * = all year
C skimmed	25%	300 g	soft	natural with ash	3 months in wood ash	disc	125 d 25 mm	2 3

Flavour: f and strong in every way

Wine: St Joseph or Beaujolais Villages

PATAY

Milk	Percentage fat	Weight	Type	Rind	Curing period	Form	Dimensions	Best season * = all year
C	45%	460 g	soft	natural with ash	6 weeks in ash	disc	250 × 25 mm	2 3 4

Flavour: e

Wine: Vins Gris of Orléanais

41

Milk	Percentage fat	Weight	Type	Rind	Curing period	Form	Dimensions	Best season * = all year
PENNES								
C	20-30%	250 g	soft	natural	1 month humid	disc	125 × 30 mm	2 3

Flavour: c^2 savoury
Wine: Dry white wines of the Loire

Milk	Percentage fat	Weight	Type	Rind	Curing period	Form	Dimensions	Best season * = all year
POULIGNY-ST-PIERRE								
G	45%	225 g	soft	natural blue	5 weeks dry	pyramid	75 × 75 × 90 mm	1 2 3

Flavour: c^2 with bouquet and strong taste
Wine: Sancerre Rouge

Milk	Percentage fat	Weight	Type	Rind	Curing period	Form	Dimensions	Best season * = all year
ST-BENOIST								
C partly skimmed	40%	400 g	soft	natural	1 month	disc	125 × 25 mm	1 2 3

Flavour: c wholesome
Wine: Vins Gris

Milk	Percentage fat	Weight	Type	Rind	Curing period	Form	Dimensions	Best season * = all year
SANTRANGES-SANCERRE								
G	45%	175 g	soft	natural and blue	4 weeks dry	flattened ball	60 × 35 mm	1 2 3

Flavour: c^2 with tang
Wine: Sauvignon and Pinot Gris
Similar but not identical to Chavignol-Sancerre; this cheese is cured longer.

Milk	Percentage fat	Weight	Type	Rind	Curing period	Form	Dimensions	Best season * = all year
SELLES-SUR-CHER/ROMORANTIN								
G	45%	150 g	soft	natural + powdered charcoal	3 weeks dry	truncated cone	75 × 75 mm	1 2 3

Flavour: c
Wine: Chinon Rouge or Vins Gris

Milk	Percentage fat	Weight	Type	Rind	Curing period	Form	Dimensions	Best season * = all year
TOURNON-SAINT-PIERRE								
G	45%	150-300 g	soft	natural and blue	3 weeks dry	truncated cone	100 × 100 × 90 mm	1 2 3

Flavour: c with slight bouquet
Wine: Château wines of Amboise and Azay-le-Rideau

Milk	Percentage fat	Weight	Type	Rind	Curing period	Form	Dimensions	Best season * = all year
VENDÔME BLEU								
C	50%	50 g	soft	natural	1 month humid	disc	110 × 40 mm	2 3

Flavour: c² with bouquet

Wine: Château Amboise or Savennières or Rosé d'Anjou

Milk	Percentage fat	Weight	Type	Rind	Curing period	Form	Dimensions	Best season * = all year
VENDÔME CENDRÉ								
C	50%	225 g	soft	natural and ashes	3 months in ashes	disc	110 × 40 mm	2 3 4

Flavour: d

Wine: Chinon Rouge

Milk	Percentage fat	Weight	Type	Rind	Curing period	Form	Dimensions	Best season * = all year
VILLEBAROU								
C	45%	450 g	soft	natural bluish	3 weeks dry	disc + plane tree leaves	175 × 25 mm	2 3

Flavour: c² with bouquet

Wine: Château Azay-le-Rideau or Vin Gris

3. BURGUNDY

Although there are thirty-nine Burgundy cheeses, few if any of them are so outstanding as the famous wines. Montrachet and Vézelay have resounding names but, although very good indeed, they do not quite live up to the wine, or the churches. Many of the goats' cheeses are very agreeable and even subtle and mysterious, but none are of a classical stature, like Roquefort, Brie or Camembert. Epoisses is outstanding. Strong, uncompromising, and resonant, it has a splendid bouquet. The Burgundians, aware of this, eat it throughout the year, macerating it when it ages with Burgundy *marc*. Most of the goats' cheeses can be bought in the marketplaces as well as shops all over the province, and also at the farms where they are made. Farmers' wives are usually quite willing to show how they make their cheeses. To walk through the wine villages tasting is exciting, but to visit the farms and the marketplaces as well, eating cheeses and the *charcuterie* is even more satisfying. Burgundy is a whole world in itself, and needs as much time as you can get for it. In going there to enjoy wine and cheese you also need to look at the Romanesque churches, which have some of the most important sculpture in all France. Gislebertus, for example, at Autun is of world stature.

Burgundy, not a natural region like the Alps or the Paris basin, is composed of several areas, three of which happen to have the right geological base for vineyards. The fourth is the Morvan, a wild area where nothing can grow except the people, who have to be strong simply to survive. Weak babies of rich Parisians were taken to the Morvan in the 19th century, where wet nurses put some life into them.

Burgundy, home of some of the best wines in the world, has a history linked with kings of France. It also contains abbeys like Cluny which were the spirit, head and heart of European civilization in the Middle Ages. Crossroads of routes and racial migrations, it has encountered the most diverse influences. In 60 BC Vercingetorix was there, gathering together all the tribes of Gaul at Bibracte on the summit of Mont Beuvrey, with the forlorn hope of stopping Julius Caesar. From the first to third centuries AD, Autun (the name derives from

Augustodonum) became the Roman capital of north-eastern Gaul. Autun is noted today for its Romanesque church, serene atmosphere, and the fabulous sculptures of Gislebertus, on the tympanum of the Cathedral of Saint-Lazare, produced between 1130 and 1135. This church was built to receive the relics of Saint Lazarus, given by Gérard de Rousillon, and for medieval pilgrims to pray in when travelling in their thousands to the tomb of Santiago de Compostela and other holy places. In Roman times, however, Autun was larger, with a theatre to seat 15,000, and two fortified gateways, as it was on the Roman road from Boulogne to Lyon. Autun suffered fearful invasions and pillages when the Romans left so that remarkably little, vestiges only, of their civilization can now be seen. There is a weird and dispiriting wind which blows in Burgundy named the Autun after the disasters that happened there at the time of the Goths and the Visigoths. The Burgundians arrived from the Baltic and settled in the plain of the Saône, in the 5th century AD. Historians say that the Burgundians were more advanced than many of the other barbarians – Vandals, Goths, Visigoths and Huns; consequently the Burgundians never figure in the catalogue of the more destructive invaders. In the 8th century the Burgundians became part of the Frankish empire of Charlemagne.

The first duchy of Burgundy (Bourgogne) was created in 1031. The summit of its power and magnificence occurred in the 14th and 15th centuries. The Valois king of France, Jean le Bon, gave the duchy to his fourth son, Philippe le Hardi, who married Margaret (Marguerite) of Flanders, the richest heiress of Europe in 1369, which extended the duchy as far as Holland, through Picardy, Luxembourg and Flanders. Franche-Comté was already part of the duchy, and when Philippe's brother Charles became king, one family was ruling most of France.

The Grand Dukes of the West, as they were called, had one of the most brilliant courts in Europe during the 14th and 15th centuries, patronizing the arts, inviting master builders, artists, sculptors, troubadours and musicians, mainly from Italy. Dijon, home of these Grand Dukes, still retains a souvenir of this magnificence in the Musée des Beaux Arts, which has been formed within the ducal palace. The lowest storey includes a vaulted kitchen with six chimneys for roasting six whole beasts simultaneously, actually a common everyday occurrence in palaces of that time. Records of the feasts show that they were spectacular to the point of surrealism. Percheron horses brought in parade floats bearing elephants, and dwarfs, weeping martyrs and naked ladies, musicians and troubadours, dancers and acrobats. The meals themselves were brought in carriages. We can get some idea of the food from one of the first books on cuisine called *La Viander* (1375), written by Guillaume Tirel, which shows that they relied heavily on ginger, cinnamon, cloves and nutmeg. Sauces were made with bread as a base and there was more concern with novel ideas than cooking. Cheese gets no mention at all in this cook book (see Chapter I).

It is impossible to over-estimate the importance of the monastic movement in the development of medieval Europe in almost all fields. France was always in the avant-garde of this movement, and Burgundy was at the heart of it: Saint Bernard of Clairvaux was born near Dijon at the Château de Fontaine; and Cluny, centre of the Benedictine order, was also in Burgundy. The wines of Burgundy were created by the monasteries, who planted the vines and spent centuries of research in the work of viticulture, concerning themselves with every detail. They also made cheeses. The houses of the present wine growers are simple, stone-built and beautiful. Architecturally they are very much better than the farms. Wine growers consider themselves in a class apart from sheep, cow and corn farmers, an élite with a more important function altogether, and their houses emphasize the fact. There is a wine museum at Beaune, and the whole town is full of interest, having been the capital of Burgundy until the 14th century. The route to Beaune, on D981 starting at Mâcon, passes Pouilly-Fuissé, Cluny, Montagny, Gevry, Mercurey, Rully, Santenay, Saint-Aubin, Meursault, Volnay, Pommard, Beaune, and goes on through Alox-Corton, Nuits-Saint-Georges, Vosne-Romanée, Vougeot, Chambolle-Musigny and Gevry-Chambertin – this is La Côte, the region of the Grands Crus. The same road going south passes through similarly memorable names to Beaujolais. The places known for their cheeses, Autun, Soumaintrain, Rouy, Vézelay and others, are nowhere near so resounding, but the cheeses have variety and make perfect partners for the wines.

The thirty-nine cheeses of Burgundy are all fairly small, none of them weighing more than a kilogram, and most are the size of the palm of your hand. The goats' cheeses are even smaller. Burgundy is wine country and the farms small. Goats can exist almost anywhere, however, and they produce milk that makes cheeses much appreciated by grape harvesters, such as the Chevrotins de Conne, Moulins, Souvigny and Bourbonnais, which are all one and the same cheese, also called simply Conne. Goats' milk cheeses have blue rinds, but as they age the rind turns brown. Boutons-de-Culotte are small pieces of Mâconnais cheese the size of trouser buttons which are kept in the drawers of kitchen dressers, and become very dark brown. The taste has quite an edge, but seems to soothe the farmers' wives who chew it through their various daily crises. Claquebitou is a fresh goats' milk cheese, flavoured with parsley and garlic, more piquant than most fresh cheeses. Epoisses, the favourite of Porthos of the Three Musketeers, is the apotheosis of Burgundy: rich, resonant, with a cheese bouquet comparable with one of the Grand Cru Burgundies and fit to be eaten with most of them.

Milk	Percentage fat	Weight	Type	Rind	Curing period	Form	Dimensions	Best season * = all year
AUTUN/CHAROLAIS								
G or CG	40-45%	G 100 g CG 200 g	soft	natural	2-3 weeks dry	cylinder	50 × 75 mm	2 3
Flavour: d								
Wine: White Mâcon or Aligotés of Burgundy								
BOULETTE DE LA PIERRE-QUI-VIRE/BOULETTE DE PRÉMONT (similar)								
C	45%	150 g	fresh		drained flavoured with herbs	ball	75 mm	
Flavour: c								
Wine: Mâcon-Villages								
BOUTONS-DE-CULOTTE/CHEVRETON DE MÂCON/MÂCONNAIS/CABRION DE MÂCON								
G or CG	40-45%	50 g	soft	natural	2 weeks dry	cone	50 × 40 mm	1 2 3
Flavour: f to g								
Wine: Mâcon Rouge								

Boutons-de-Culotte are little pieces of this cheese (trouser buttons) which are stored in cupboards for winter use and become hard and dark brown. Small drawers on kitchen dressers are often full of them; eaten at odd moments by the farmer's wife when irritated. Later, when harder still, they are grated into the *fromage fort*.

Milk	Percentage fat	Weight	Type	Rind	Curing period	Form	Dimensions	Best season * = all year
CABRION/CHEVRETON								
G or CG	45%		soft	natural				
Flavour: c								
Wine: Fruity red wines of the region								

Milk	Percentage fat	Weight	Type	Rind	Curing period	Form	Dimensions	Best season * = all year
CENDRÉ D'AISY								
C	45%	350 g	soft	washed in *marc*	2 months in *marc*, 1 month in ashes	disc or cone	100 × 60 mm	1 3 4

Flavour: e with an aroma rather than a bouquet and quite a tang

Wine: Good strong reds, like Aloxe-Corton or Chambertin

Milk	Percentage fat	Weight	Type	Rind	Curing period	Form	Dimensions	Best season * = all year
CHAMBERTAIN								
C		250 g			6 weeks to 2 months			

Flavour: d

Milk	Percentage fat	Weight	Type	Rind	Curing period	Form	Dimensions	Best season * = all year
CHEVROTIN DU BOURBONNAIS/CHEVROTIN DE CONNE/CHEVROTIN DE MOULINS/CHEVROTIN DE SOUVIGNY/CONNE								
G	45%	100 g	soft	natural	1-2 weeks	truncated cone	70 × 60 mm	2 3

Flavour: d

Wine: Chablis. Most Burgundies go well with Conne

Milk	Percentage fat	Weight	Type	Rind	Curing period	Form	Dimensions	Best season * = all year
CÎTEAUX/TRAPPISTE DE CÎTEAUX								
C	45%	1 kg	pressed uncooked	washed	2 months	disc	175 × 40 mm	2 3

Flavour: c

Wine: Montagny and St-Aubin

Milk	Percentage fat	Weight	Type	Rind	Curing period	Form	Dimensions	Best season * = all year
CLAQUEBITOU								
G	45%		fresh					

Flavoured with parsley and garlic.

Flavour: b to c, slightly sharper than most fresh cheeses, reflected in the onomatopaeic name

Wine: None necessary

Milk	Percentage fat	Weight	Type	Rind	Curing period	Form	Dimensions	Best season * = all year
COULANDON/CHAUCETTER								
C	45%	450 g	soft	bloomy	1 month dry	disc	10 × 20 mm	1 3 4

Flavour: c and rich

Wine: Beaujolais-Villages

Milk	Percentage fat	Weight	Type	Rind	Curing period	Form	Dimensions	Best season * = all year
COULANDON/CHAUCETTER								

Flavour: b

A partly skimmed cows' milk fresh cheese

Milk	Percentage fat	Weight	Type	Rind	Curing period	Form	Dimensions	Best season * = all year
DORNECY								
G or GC	45%	250 g	soft	natural	3-4 weeks dry	truncated cone	75 × 60 mm	2 3

Flavour: c^2 with bouquet

Wine: Sancerre

Milk	Percentage fat	Weight	Type	Rind	Curing period	Form	Dimensions	Best season * = all year
DUCS								
C	50%	225 g	soft	bloomy	2 weeks humid	cylinder	75 × 50 mm	*

Flavour: c

Wine: Francy Rosé

Milk		Weight	Type	Rind	Curing period	Form	Dimensions	Best season
EPOISSES								
C	45%	250 g	soft	washed	3 months humid + 1 month washing in *marc*	disc	100 ×	2 3 4

Flavour: e^2, bouquet plus strong smell like a young *fromage fort*

Wine: Nuits-St-Georges

Milk		Weight	Type	Rind	Curing period	Form	Dimensions	Best season
LES LAUMES								
C	45%	1 kg	soft	washed	3 months humid + washing with coffee wastes and wine	brick	125 × 75 × 75 mm	3 4

Flavour: e^2 spicy

Wine: Côte de Beaune-Villages

Milk		Weight	Type	Rind	Curing period	Form	Dimensions	Best season
LORMES								
G or CG	45%	250 g	soft	natural	3-4 weeks dry	truncated cone	75 × 50 mm	1 2 3

Flavour: d^2 with bouquet, subtle and goaty

Wine: Pouilly-Fumé, Rosé d'Anjou

Milk		Weight	Type	Rind	Curing period	Form	Dimensions	Best season
MONTRACHET								
G	45%	100 g	soft	thin blue	1 week draining + 1 week dry cellar	cylinder wrapped in chestnut or grape leaves	100 ×	1 2 3

Flavour: c^2 with bouquet and very subtle

Wine: Montrachet

Milk	Percentage fat	Weight	Type	Rind	Curing period	Form	Dimensions	Best season * = all year
PETIT BESSAY								
C	40-45%	200 g	soft	natural	3-4 weeks humid	disc	90 × 25 mm	2 3

Flavour: d² with bouquet

Wine: Touraine, Amboise Rosé, Savigny-les-Beaunes

Milk	Percentage fat	Weight	Type	Rind	Curing period	Form	Dimensions	Best season * = all year
PIERRE-QUI-VIRE								
C	45%	200 g	soft	washed	2 months humid with washings	disc	100 × 25 mm	2 3

Flavour: d and penetrating smell

Wine: Beaujolais

Milk	Percentage fat	Weight	Type	Rind	Curing period	Form	Dimensions	Best season * = all year
POURLY								
G	45%	300 g	soft	natural	1 month dry	cylinder	100 × 60 mm	1 2 3

Flavour: c

Wine: Chablis or Aligotés

Milk	Percentage fat	Weight	Type	Rind	Curing period	Form	Dimensions	Best season * = all year
ROUY								
C	45%	250 g	soft	washed	1 month humid	square	100 × 100 × 25 mm boxed	*

Flavour: d sharp

Wine: Beaujolais

Milk	Percentage fat	Weight	Type	Rind	Curing period	Form	Dimensions	Best season * = all year
ST-FLORENTIN								
C	45%	450 g	soft	washed	2 months washing with salt	disc	140 × 25 mm	2 3 4

Flavour: d, with washed rind tang

Wine: Mâcon-Villages

Milk	Percentage fat	Weight	Type	Rind	Curing period	Form	Dimensions	Best season * = all year
ST-MARIE (rare)								
C	45%	450 g	fresh	no rind	none	cone	125 × 75 mm	1 2

Flavour: a and lactic

Wine: None necessary

OPPOSITE Goats being milked, Burgundy.

Milk	Percentage fat	Weight	Type	Rind	Curing period	Form	Dimensions	Best season * = all year
SOUMAINTRAIN								
C	45%	300 g	soft	washed	6 weeks washing with brine	disc	125 × 25 mm	1 2 3

Flavour: e with washed-rind tang and smell

Wine: Blagny, Mâcon

SUPRÈME DES DUCS

Suprème des Ducs is made in Burgundy by Establissements Renard from pasteurized milk. A boxed, oval, bloomy rind cheese, cured dry for 2 weeks. The taste is very mild.

Milk	Percentage fat	Weight	Type	Rind	Curing period	Form	Dimensions	Best season * = all year
VERMENTON								
G	45%	50 g	soft	natural blue	2 weeks dry	cone	50 × 50 mm	1 2 3

Flavour: c and subtle

Wine: Chablis or rosés

Milk	Percentage fat	Weight	Type	Rind	Curing period	Form	Dimensions	Best season * = all year
VÉZELAY								
G	45%	100 g	soft	thin blue	2 weeks dry	cylinder leaf-wrapped	100 × 50 mm	1 2 3

Flavour: c^2 with bouquet

Wine: Chassagne Montrachet, Volnay

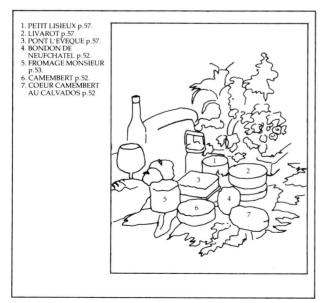

1. PETIT LISIEUX p.57.
2. LIVAROT p.57.
3. PONT L'EVEQUE p.57.
4. BONDON DE NEUFCHATEL p.52.
5. FROMAGE MONSIEUR p.53.
6. CAMEMBERT p.52.
7. COEUR CAMEMBERT AU CALVADOS p.52

OPPOSITE A selection of Normandy cheeses.

4. NORMANDY

The plain that stretches across much of Normandy, cleft by the Seine, is one vast farm. The geological structure of chalk is covered by a deposit of loamy soil reputed to be hundreds of feet thick. This loess set in well-drained chalk makes superb growing land, so here is the dairy for a quarter of France's needs. To the west of the Seine are Jurassic rocks and Armorican granite which make for a rolling landscape with sharp valleys. Everywhere there are farms, varying considerably between the regions of Bray, Caux, Auge and the Cotentin peninsula.

Cream is the dominant feature in Normandy cuisine, so the cow is queen. Six million cows produce the milk which becomes cream, butter and cheese and they have been scientifically researched and artificially inseminated under the auspices of a milk control board since 1965. The milk volume and fat content of each and every cow is measured against its food ration – namely, the acreage of grazing related to the type of grass, and the content of the cattle cake eaten in winter. The result is a technological success, in contrast to the calm acceptance of Mother Nature and her largesse in the alpine pastures of the Jura and the Haute-Savoie. Either way, a good cow gives 30 litres (6.6 UK, 8 US gallons) of milk a day.

The Normandy breed of cow, named after the province, is unmistakable. The hides of white, cream and dark brown are noticeable enough, but there are also 'spectacles' of brown, like wild mascara, around the eyes.

The various regions have different characteristics and produce. The Bray region is the larder of Paris. It sends 180 million litres (40 million gallons) of milk and nearly 1.15 million litres (a quarter million gallons) of cream a year to the capital, as well as fresh cheese. Gournay en Bray produces the major part of the fresh cheese consumed in France, the Gervais factory alone turning 40,000 gallons of milk a day into their product. Bondard, Bondon de Neufchâtel, Carré and Cœur de Bray, Brillat-Savarin, Fin-de-Siècle, Gournay and Magnum are also all made in the Bray region.

The Auge region is the home of Camembert, Livarot, Petit Lisieux, Pont l'Evêque, Mignot and Pâvé d'Auge. Cider and Calvados are also made there. Cider is pure apple juice fermented; Calvados is an apple brandy matured for up to fifteen years and it plays a dominant role in the regional cuisine.

The farmsteads of the Auge region, some of them old manor houses, are set around with orchards, apple stores, cider presses, cattle stalls, dairies and cheese cellars; but most of the cheese is now sent to *affineurs* (called *cavistes* in Normandy) to complete.

The Neubourg plain, and Roumois, where the cheese Monsieur Fromage originated, has not yet been visited by tourists and has a quiet beauty together with a number of small castles. Tilly castle (1500), Harcourt (13th/14th century) with an arboretum, and Champ de Bataille castle, which has a deer park, are here.

The southern part of the Cotentin peninsula contains a plain, watered by three small rivers, which resembles an enormous park where cows graze and horses are bred. The Val de Saire, in fact, has such a mild climate that cows are left out of doors for nine months of the year. Carentan is the largest centre of the dairy industry in the peninsula, and there is a butter market near the Church of Notre Dâme with its unusual octagonal belfry.

The granite north-western corner of the Cotentin peninsula is different altogether and a foretaste of Brittany.

A great deal can be learned about Normandy, its history, customs, and regional cooking by attending the numerous fairs and festivals held throughout the year. These have been a part of the life of the region since the 7th century. The church always encouraged the minstrels and troubadours. The robust mixture at today's fairs of auctions, conjurers, cheese stalls and shooting galleries is enlivened by discos and concertinas.

Sainte-Croix or Holy Cross fair (9-12 September) at Lessay centres around cattle, dairy produce and craftwork such as cowbells and harness.

The Alençon festival (end of September and early October) is a serious occasion for farmers buying and selling stock, with deep thought, anxiety, and heavy eating.

At Caudebec-en-Caux there is a cider festival (last Sunday in September) which includes folk dancing, processions with traditional costumes, and a lot of cider and Calvados to accompany the regional cooking and cheeses.

Other festivals include the Blessing of the Ships at Honfleur, (Whit Sunday and Monday) and the Joan of Arc festival at Rouen (last Sunday in May). There are horse shows at Cabourg Harcourt, and a Grand Prix at Deauville for thoroughbreds (last Sunday in August). The festival of the Archangel Gabriel in the cathedral at Mont-Saint-Michel (last Sunday in September) includes mass and concerts of 16th-century music. There are three festivals at Lisieux, in July, August and September, all concerned with Saint Theresa whose shrine and relics reside there. Theresa was the saint who said: 'It is in the kitchen, among the pots and pans, that the Lord walks.' Not surprisingly, Saint Theresa is a favourite beyond her region, for this quotation brings smiling approval all the way to Provence.

Normandy cuisine is rich. Auge valley chicken, Avranchin pudding, Dieppe sole, Rouen duck, Vire chitterlings, Duclair duckling, Courseulles oysters, lobsters from Barfleur and La Hague, mussels from Villerville and Isigny, and Caen *chiques* (boiled sweets).

Cheeses, an integral part of the meal, are of such variety that they can be chosen to follow steak or duck, fish, lobster or chicken. There is a pause, which is called the Trou Normand, after the main course and before the cheese, for a long drink of Calvados.

The only sadness is that 'Angelot', William the Conqueror's favourite, and also mentioned in the Roman de la Rose, is no longer available. Some say it is Pont l'Eveque, others insist that it is Livarot.

There have been links between England and Normandy for hundreds of years, not least during the Allied invasion of 1944, but the Norman Conquest linked England to the cultural developments of France and the Mediterranean countries. England would now be a very different country if Harold had lost that battle against his Norwegian namesake at Stamford Bridge, and we had been further influenced by the Scandinavians, instead of the French-speaking Normans. William the Conqueror also brought a quality of leadership which England needed at that time to avoid imminent chaos. There are many in England who feel that the Conqueror was a tyrant, and others who say that in the long run the Norman iron fist killed off much of the Anglo-Saxon poetry; that we may well have had more Shakespeares and John Donnes without him. This may be true, but he also brought Lanfranc with him, one of the best minds of Europe. Between them, they not only re-organized England but made it aware of the much more developed civilization of mainland Europe, and the ways and means of becoming a part of it. Duke William had trained hard to become the Conqueror. First he manhandled the rebellious knights of the Cotentin peninsula into submission. In doing so, he was so heavy-handed that the sons of Tancrède de Hauteville, William, Guiscard and Roger, left Brittany altogether and took the pathway to the holy places. On the way, they conquered Sicily and set up a Norman kingdom there. Complete with Romanesque castles and churches, it lasted until 1265.

After dealing with Tancrède and his sons, Duke William laid siege to the castle of Brionne, held by the Duke of Burgundy. Sieges can be monotonous, and William wandered off one day to Le Bec-Hellouin, where Count Gilbert of Brionne (later called Herlvin) had founded a Benedictine monastery with study as one of its main rules. There, William met Lanfranc, an Italian whose intellectual brilliance had brought him to pre-eminence in many centres. An immediate bond sprang up between them, and Lanfranc became the Duke's friend, and *éminence grise*. With such a spiritual and political adviser, William shaped a fair amount of destiny.

After the siege of Brionne, William began to consider matrimony. He had seen a painting of Matilda, daughter of Baldwin, Count of Flanders, and sent her an offer of marriage. Her reply that she would rather take the veil than marry a bastard had immediate results. It was true that William had been born out of wedlock. His mother, the beautiful Arlette, was a woman of real quality whose second son, by a different father, became Odo of Bayeux. William's father, Duke Robert of Normandy, variously called the 'Magnificent' and the 'Devil', provided the violent side, together with their lineage back to Rollo the Viking. The Chronicler of Tours is explicit about Duke William's actions. Mounting his Percheron, he went to Flanders, rode up the castle steps, dragged Matilda round the great hall by her plaits, and kicked her violently. Machismo run riot, or love overcoming obstacles – call it what you will, Matilda followed him to Normandy and after a difficulty with the Pope concerning their distant relationship, solved by Lanfranc, they were married. They were apparently so contented with their marriage that they both founded abbeys in Caen to commemorate it. He, the Abbaye aux Hommes, she the Abbaye aux Dames (badly damaged in World War II).

It is usually thought that Lanfranc was made Archbishop of Canterbury due to William's influence but this was not the case. Pope Alexander II had been one of Lanfranc's students at Bec, and he appointed him, as he also made Anselm archbishop later, another student of Bec. So also was Gundulf, architect of the Tower of London and designer of the prefabricated forts that William brought over in his invasion boats. These sectionalized wooden walls were made to bolt together strongly, and were used at Hastings and frequently afterwards in the conquest of England. It would appear that the Normans have often had precocious ideas on design in many fields. In 1890 a Monsieur Ridel of Vimoutiers designed the lightweight yet strong chipwood box, without which Camembert would have remained a local, unexportable soft cheese of Normandy and not a name of global recognition. Camembert is made under licence in enormous quantities in every country in Europe and all over America; the chipwood box is an essential part of it, guarding Marie Harel's delicate mould flora. The total production of French cheese is in the region of 900,000 tons a year and Camembert represents a quarter of it.

Milk	Percentage fat	Weight	Type	Rind	Curing period	Form	Dimensions	Best season * = all year
BRICQUEBEC/TRAPPISTE DE BRICQUEBEC/PROVIDENCE								
C	45%	1.5 kg	pressed uncooked	washed	2 months humid	disc	220 × 40 mm	*

Flavour: c

Wine: St-Emilion

Made at the abbey of that name in the Cotentin peninsula all the year round from cows' milk, with the inevitable smooth yellow rind. *Croque-madame* demands it.

Milk	Percentage fat	Weight	Type	Rind	Curing period	Form	Dimensions	Best season * = all year
BRILLAT-SAVARIN								
C	75%	250 g	triple cream	bloomy	3 weeks	disc	125 × 40 mm boxed	*

Flavour: b[2]

Wine: Champagne or Vins Mousseux

Invented by Henri Androuët in the 1930s. The taste is buttery, lactic and similar to Excelsior.

Milk	Percentage fat	Weight	Type	Rind	Curing period	Form	Dimensions	Best season * = all year
BONDARD								
C	60%	225 g	double cream	bloomy	4 months dry	cylinder unwrapped or foil	65 × 75 mm	3

Flavour: e[2]

Wine: Anjou, Chinon or Bourgueuil

It was traditionally made from evening milk only. The name arose because the shape resembled a cider barrel bung.

Milk	Percentage fat	Weight	Type	Rind	Curing period	Form	Dimensions	Best season * = all year
BONDON also known as NEUFCHÂTEL								
C	45%	84 g	soft	bloomy	3 weeks	cylinder unwrapped or straw	50 × 60 mm	2 3 4

Flavour: c

Wine: Rosé d'Anjou or Saumur-Champigny

Normandy has been making this cheese since long before the Conquest. The taste is fruity, the paste is smooth textured and the rind should have touches of red pigment: if it is grey or dry at all, avoid it.

Milk	Percentage fat	Weight	Type	Rind	Curing period	Form	Dimensions	Best season * = all year

CAMEMBERT AND DEMI-CAMEMBERT: ½ DISC

Milk	Percentage fat	Weight	Type	Rind	Curing period	Form	Dimensions	Best season * = all year
C	45-50%	250 g	soft	bloomy	1 month dry	disc	110 × 30 mm boxed	1 2 3

VCN signifies 'Véritable Camembert de Normandie'

Flavour: c^2

Wine: All Médocs, such as Talbot St-Julien, Pontet Canet, Palmer

One of the classic bloomy rind cheeses, which can be traced to the 12th century and is also recorded in the 18th-century dictionaries. Improved by Marie Harel of Vimoutiers in 1790 and Roget in 1910, who introduced the innoculation with *Penicillium candidum*. Ridel designed the chipwood box in 1890 which has facilitated export. The cheese should have no trace of ammonia, in fact it should have no smell (Léon-Paul Fargue compared it with *'Les pieds du Dieu'*). It should not be cracked or tacky.

CARRÉ DE BRAY

Milk	Percentage fat	Weight	Type	Rind	Curing period	Form	Dimensions	Best season * = all year
C	45%	75 g	soft	bloomy	2 weeks humid	square	70 × 70 × 20 mm unwrapped or straw	1 2

Flavour: c

Wine: Beaujolais-Villages, Rosé d'Anjou or cider

CŒUR DU BRAY

Milk	Percentage fat	Weight	Type	Rind	Curing period	Form	Dimensions	Best season * = all year
C	45%	100-400 g	soft	bloomy	3 weeks dry	heart	varying sizes	2

Flavour: c^2

Wine: Anjou, Borgueuil, Chinon

Similar to Carré de Bray but with slightly more flavour.

CŒUR DE CAMEMBERT/CALVADOS

Cœur de Camembert/Calvados is a cows' milk cheese of Camembert type with the addition of Calvados; flavour c.

DEMI-SEL

Milk	Percentage fat	Weight	Type	Rind	Curing period	Form	Dimensions	Best season * = all year
C	40-45%	250 g	fresh			sold in foil-wrapped squares	75 × 75 × 25 mm	

Flavour: b^2

Wine: None

Originated by M. Pommel in the 19th century. A 'descendant' of Carré de Bray.

Milk	Percentage fat	Weight	Type	Rind	Curing period	Form	Dimensions	Best season * = all year

EXCELSIOR

Milk	Percentage fat	Weight	Type	Rind	Curing period	Form	Dimensions	Best season
C	72%	225 g	double cream	soft bloomy	2 weeks dry	cylinder	100 × 25 mm box	2 3

Flavour: b^3

Wine: Beaujolais or Bouzy Rouge

This 1890s cheese is the progenitor of many similar modern cheeses, such as Brillat-Savarin, Fin de Siècle and Suprème. Its flavour (b^3) is what you would expect from the Nineties, with those twelve-stone beauties in enormous hats and feather boas eating it for breakfast. It is at its best in summer and autumn; at its worst (concealed by the box) it is unpleasant in every conceivable way.

FEUILLE DE DREUX/DREUX À LA FEUILLE

Milk	Percentage fat	Weight	Type	Rind	Curing period	Form	Dimensions	Best season
C partly skimmed	30%	100, 200 or 500 g	soft	bloomy	3 weeks	disc 3 chestnut leaves on each side	various sizes	3 4

Flavour: d

Wine: Chinon or Rosé d'Anjou

FIN DE SIÈCLE/PARFAIT/SUPRÈME

Milk	Percentage fat	Weight	Type	Rind	Curing period	Form	Dimensions	Best season
C	72%	225 g	double cream	soft bloomy	2 weeks dry	disc	100 × 25 mm unwrapped	1 2 3

Flavour: b^3

Wine: Beaujolais

Almost identical to Excelsior, but as it is unwrapped, it is possible to see, touch, and smell it.

GOURNAY OR MALAKOFF (Affiné)

Milk	Percentage fat	Weight	Type	Rind	Curing period	Form	Dimensions	Best season
C	45%	100 g	soft	bloomy	1 week	disc	75 × 25 mm unwrapped	1 2 3

Also obtainable fresh

Flavour: c

Wine: Rosé d'Anjou

The ancestor of all the Caserette (pronounced Cagerette in Normandy) cheeses, drained in rush or straw baskets. Displayed on straw mats, the bloomy rind is a *very* fine white down compared with some of the others.

LA BOUILLE

Milk	Percentage fat	Weight	Type	Rind	Curing period	Form	Dimensions	Best season
C	60%	25 kg	double cream	bloomy	10 weeks dry or 12 weeks	cylinder unwrapped	75 × 50 mm	2 3 4

Flavour: d^2

Wine: Bourgueil or Anjou Rouge

Really another Monsieur Fromage, with a richer flavour due to a longer curing period, and the fact that it is a double cream.

Milk	Percentage fat	Weight	Type	Rind	Curing period	Form	Dimensions	Best season * = all year

LIVAROT

Milk	Percentage fat	Weight	Type	Rind	Curing period	Form	Dimensions	Best season
C	45%	450 g	soft	washed	3 months humid	cylinder	120 × 50 mm	1 3 4

Flavour: e²

Wine: Calvados or vintage cider

One of the oldest and greatest of the Normandy cheeses, named after the town of Livarot (in Seine-Maritime) and no doubt the 'Angelot' of Guillaume de Lorris's 13th-century *Roman de la Rose*. *Affineurs* and knowledgeable cheese-tasters say the word with a lilt, showing that they like it. There are usually five strips of sedge round the outside of the cheese, 'insignia' giving rise to the nickname *Colonel*. It can have a really putrid odour when you first open the box, *and* a tacky rind, both of which are advertisements of doom, as far as cheese flavour goes, so open the box before you buy.

MAGNUM

Milk	Percentage fat	Weight	Type	Rind	Curing period	Form	Dimensions	Best season
C	75%	460 g	soft triple cream	bloomy	3-4 weeks	disc	140 × 40 mm	*

Flavour: c

Wine: Vins Mousseux

This is the same cheese as Brillat-Savarin, aged slightly longer and with more flavour.

MIGNOT

Milk	Percentage fat	Weight	Type	Rind	Curing period	Form	Dimensions	Best season
C	40%	400 g	soft	natural	1 month humid	disc	120 × 35 mm unwrapped	3 4

Flavour: d³

Drink: Cider

Made exclusively on farms. The red and oily rind is pleasant and the white paste firm with a good texture. It really does find cider, or apple juice, to be exactly the right drink.

'MONSIEUR' OR MONSIEUR FROMAGE

Milk	Percentage fat	Weight	Type	Rind	Curing period	Form	Dimensions	Best season
C	60%	120 g	soft	bloomy	6 weeks dry	cylinder	75 × 50 mm boxed	1 2 3

Flavour: d²

Wine: Châteauneuf-du-Pape

A farmer named Fromage produced this cheese at the end of the 19th century, and it has been slowly perfected. A classic cheese, it is in the same class as Chaource. The flavour is fruity and with a remarkable bouquet, the red dots on the bloomy rind are similar to a good Brie, and the strong smell does not undermine its quality in the least. The size is 75 mm × 50 mm, and as the curing period is only 6 weeks, the flavour is less resonant than its lustier relation, La Bouille.

Milk	Percentage fat	Weight	Type	Rind	Curing period	Form	Dimensions	Best season * = all year
PAVÉ D'AUGE/PAVÉ DE MOYAUX/CARRÉ DE BONNEVILLE								
C	50%	700 g	soft	washed	2½ to 3 months humid	slab	110 × 110 mm unwrapped	2 3 4

Flavour: d

Wine: L'Evangile, Clos de l'Eglise, Beauregard

The rind can get leathery, by which time the taste is rather too sharp. An ancestor of the Pont l'Evêque cheeses and related to Livarot.

Milk	Percentage fat	Weight	Type	Rind	Curing period	Form	Dimensions	Best season * = all year
PETIT LISIEUX/DEMI-LIVAROT								
C	40-45%	280 g	soft	washed	2 months humid	cylinder	120 × 25 mm	1 2 3

Flavour: d

Wine: Cider or Saumur Mousseux

Watch out for putrid odour or dried-out rind.

Milk	Percentage fat	Weight	Type	Rind	Curing period	Form	Dimensions	Best season * = all year
PONT L'ÉVÊQUE/TROUVILLE (farm-produced version)								
C	50%	300 g	soft	washed brushed	6 weeks humid	slab	100 × 100 × 25 mm	2 3 4

Flavour: d^2 with bouquet and pleasant smell

Wine: Volnay, Pomerol

There are Pont l'Evêque fans who say that this is the 'Angelot' cheese of the Roman de la Rose, *not* Livarot.

Camembert being made, c. 1870, before the advent in 1890 of the lightweight chipwood box.

5. BRITTANY

The cheeses of Brittany do not have the same impact on French gastronomy as the region's Belon oysters, fish, crustaceans, *charcuterie*, or even vegetables. Fromage du Curé with its bouquet is a fine, wholesome cheese, and so is Crême Nantais, the fresh unsalted cheese served with fresh fruit, sugar and whipped cream. Saint Gildas-des-Bois has a velvety texture which almost deserves its 'Le Roi' trademark, but none of the Breton cheeses has the cachet of Banon; and by no stretch of the imagination could anyone say that they are extraordinary in the way that Roquefort is.

The Brittany peninsula, pointing 290 km (180 miles) out to sea, was originally cut off from France by desolate moorlands and forests. It still remains something of a separate entity, a place of mystery – the most overwhelming being the menhirs, of which there are 3000 in the Carnac district alone, erected between 5000 and 2000 BC by a people about which the archaeologists know exasperatingly little. Astronomically set, with an error of only one degree, to the cardinal points of the compass, the stones themselves weighing up to 350 tons, they are evidence of minds more formidable and far-seeing than most of those that have looked at them subsequently. Successive cults and religions have scratched their surfaces with what amounts to graffiti over the centuries: the Celts in the 6th, the Romans from the 1st century BC onward, and the Christians in the 5th century AD; but the stones remain adamant and infinite.

The missionaries from Ireland and Wales who came with the Celtic refugees from Britain in the 5th century had an effect on the Bretons that is still evident. They made saints of the missionaries and named places after them: Saint-Malo, Saint-Briévac, Saint-Pol-de-Léon and others. It was a region where Catholicism came to be accepted completely and absolutely. At the time of the French Revolution, Brittany was a centre of revolt against the reorganization of the Roman Catholic Church. Throughout the 19th and 20th centuries, Brittany has remaîned a conservative area of France, keeping to old social structures and religious feelings, and preserving its own Celtic language.

The soil of Brittany varies from the moorland crests of quartzite to the rich loam of the Ceinture Dorée, but in general it is poor siliceous clay which needs all the enriching it can get – in the past from marine fertilizers, and at present from modern chemicals. They used seaweed and algae for hundreds of years, but in particular a shelly sand, which includes Maerl (calcified algae). The Bretons used to say that this shelly sand would change gorse to clover.

The Ceinture Dorée, a sheltered rich alluvial coastal area between the mouth of the Loire and Saint-Malo, provides 40 per cent of the national total of market garden produce. There are the strawberries of Plougastel-Daoulas, 69 per cent of France's artichokes, and 66 per cent of its seed potatoes, as well as every other imaginable vegetable.

Arable farming occupies almost half of the land under cultivation, with wheat, maize, rye and fodder crops grown. The industry based on these cereals represents half of the total output of France. The orchards produce apples which are mainly used for cider, but there is also a thriving trade in mistletoe, sacred to the ancient Celts, which grows in profusion on the apple trees.

Brittany is the most important fishing region in France both in size of catch and value, its percentage of the total catch being 41 per cent of the fish and 67 per cent of crustaceans. This is achieved through modern methods with refrigeration plants and tanks on board the ships, and by sailing enormous distances in search of fish. Brittany has always been known for its Belons, but *conchyliculture* – oyster and mussel breeding – has been developed since 1950, producing a striking increase in quantity. Oysters are harvested in 3 to 5 years, and mussels take 1½ to 2½ years to mature. In fish canning Brittany produces 66 per cent of the national total, and meat, including pork products, and vegetables are also canned.

Intensive pig rearing with units of 300 animals has resulted in Brittany producing a third of the *charcuterie* for all France. Scientific interest in stock raising has increased both milk and meat yields, but has changed the breeds of cattle. The old pie-bald Pie Noire for example is now under special protection measures. The Armorican has been crossed with other breeds to produce the Pie

Rouge, but the Friesian is actually the most common breed.

Brittany, then, is essential to, and very much a part of, France with its fish, dairy produce, cheese and *charcuterie*, but it is still something of an odd ball in that it lacks a sense of style. The fish are the best, but the fishmonger slaps them down on the slab with no artistry. Next door in Normandy the same fish would be arranged with an innate sense of design. It is the same with Breton wrestling, often seen at festivals. They give each other three loud kisses then try to break each other's back with gusto, but with only five known medieval throws. Bullfighters in Provence achieve more grace even when running away from the bull towards the barricade.

(On a more positive note, Brittany provided more men for General de Gaulle's Free French Army than any other province.)

There is one splendid exception to this lack of style, and that is Anne, daughter of Duke François II of Brittany. Described by contemporaries as a slight girl with a limp, Anne must have had style, and other extraordinary qualities.

After a marriage by proxy to Maximilian of Austria, she actually married Charles VIII of France, and when *he* died, she married Louis XII. When *she* died, her daughter Claude (Reine Claude greengages were named after her) also became Queen of France by marrying François of Angoulême, the future François I. Queen Claude died at 25 of anaemia, caused by giving François I seven children in only eight years.

The Château Ducal at Nantes was begun in 1466 by Duke François II, and from Charles VIII to Louise XIV nearly all the kings of France have spent some time in it. There are two museums there that contain material crucial to an understanding of Brittany. One has furniture, costumes and objects of folklore; the other, the Musée des Salorges, shows models of fishing boats from the 17th to the 19th century, and also slave trade boats, on which

the wealth of Nantes in the 18th and 19th centuries was founded. The 'Ebony trade', as it was called, brought sugar to France on the return voyage, which helped to start the well-known Nantes biscuits. Fromage du Curé was also originated in Nantes, which is quite different in almost every way from the rest of Brittany, to the north. Nantes took to the new bourgeois way of life readily in the 18th century while the rest of the region remained isolated.

The festivals of France give a vital indication of the life of each province. In Provence for example there are 43, of which only 9 are religious. In Brittany there are 39 festivals, of which 9 are about the sea, and 30 are *Pardons*: religious meetings concerned with the forgiveness of sins. No other region has so many religious festivals.

One of the most distinctive and unspoiled of these *pardons* takes place on 15 August at Quelven, 50 km (31 miles) north-west of Vannes. A continuous mass is held from 6.00 am to 3.00 pm, after which a fountain of healing water in a Romanesque chapel is visited. A wooden statue of the virgin is carried to the village green, where a mitred bishop stands. A wooden figure of an angel with wings outstretched then 'flies' (it is attached to a rope) from the church tower to the standing bishop. A bonfire is then lit, with fireworks. In the past, the older ladies waited until the fire went out and then poked in the ashes for omens, with which to carry on a pagan seance, but this has now ceased. Instead, there is a feast of Morlaix ham, black puddings, smoked sausages from Guémené, the wine of Rhuys, cider from Beg Meil, crêpes, *palourdes farcies* (stuffed clams), bowls of La Cotriade (Brittany's bouillabaisse), and Fromage du Curé or Campenéac.

Last of all there is dancing to bagpipes and concertinas, which is an excruciating experience. While all the rgions of France are different, Brittany is almost an island in its determination to remain isolated and free from external influences.

Milk	Percentage fat	Weight	Type	Rind	Curing period	Form	Dimensions	Best season * = all year

CAMPENÉAC/TRAPPISTE DE CAMPENÉAC

Milk	Percentage fat	Weight	Type	Rind	Curing period	Form	Dimensions	Best season
C	42%	2 kg	pressed uncooked	washed	2 months humid	disc	250 × 40 mm	*

Flavour: c lactic and very quiet

Wine: Muscadet

Made by nuns of the Campenéac convent.

CRÉMET NANTAIS

Milk	Percentage fat	Weight	Type	Rind	Curing period	Form	Dimensions	Best season
C	50%		fresh	unsalted	drained only			

Flavour: a

Wine: none

Served with fresh fruit and sugar or whipped cream.

FROMAGE À LA PIE/FROMAGE BLANC

Milk	Percentage fat	Weight	Type	Rind	Curing period	Form	Dimensions	Best season
C		6 kg	fresh			disc		*

LA MEILLERAYE DE BRETAGNE/TRAPPISTE DE LA MEILLERAYE/ABBAYE DE LA MEILLERAYE

Milk	Percentage fat	Weight	Type	Rind	Curing period	Form	Dimensions	Best season
C	40%	0.2 kg	pressed uncooked	washed	2 months humid	slab	240 × 240 × 50 mm	1 2 3

Flavour: c with the washed-rind tang

Wine: Muscadet

NANTAIS/FROMAGE DU CURÉ

Milk	Percentage fat	Weight	Type	Rind	Curing period	Form	Dimensions	Best season
C	40%	200 g	pressed uncooked	washed	1 month humid	square	90 × 90 × 40 mm	*

Flavour: c^2 with bouquet and full smell

Wine: Sancerre, Saumur, Touraine

ST GILDAS-DES-BOIS

Milk	Percentage fat	Weight	Type	Rind	Curing period	Form	Dimensions	Best season
C	75%	200 g	triple cream	bloomy	2 weeks dry	cylinder boxed as 'Le Roi'	75 × 50 mm	*

Flavour: c with velvet texture

Wine: Pouilly-sur-Loire, Sancerre

Milk	Percentage fat	Weight	Type	Rind	Curing period	Form	Dimensions	Best season * = all year
ST-PAULIN (original name Port-Salut)								
C	50%	2 kg	pressed uncooked	washed	2 months humid	disc	220 × 50 mm	*

Flavour: b lactic

Wine: Light table wines

Port-Salut was the first of the mild-flavoured monastery cheeses, now made as St-Paulin all over France and all the year round.

6. NORTHERN FRANCE: NORD, PAS DE CALAIS, PICARDY

This area has both agricultural and mineral resources, together with a wide range of industries so it is surprising to find such a profusion of cheeses. The industries span automobiles, aircraft, electrical goods, coal, metal, glass, cement, ceramics, textiles, leather, tyres, sugar and paper-making. Some of these industries are new, but coal, metal and glass have been there for hundreds of years, and the workers in these industries have an assertive and Netherlandish taste in food and cheese, which is one of the noticeable features of northern French cuisine. With the exception of Mont-des-Cats, the cheeses are all strong and remarkably smelly, starting with old Puant de Lille, Dauphin, Boulette d'Avesnes and Maroilles, which is washed in beer. Maroilles Flamiche, however, a tart served as a desert or at any hour, is a good thing for a cold wet northern day.

Beer, known since the Franks, who called it *Cervoise*, used to be made all over northern France by artisans, who grew the hops and barley, added pure water to the malt, and mixed it all together with a *Fourquet* – a sort of pointed spade. One man and a boy could make gallons of outrageously strong beer, but now it is a huge industry concentrated in the north of France.

The Flanders cuisine is accompanied by beer, a glass of gin, or a *bistouille* – coffee with alcohol. Typical menus would include: hochepot, a jolly pot mixture consisting of pieces of mutton, pork, veal and vegetables; potjeflesh, a pâté of rabbit, chicken, and veal; and carbonnades, beef braised in beer, with a rich mixture of onions, spices and other vegetables, which is very good indeed.

Cooking varies from one area to another; Picardy and Artois have many interesting soups, and dishes using tripe, frogs, pumpkins and, in particular, their famous vegetable soup. Vegetables are important in these areas, especially the Saint-Omer cauliflowers, Laon artichokes, Saint-Valéry carrots, and the *petits pois* of Vermandois. They have been making duck pâté at Amiens since the 17th century, and snipe pâté at Montreuil, eel pâté at Péronne, and chitterlings at Arras and Cambrai. A *ficelle picardie* is a ham pancake with Béchamel sauce and mushrooms. (*Ficelle* means tricky or knowing in this context; as in *avocat ficelle*, a knowing lawyer.) Plovers' eggs, snipe, wild duck, trout, eels, carp and pike are all available inland to make a variety of menus, and from the sea there is sole, turbot, herring, cod, shrimps and mussels.

So the north of France is certainly not all beer and cheeses that are obnoxiously smelly, nor are we suggesting that hand-made beer of the misty past was better than the technologically manufactured beer of today – the reverse is probably true. Nor are the men all miners and industrial workers: they have included men of action like the pioneers of aviation, Blériot, Caudron and Mermoz, and they have also bred a few revolutionaries. Authors include Jean Froissart (c. 1337-c. 1410) who had an edge of malice in his descriptions of the Hundred Years War; Abbé Prévost (1697-1763) wrote *Manon Lescaut*; and Pierre de Laclos (1741-1803), *Les Liaisons Dangereuses*. Intellectuals with their eyes open, and showing sharp teeth in their work. Maximilien de Robespierre, the 'Incorruptible', was born at Arras; and so was Joseph Lebon, who became Mayor of Arras during the Terror and set up the guillotine in the Place de Théâtre there. The people themselves are hard-working, look a little reserved but have courtesy and generosity. Their houses are plain but scrupulously clean and shining. There are many similarities with Northumberland and Durham in England.

The large farms in Flanders and Artois are arranged around a courtyard with a large entrance: those that have survived the two world wars, that is. The north of France, its people and buildings, have suffered terribly in these wars. There used to be many windmills here – wooden in Picardy, brick in Flanders – now they are all gone. Once there were 500 in the Somme, and 250 in the Lille region.

The northern festivals are concerned with regattas, horses and flowers, fishermen, beer, and carillons of bells, several religious pilgrimages to cathedrals, and promenades to giants, all with folklore in profusion. These giants are legendary, and there are few towns in the north without one; Gayant of Douai, Gargantua of Bailleul, Martin and Martine of Cambrai, Lyderic and Phynaert of Lille. Pigeon racing is a favourite sport, as it is also in the north of England. Archery is popular, with fantastically high standards, and not without a semireligious acknowledgement to the patron of archery, Saint Sebastian.

The regions of France, all different from one another, have a certain pecking order and there is a tendency for Northern France, sadly, to emerge at the bottom of the pile: too flat, too industrial and too ravaged by the two world wars. In a country that produces the best wines in the world, it is surprising to say the least to find a region that drinks beer and gin all the time. In a country renowned for its art, it is spread so thin that it is difficult to find, but worth the effort. The cheeses have some of the same problems as the landscape, which is rarely as beautiful as the Dordogne, the Auvergne, Burgundy, Alsace, or Provence. Most of the cheeses have this strong smell.

Maroilles, historically impeccable as it dates to the 10th century, and even called a miracle at one period, has the deuce of a smell, but the flavour is something that has been acceptable to all the kings of France, and now to President Mitterand. I like the local northern name for it, *craquegnon*.

Then there is Gris de Lille, 'old Puant', its splendid flavour also encapsulated in an inescapable smell. Dauphin has a bouquet and a d² flavour which deserves Gevrey-Chambertin, but this would be considered weird and affected by the locals, who drink beer with it. Cœur d'Arras is a splendid, tasty and wholesome heart, and Sorbais deserves Bouzy Rouge. Boulette d'Avesnes with its tinted red rind has a doughy paste which really *needs* gin, but Mont-des-Cats, lactic and delicate, gets Muscadet when I eat it. With home-made Fromage Fort de Béthune we are back with the gin bottle, and a taste that will last a week. They use beer again for poaching the eels caught in the inland marshes and meres. Soupe à la bière seems to be really beer thickened with egg and cream. There are a few places, however, and Château de Montreuil is one of them, where the food is as good as anywhere in France. Wild duck can come to the table there as *á l'orange, au vin, en terrine*, and especially as Pâté de Caneton d'Amiens, which is stuffed and boned duck baked in pastry. A dish unique to the region served there is subtle, fabulous even, for the way it disguises that old rabbity flavour: Lapin de Garenne aux Pruneaux.

On the whole, the food and cheeses of the north, Picardy, Artois and Flanders, are good. They suit the climate, the people and the local way of life, and there are several that deserve accolades, such as Anguille au Vert à la Flamande, sautéed eel in a bitter green salad; Perches du Menon, poached perch in still Champagne; Pied de Porc à la Sainte Ménehould, grilled and breaded pigs' trotters; and the subtle, refined Cailles sous les Cendres, quails wrapped in vine leaves and bacon, and roasted in wood ash.

Milk	Percentage fat	Weight	Type	Rind	Curing period	Form	Dimensions	Best season * = all year
BELVAL/TRAPPISTE DE BELVAL								
C	40%	2 kg	pressed uncooked	washed	2 months humid	disc	230 × 35 mm	*

Flavour: c and lactic

Wine: Bouzy Rouge, Beaujolais

Milk	Percentage fat	Weight	Type	Rind	Curing period	Form	Dimensions	Best season * = all year
BERGUES								
C skimmed	15%	2 kg	soft	washed	2 months humid, washing with brine and beer	disc	175 × 45 mm	*

Flavour: f sharp

Drink: Beer

BÉTHUNE/FROMAGE FORT DE BÉTHUNE

C	45%							

This *fromage fort* is home-made and not marketed. It has a remarkably strong smell and they drink gin with it in the north. Maroilles cheeses are put in a crock, seasoned with pepper, tarragon and parsley, and left there fermenting for three months. It has no shape, being spooned out loose when strong enough. A favourite cheese with miners. The flavour is g and sticky. When the cheese has reached a deep colour, almost black, it may well be digestively dangerous. *See* Maroilles.

BOULETTE D'AVESNES

C	50%	300 g	soft	tinted red	3 months humid	cone	75 × 100 mm	2 3 4

Flavour: f sharp and with a strong smell; the paste is doughy

The curd is mashed, kneaded and flavoured with herbs and pepper.

Drink: Gin

BOULETTE DE CAMBRAI

C	45%	280 g	fresh					

Fresh and flavoured with herbs – parsley, tarragon, chives.

Made in hard moulded balls, about 75 mm diameter, weight 280 g. The flavour is b and best when newly made.

CŒUR D'ARRAS

C	45%	200 g	soft	washed	2 months humid	heart-shaped	90 × 90 mm	1 2 3

Flavour: d and wholesome

Wine: Beajolais

DAUPHIN

C	50%	150 g to 1 kg	soft	washed	2-3 months + tarragon and vinegar	shield, heart, fish, loaf	150 × 50 mm	2 3 4

Flavour: d² with bouquet

Drink: Beer locally but it deserves Chambertin

This is really a variant of Maroilles, created because of the visit of Louis XIV and his son the Dauphin. This cheese was exempted from the normal duties paid by the cheese carters.

Milk	Percentage fat	Weight	Type	Rind	Curing period	Form	Dimensions	Best season * = all year

EDAM FRANÇAIS/EDAM GALANTINE FRANÇAIS (a copy of Dutch Broodkaas)

Milk	Percentage fat	Weight	Type	Rind	Curing period	Form	Dimensions	Best season
C	40%	1½ kg	pressed	tinted red and paraffin-waxed	2-3 months dry	flattened ball	125 × 110 mm	*

Flavour: b

Drink: Lager

The first French Edams were made in 1670, after a treaty against France by the Netherlands, Sweden and England which made Dutch Edam unobtainable.

FROMAGE D'HESDIN

A cows' milk cheese made in the Pas de Calais, similar to the Trappist cheeses with a strong smell and taste d.

GRIS DE LILLE/PUANT DE LILLE/PUANT MACERÉ

Milk	Percentage fat	Weight	Type	Rind	Curing period	Form	Dimensions	Best season
C	45%	350 g	soft	washed	2 months with washings + immersed in brine for 3 months	slab	120 × 120 × 60 mm	1 3 4

Flavour: e and powerful smell

Drink: Gin

LARRON D'ORS

Milk	Percentage fat	Weight	Type	Rind	Curing period	Form	Dimensions	Best season
C skimmed	30%	500 g	soft	washed	6-7 weeks humid	square or cross	100 × 100 × 50 mm	1 4

Flavour: d and sometimes a bouquet

Wine: Côtes-du-Rhône

MAROILLES

Milk	Percentage fat	Weight	Type	Rind	Curing period	Form	Dimensions	Best season
C	45-50%	500 g	soft	washed	4 months humid	slab	125 × 125 × 65 mm	2 3 4

Flavour: e with a strong smell

Invented a thousand years ago at the monastery of Maroilles and called 'The Miracle of Maroilles'; the country people simply called it *craquegnon*. Popular with French kings – Philippe-Auguste, Louis IX, Charles VI, François I – and also President Mitterand. There are small versions of it: Mignon de Maroilles, Quart de Maroilles.

MIMOLETTE FRANÇAISE/BOULE DE LILLE/VIEUX LILLE

Milk	Percentage fat	Weight	Type	Rind	Curing period	Form	Dimensions	Best season
C	45%	3 kg	pressed and reheated	natural brushed and coloured orange	6-18 months	flattened sphere	200 × 175 mm	*

Flavour: c^2 and nutty, with a fruity aroma

Wine: Port, Madeira; also Beaune, Beaujolais-Villages

Mimolette Français, also called Boule de Lille and Vieux Lille, is a copy of the famous Dutch cheese of the same name, from Alkmaar, where they also drink beer with it.

Milk	Percentage fat	Weight	Type	Rind	Curing period	Form	Dimensions	Best season * = all year
MONT-DES-CATS/ABBAYE DU MONT-DES-CATS/TRAPPISTE DU MONT-DES-CATS								
C	40-45%	2 kg	pressed uncooked	washed	2 months humid	disc	250 × 40 mm	2 3

Flavour: c and lactic

Wine: Muscadet

PAVÉ DU BLESOIS/DE SOLOGNE

Pavé du Blesois/de Sologne is a square, 100 × 100 × 25 mm, goats' milk cheese with a nutty flavour c, packed on straw, in wooden boxes.

Wine: Beaujolais

ROLLOT/GUERBIGNY

Milk	Percentage fat	Weight	Type	Rind	Curing period	Form	Dimensions	Best season * = all year
C	45%	200 g	soft	washed	2 months humid	disc or heart	75 × 35 mm	1 2 3

Flavour: d^2 with bouquet and mild tang

Wine: Côtes Grand-Mayne, Côtes Haut-Cadet

SORBAIS

Milk	Percentage fat	Weight	Type	Rind	Curing period	Form	Dimensions	Best season * = all year
C	45-50%	500 g	soft	washed	3 months humid	slab	120 × 120 × 45 mm	1 2 3

Flavour: e with bouquet and smell

Wine: Beaujolais, or Bouzy Rouge

LES VIGNOTTES

A triple cream cheese, made in commercial dairies in Lorraine and Champagne from pasteurized milk; the size is 200 × 75 mm. Also obtainable made from unpasteurized milk.

Wine: Muscadet

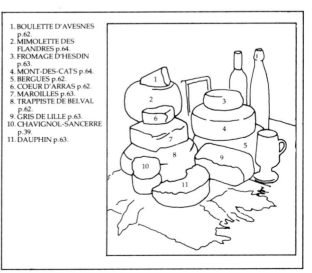

1. BOULETTE D'AVESNES p.62.
2. MIMOLETTE DES FLANDRES p.64.
3. FROMAGE D'HESDIN p.63.
4. MONT-DES-CATS p.64.
5. BERGUES p.62.
6. COEUR D'ARRAS p.62.
7. MAROILLES p.63.
8. TRAPPISTE DE BELVAL p.62.
9. GRIS DE LILLE p.63.
10. CHAVIGNOL-SANCERRE p.39.
11. DAUPHIN p.63.

OPPOSITE Cheese from northern France.

7. CHAMPAGNE AND THE ARDENNES

Champagne, the wine, dominates the scene in this region so completely that cheeses get slight consideration. Grape harvesters, however, invariably eat ash-covered cheeses. These Cendrés d'Argonne include Noyer-le-Val and Heiltz-le-Maurupt, which are becoming rare. This is a pity because they have a spicy flavour (e^2), no smell to speak of, and go well after pâté, cold meats, or at the end of *auberge* meals. There is another Cendré, named 'de Champagne' or 'des Riceys', which varies in flavour from d to g, depending on many factors; made from skimmed cows' milk, it varies with the unpredictable taste buds and habits of the individual farmers' wives who make it.

Chaource, with an *appellation d'original*, is a cheese that merits a place at the table with the Champagne. A soft, bloomy-rind cows' milk cheese, it is cured semi for 3 weeks, or fully for 8 weeks and the flavour varies from a milky c to d^2 with a full bouquet. The paste is tender, with a suggestion of mushrooms, and the rind is downy. There is another cheese that could accompany Champagne, which is Langres, made in the Bassigny area. It has a real bouquet and a rich, spicy e^2 flavour that makes it one of the basic, classical cheeses of France.

Champagne regional cuisine varies considerably in the better restaurants, as in all rich tourist areas with a particularly refined and sophisticated clientele – in this case it includes wine merchants and buyers from foreign countries. In the *auberges*, however, you realize that the Champenois have superb ways of cooking fried chicken, kidneys, stuffed pike, trout, crayfish and escargots, which make them all taste entirely different from the same items cooked elsewhere. The basic regional peasant dish is Potée Champenoise, which is a smoked ham, bacon, sausages and a cabbage. There are also Troyes chitterlings; the special Moutarde au Champagne and Ratafia of Epernay; the Pâté de Pigeons, Croquignoles and Massepins of Reims; and Quenelles de Brochet of Marsuil – which are strong stuff, unlike most quenelles. The Champagne cuisine, however, is actually in debt to all the surrounding regions. The Gougère is copied from Burgundy, the Potée Champenoise is an

OPPOSITE Geese in the Ardennes.

imitation of Lorraine's, and the Champagne fruit brandies are very reminiscent of the eaux-de-vie from Alsace-Lorraine. Cervelas de Brochet really is a Champenoise dish, translating unattractively as pike and potato saveloy. There is a soufflé called simply Pain-à-la-Reine, which is actually pounded pike mixed with crayfish. Champagne has a local matelote with a sparkling reputation in all guides to regional cuisine.

Champagne is part of the Parisian basin, with a geological basis of Jurasic limestone, arranged in folds and sloping towards the Vosges. The upward folds are the various *côtes* and the whole arrangement might have been designed by a thoughtful and beneficient deity specially for growing vines. The limestone is invaluable, the soil is correct and the inclination towards the sun superb. Champagne wine as we know it today, with the splendid effervescence, began in the 17th century. Dom Pérignon (1638-1715), cellar master of a Benedictine abbey, was the first to provide the fascinating quality of sparkling Champagne. Before that it had a similar bouquet, but was only *pétillante*. The Gauls grew wines in this area, and Attila the famous Hun camped here for some time. The Romans, and later the monasteries, grew vines, and they were all aware of the quality of the bouquet, long before the cork-popping. 'Wine of God', the Church called it, for it was admired by bishops and popes. 'Wine of kings', others named it. Henry VIII of England actually owned the Côte des Blancs area for a while, centred around Ay and Epernay. Once, bored by an ambassador enumerating the titles of the King of Spain, said, 'Let it be known to His Majesty the King of Spain, Castille, Aragon, etc. etc. that Henry VIII is Sire of Ay, that is to say the best vineyards in Europe . . .' Casanova seemed to drink it continually, rarely mentioning other wines. La Pompadour, Richelieu and Napoleon all admired it. Talleyrand called it the 'civilizing wine', using it freely at that Congress of Vienna where, as we have seen, cheese was a subject for decision making as well as the boundaries of European countries.

The most respected regions, producing the best Champagne, are the Côte des Blancs, the Valley of the Marne, and the Montagne de Reims, where the only vines used are Pinot Noir, Meunier Noir, and Chardonnay Blanc – the marriage of *crus* laid down by Dom Pérignon. One hectare (2½ acres) of a vineyard in this area was worth 500,000 francs in 1982, but this means nothing because no one would sell it.

The growth of Champagne since World War II has been one of the success stories of the wine trade. In 1950, annual sales were 35 million bottles. By 1960, this had risen to 49 million, in 1977 it reached 170 million bottles and in 1982 it was more than 200 million bottles. This has led to an increase in the areas of vineyards under cultivation. A steady increase of this order in the area of vines has meant an increased production of *cendré* cheeses, because grape harvesters are not the sort of people to be fobbed off with processed cheeses.

The Ardennes is different from the Champagne area in almost every way. The limestone base is covered with clay, sand and silt, and with the exception of the Aisne valley, where cereals are grown, the country is covered in woods and copses, which is why Givet, Rocroi and Charleville are all noted for Pâté de Grives, and smoked ham. *Grives* are thrushes, which are roasted in sage leaves, made into terrines with juniper berries, or used to produce commercial pâtés with varying herbs. Anglo-Saxons, fond of all game, blanch at the thought of eating a songbird. There is a French proverb that might seem to rub further salt in: 'Faute de grives on mange des merles' (If there are no thrushes you eat blackbirds). But the usual translation is 'Beggars can't be choosers', or 'Half a loaf is better than no bread'.

The Ardennes cuisine is largely based on fish and game. The fish consist of river trout, pike from the lakes, and many fish, unknown in England, from the Meuse. These are all cooked in various ways peculiar to the Ardennes, but also they are made into fish quenelles. The game starts with roe deer, and includes wild boar (*pére et fils*, the little ones being particularly tasty). These are also made into pâtés with herbs. And here come those thrushes again: it must take a dreadful lot of thrushes to make *one* Pâté de Grives, let alone hundreds.

Most of the regions of France have produced at least one genius in the arts, as well as wines, cheeses, cuisine, political leaders and generals, and in the case of the Ardennes it was Arthur Rimbaud 1854-91, born at Charleville, and inspired, so he said, by the mysterious forests.

Milk	Percentage fat	Weight	Type	Rind	Curing period	Form	Dimensions	Best season * = all year
BARBEREY/FROMAGE DE TROYES/TROYEN CENDRÉ								
C skimmed	20%	250 g	soft	ash natural	1 month humid in ash	cylinder boxed		1 2 3

Flavour: d and a musty smell

Wine: The Riceys

Milk	Percentage fat	Weight	Type	Rind	Curing period	Form	Dimensions	Best season * = all year
CAPRICE DES DIEUX								
C	60%	200 g	soft double cream	bloomy	3 weeks dry	loaf boxed	140 × 60 × 35 mm	*

Flavour: b

Wine: Light and *mousseux* wines

Milk	Percentage fat	Weight	Type	Rind	Curing period	Form	Dimensions	Best season * = all year
CARRÉ DE L'EST								
C	50%	100-200 g	soft	bloomy	3 weeks dry	square boxed	100 × 100 × 30 mm	*

Flavour: c

Wine: Blanc de Blanc

Milk	Percentage fat	Weight	Type	Rind	Curing period	Form	Dimensions	Best season * = all year
CENDRÉ D'ARGONNE/HEILTZ-LE-MAURUPT/NOYERS-LE-VAL								
C	35%	280 g	soft	ash natural	2-3 months dry in ashes	disc	125 × 40 mm	2 3

Flavour: e^2 and spicy

Wine: Bouzy Rouge

A grape harvest cheese.

Milk	Percentage fat	Weight	Type	Rind	Curing period	Form	Dimensions	Best season * = all year
CENDRÉ DE CHAMPAGNE/CENDRÉ DE RICEYS/LES RICEYS								
C	20-30% skimmed	250 g	soft	ash	6-8 weeks dry ashes	disc	210 × 30 mm	2 3

Flavour: e-g, depending on age

Wine: Bouzy Rouge

Milk	Percentage fat	Weight	Type	Rind	Curing period	Form	Dimensions	Best season * = all year
CHAOURCE								
C	45-50%	700 g	soft	bloomy	2-3 weeks or 1-2 months	basin shape	120 × 70 mm	2 3

Flavour: c lactic semi-cured, or d^2 + bouquet fully cured

Wine: Coteaux Champenois, Blanc de Blanc, or Bollinger

Milk	Percentage fat	Weight	Type	Rind	Curing period	Form	Dimensions	Best season * = all year
CHAUMONT								
C	45%	250 g	soft	washed	2 months	truncated cone	75 × 50 mm	2 3

Flavour: d and spicy with strong smell

Wine: Bouzy Rouge or Cheval Noir

Milk	Percentage fat	Weight	Type	Rind	Curing period	Form	Dimensions	Best season * = all year
ERVY-LE-CHÂTEL								
C	45%	250 g	soft	washed	3 months humid. 1 month washing with *marc*	cylinder	100 × 60 mm	2 3 4

Flavour: e^2 with bouquet, and good smell

Wine: Nuits-St-Georges, Aloxe-Corton

Milk	Percentage fat	Weight	Type	Rind	Curing period	Form	Dimensions	Best season * = all year
IGNY/TRAPPISTE D'IGNY								
C	45%	1-2 kg	pressed uncooked	washed	2 months humid	disc	200 × 40 mm	1 2 3

Flavour: c and spicy

Wine: Coteaux Champenois, Blanc de Blancs

Milk	Percentage fat	Weight	Type	Rind	Curing period	Form	Dimensions	Best season * = all year
LANGRES								
C	45%	300 g	soft	washed	3 months and washings	truncated cone paper-wrapped	100 × 50 mm	1 2 3

Flavour: e^2 bouquet and strong wholesome smell

Wine: Côte de Beaune-Villages

Milk	Percentage fat	Weight	Type	Rind	Curing period	Form	Dimensions	Best season * = all year
ROCROI								
C	20%	400 g	soft	ash natural	1-2 months in ashes	disc or slab	130 × 25 mm	2 3

Flavour: f and strong

Wine: Morgon, Moulin-à-Vent

8. ALSACE, LORRAINE AND THE VOSGES

The high natural meadows in the Vosges provide pasture for large herds of cows. The milk is made into cheese in *Marcaireries*, which are small mountain farmhouses divided into a large area for making cheeses, and a smaller part for living quarters. Pigs kept in large sties live on the whey, and later provide various kinds of sausage. The cows still follow the medieval timetable of going up the mountain on 25 May, Saint Urbain's day, and returning to the valley on 29 September, Saint Michael's day. The pastures in the Vosges, especially in spring, are full of rare flowers and herbs, and are thus similar to such other unspoiled areas of France as the Haute-Savoie.

The plain of Alsace is a beautiful corridor between the Vosges and the Black Forest mountains, created by an earth movement 60 to 30 million years ago, and beneficial to farmers and wine growers ever since. The Rhine runs down the middle of it, separating Alsace from Germany. Right from the beginning, Nature has continuously poured largesse into this fabulous valley. There have been three tragic wars but there is now little sign of them; the scars in the landscape have healed, and the conscientious, hard-working people of Alsace, have carefully rebuilt their houses after each war.

Protected by the Vosges and the Black Forest mountains, Alsace not only has a rare situation, it has the loess (also found in Normandy) – a soil metres deep and mixed by Nature and luck to contain every element needed to grow any kind of plant to its full potential; together with the streams, rivers, springs and torrents to keep it so for ever. And the farmers of Alsace do grow every conceivable plant in it exceedingly well.

Somehow people of Alsace do not look, act, or talk like Frenchmen. They *talk* a kind of German. This sing-song German dialect with French words casually sprinkled in it is part of Alsace. The people are neat, calm, quiet, reserved, cautious – and perhaps more like Austrians? What is more, they are aware of the fact and even have an old song about it called 'Le Jeannot-du-Nid-aux-Moustiques': 'Qui a tout ce qu'il peut désirer, mais ne possède pas ce qu'il désire, et ne désire pas ce qu'il possède.' Psychologists say that this general mental malaise is due to the unease produced by the many wars that have swept over them in the past, coupled with the fact that their country *is* covetable, and the fear that it may all happen again.

The Alsace cuisine is different from, and more diverse in origin than, that of other provinces, due partly to an old Jewish colony in Strasbourg which brought dishes from Poland, Austria, and Russia. Alsace also has important wine districts which attract knowledgeable tourists, interested in gastronomy. This means that the restaurants and their chefs work at it, rather than just relaxing and serving well-known regional dishes. On this level, the *foie gras*, studded with truffles, is served pure and alone, as an hors d'œuvre. It is remarkably expensive even in its home town, Strasbourg.

With Germany so close, it would be logical to expect an influence from there, but the cuisine of Alsace shows very little. You can find it in the brasseries, in the Choucroute Garnie with frankfurters and lager. There are dishes served in Alsace that do not occur anywhere else. 'Coq au Coutes d'Ecrivisses' is chicken cooked very simply, but surrounded by a rose-pink sauce of river crayfish, with rice. There is also a terrine with these same crayfish – Terrine d'Ecrivisses aux Petit Légumes – that actually includes truffles poached in dry white wine or Champagne, although this gets no mention in the title. Aiguillettes de Canard aux Pieurottes shows the Alsatian's cool subtlety and perfection. *Aiguillettes* means thin strips of duck breast, and *pieurottes* are oyster mushrooms. The sauce is usually a duck stock and red wine, shallots, flour and butter plus fresh cream and cognac.

Frogs' legs, one of the French delicacies since at least the 16th century, appear in many of the menus of Alsace. Incidentally, these legs are bought fresh by the dozen, on skewers, and six are considered enough for one person. Sometimes they are marinated in white wine and herbs, sometimes casseroled in butter, wine and cream, but most often just dipped in butter and fried: so much for everyday cooking. However, the *toques* (this word, meaning a chef's hat, has become a collective term for the profession) make it much more of an act, cutting off the feet and putting them in cold water, changing the water every two hours. Then they cook them in a fish *fumet* with Riesling and shallots, and boning them and putting them to one side while they make a mousse of sole or pike and put it in buttered ramekins. Then they make another *fumet* with the sole or pike pieces and Riesling again, and warm the frogs' legs in it. When just right, the frogs' legs are then ladled into the ramekins, covered with the fish mousse and poached in a bain-marie. When the ramekins are turned out on plates, more Riesling sauce is added with finely chopped chives. (Later in the day, or the day after perhaps, it is possible to have a gâteau of frogs' legs.)

Lorraine is completely different from Alsace, being simply a continuation of the Paris basin. If you drive from the Île de France towards the Vosges, there is a repetitive arrangement of *côtes*, always followed by pastures and forests. First, the Côte de Champagne, followed by the Côtes de Bars, the Meuse and finally the Côte de Moselle, the Côte in each case being followed by pasture and then forest. As you near the Vosges it is the forests that finally predominate, but with natural valley pastures, and views of more mountain ranges. In the 10th century AD there were still European bison in these pastures, and wild horses roamed there until the 16th.

Lorraine is divided into two strongly contrasted regions, the north with various industries, and the agricultural south with vineyards. The wines of Lorraine have no *grand crus*, but the dry flinty taste is agreeable, when served fresh. Nancy, the capital, has an extraordinary magnificence. Louis XV gave it to his father-in-law, Stanislas Leszczyński, the dethroned King of Poland. What an incomparable gift. There was also a revenue to go with it, which Stanislas used very purposefully to turn Nancy into a beautiful Polish city. With the help of Emmanuel Here, architect, and Jean Lamour, designer of the wrought-iron grilles and gates, he created an architectural complex of quite exceptional quality and grace.

Also in Lorraine there is Vittel, the thermal used by the Romans and rediscovered by Stanislas, and the Vosges has lakes like Gérardmer, Blanc, Noire, the Lac des Corbeaux, and Longemer. Baccarat is known for its crystal decanters, wine goblets and chandeliers.

The great covered marketplaces of France are all overwhelming, and Nancy is no exception. *Charcuterie* of every sort: smoked sausages and hams; terrines and pâtés of duck, tongue and pork: deep dishes of *porcelet en gelée*, an elegant brawn of sucking pig embedded in a crystal-clear jelly; and pale-pink mild-cured hams from Luxeuil. Amber-green *choucroute*, centrepiece of Alsatian cooking, is also for sale in the markets here. Through an archway there is a separate hall with more flowers than you could imagine, but first the cheese stalls have to be inspected – and yes, they are all there, all fifteen of them, each one impeccable.

The regional festivals of Lorraine express many interests: flowers, roses, music, theatre and folklore, as well as religious pilgrimages to the churches. At this point it should be said that, as usual, this province is different from all the others – from Brittany, Provence, Champagne, the Loire valley or the Île de France – but that it is still unquestionably French. Neighbouring Alsace is something else altogether.

Lorraine has a Regional Park of about 2000 square kilometres (770 square miles) between the Meuse and the Moselle, opened in 1974 expressly to preserve the flora.

It is suggested that your route across Lorraine might start from Paris and then the Champagne region, in which case the first city you enter driving east would be Bar-le-Duc, ancient capital of the Dukes of Bar and Lorraine. It is the home, among many other things, of those miniature glass jars of translucent preserves, seen in the luxury Paris shops: red currants, white currants, strawberries and stoned gooseberries (gooseberry fool). At Commercy, there is a forest and one of Stanislas' favourite châteaux. Commercy also originated *madeleines*, the shell-shaped cakes of which all French children are passionately fond.

Many more cheeses are made in Lorraine than in Alsace, for the usual French reason: the soil of the latter province is more usefully employed growing vines than grass for cows to eat.

The world is now so full of exciting-looking cheesecakes, almost invariably with a topping of tinned blackcurrants, that there may be some merit in returning to first essentials and seeing how the original cheesecakes were made – in Alsace, of course.

The ingredients are:

¼ cup dried breadcrumbs	4 eggs
½ tsp. sugar	1 cup thick cream
½ tsp. cinnamon	2 tbsp. flour
450 g (1 lb) cream cheese	1 tsp. vanilla
¾ cup granulated sugar	

Method: Grease pan with butter. Combine breadcrumbs, sugar and cinnamon and place in pan, turning so that the sides and bottom are well coated with the crumb mixture. Beat cream cheese with the ¾ cup of sugar (in an electric mixer). Slowly beat in the eggs, then the cream, flour and vanilla, never stopping the beating. Pour into pan and bake in preheated oven at 350°F for 45 minutes. Turn off oven and leave to cool.

Most of the regional festivals of Lorraine and Alsace, whether religious or secular, have been held since the Middle Ages.

Alsace

1 May, Molsheim Wine fair

1 May, Neuf-Brisach Lily of the valley festival

Whitsun, Wissembourg Week-long gourmet festival, with regional costumes, dancing, folklore, horse racing

June, Strasbourg International music festival

30 June, Thann Fir tree ceremony: burning three trees

1st weekend in July, Ribeauvillé Wine fair and tasting, with folklore

2nd Sunday in August, Sélestat Floral festival, wine fair, regional costumes

15 August, Colmar Wine fair, with folklore and costumes

Early September, Colmar Sauerkraut *(choucroute)* festival

1st Sunday in September, Ribeauvillé The *Pfifferdaj* festival of strolling musicians, singers and storytellers, with music and folklore; free wine from a wine fountain

Late September, Hagenau Beer festival, with folklore and costumes

Late September, Strasbourg European fair

1-24 December, Strasbourg Sale of Christmas trees in the Place Brogue

Lorraine

Wednesday before Easter, Epinal Children's religious festival; they sing in local patois and carry lights

20 April (nearest Sunday), Gérardmer Flower and music festival, with wagons of jonquil, regional costumes

8-19 May, Nancy Festival of the theatre

Early June, Epinal Picturesque festival of regional costume, music, folklore and crafts

1st Saturday in June, Metz Fires of St John, with songs and dancing (carrying torches)

14 July, Bar-le-Duc National holiday celebrated with a wine fair

14 August, Gérardmer Fairy festival on the lake, with *son et lumière* (Girls dressed as fairies)

Last Sunday in August, Metz Mirabelle (plum) festival, with floats and wagons of fruit, regional costumes and dancing

1st Sunday in October, Bar-le-Duc Vintage festival, with floats and wagons of regional costumes; free wine from a wine fountain

Milk	Percentage fat	Weight	Type	Rind	Curing period	Form	Dimensions	Best season * = all year

BIBBELSKÄSE

Bibbelskäse is a fresh cows' milk cheese with a mild flavour b[2] sparkled by the herbs and horseradish that are added. The fresh drained cheese is salted and beaten with finely chopped horseradish and herbs, then put in a cool place for two days to allow the herbs to penetrate.

BROCQ

Brocq, also called Brockel and Bracq depending on the district, is a fresh cows' milk cheese made from slowly drained curdled milk which is then mixed with fresh milk and eaten with bread soaked in it. The flavour is very mild – a.

FREMGEYE

Fremgeye is fresh cows' milk cheese, but with a much stronger than usual flavour, e[2] or even f[2], because after draining and seasoning it is left to ferment in a closed crock for a month. It needs the minced shallots or onions with which it is usually served.

FROMAGE CUIT

Fromage Cuit has a reasonably strong flavour, d, and it is exactly what its name states – a cooked cheese. Undrained cows' milk cheese is cooked for five minutes, after which the whey is drained off and the cheese hung up in a cheesecloth for about five days. It then goes into an earthenware crock, salt is added, and the crock is covered. After two weeks this fermented cheese is put in a pan with butter and milk, egg yolks, seasoning, and heated. A pleasant enough dish for a cold morning.

FROMAGE EN POT

Fromage en Pot is made around Metz from cows' milk. It is another of those northern French recipes that produces a strong flavour – f[2]. Fresh cheese drained for about a week is put in a crock to a depth of some 25 mm with fennel seeds and seasoning. This is continued, layers of cheese and fennel alternating, and the crock finally sealed with its lid and put in the cellar for at least six weeks. A film of interesting grey mould has to be removed before eating.

GÉRARDMER/LORRAINE/GROS LORRAINE

Milk	Percentage fat	Weight	Type	Rind	Curing period	Form	Dimensions	Best season
C	45%	6 kg	soft	washed	1 month humid	cylinder	300 × 75 mm	2 3

Flavour: d lactic

Wine: Rosé d'Alsace

GÉROME

Milk	Percentage fat	Weight	Type	Rind	Curing period	Form	Dimensions	Best season
C	45-50%	300 g	soft	washed	1-3 months humid	disc	120-200 × 25-50 mm	2 3 4

Flavour: d[2] with bouquet and very strong smell

Wine: Côtes-du-Rhône or Chambertin

There is also Gérome Anise, the same cheese flavoured with caraway seeds.

Milk	Percentage fat	Weight	Type	Rind	Curing period	Form	Dimensions	Best season * = all year

GUEYIN

Take Trang'nat after 15-20 days of hanging from the beams, put it in a crock, cover it with a cloth, and place it in a corner of the cellar. Traditionally, it was put near the livestock in the barn to keep warm. When the Trang'nat has 'turned' to a yellowish colour and quite a perfume, it is Gueyin.

MATTONS

Milk	Percentage fat	Weight	Type	Rind	Curing period	Form	Dimensions	Best season * = all year
C	0.5%		hard	no rind		lumps like nuts		

A whey cheese, almost inedible, made to produce Cancoillote as in the Franche-Comté, but in Lorraine it is called Thionville and it is made commercially.

MUNSTER

Milk	Percentage fat	Weight	Type	Rind	Curing period	Form	Dimensions	Best season * = all year
C	45-50%	500 g	soft	washed	5 weeks to 3 months due to size		120-200 mm	2 3

Flavour: e²

Wine: Pinot Rouge

Known and respected since the 7th century, this cheese was first made by Irish monks who settled in the Vosges. It is made from cows' milk both in the mountain farms (when it has a label of origin regulated by law) and in large industrial dairies. The farm cheese is sold unwrapped, the dairy variety boxed. In the Vosges villages of Alsace they make a salad including half-matured Munster, seasoned with vinegar, and drink Gewürztraminer with it – which shows how mild Munster, half matured, can be. Munster au Cumin is the same as Munster, but flavoured with caraway seeds.

OELENBERG/TRAPPISTE D'OELENBERG

Milk	Percentage fat	Weight	Type	Rind	Curing period	Form	Dimensions	Best season * = all year
C	45%	1 kg	pressed uncooked	washed	2 months humid	discs	230 × 40 mm	*

Flavour: b lactic

Wine: Sylvaner

RÉCOLLET/CARRÉ DE L'EST

Milk	Percentage fat	Weight	Type	Rind	Curing period	Form	Dimensions	Best season * = all year
C	45%	150-300 g	soft	bloomy	3 weeks dry	square	75-100 × 25-30 mm	*

Flavour: c

Wine: Rosé d'Alsace

ST-RÉMY

Milk	Percentage fat	Weight	Type	Rind	Curing period	Form	Dimensions	Best season * = all year
C	40-45%	250 g	soft	washed	6 weeks humid	square	100 × 100 × 25 mm	1 2 3

Flavour: d, spicy and strong with a smell

Wine: St-Emilion

Milk	Percentage fat	Weight	Type	Rind	Curing period	Form	Dimensions	Best season * = all year
TRANG'NAT								

Trang'nat is not sold; it is made in the home, as follows. Fresh cows' milk cheese is salted, peppered and cured in cellars for 3 weeks until it is slightly crusted, and then hung from beams and eaten as required. When it has gone a little too far, it is turned into Gueyin.

Milk	Percentage fat	Weight	Type	Rind	Curing period	Form	Dimensions	Best season * = all year
VOID								
C	40-45%	600g-1kg	soft	washed	2 months humid	loaf	180 × 60 × 60 mm	2 3

Flavour: d^2 with bouquet and remarkable smell

Wine: Rauzin Gassies, St-Emilion

9. FRANCHE-COMTÉ AND THE JURA

The Jura mountains do not have points like the Alps, nor rounded tops like the Vosges; they are arranged in chains. Goethe, Ruskin and Lamartine have all written of their romantic splendour. They are covered with forests, and from the 6th to the 15th century there were only small clearings in this enormous area of pine and oak. Early civilizations were very dependent on wood, and there is still evidence of this, such as tree trunks made into water drains. All the tools for agriculture and dairy farming were of wood. In the case of cheesemaking many of the implements are still of wood, because it gives the cheese a particular savour.

The history of Franche-Comté is tortuous in the extreme. It was owned by various dukes and sovereigns who rarely, if ever, visited it. The province was simply passed from one ruler to another through much of its history. In the main, Franche-Comté managed to rule itself, disregarding its royal or ducal owners. The flowers grew, the cattle bred, cows made milk, and the farmers made cheese, especially Gruyère de Comté. Although it is recorded that the rulers were content to eat enormous quantities of this cheese, there are no records to show that they took any interest whatsoever in the technology of cheesemaking or stock rearing. The cattle are at present Pie Rouge, Montbéliarde and Abondance, but there is considerable research going on with new breeds. The fat little Abondance cows are becoming rare, and now fetch lower prices at the cattle markets.

Farmhouses in the Comté illustrate Frank Lloyd Wright's precept that the best architecture has such a close affinity with the landscape that the buildings might have grown there. The stone-built mountain houses have enormous shingle roofs that cover a very large area, enclosing humans, horses, cattle, carts, hay, a sausage and ham smoking area around the chimney; both kitchen and bedrooms are heated by the stove. The houses on the plateaux are similar, except that they are higher and with more wood in their construction. The vital part of the farmhouse is really the big chimney. This structure starts in the centre of the house with an enormous wood-burning stove. The chimney above it is black and made with overlapping wooden shingles, a rectangular funnel that goes right up through the building to an opening sheltered by a little hipped roof. All the way up the chimney are hooks from which hang fish, hams, and sausages, smoking being an everyday practice. Juniper wood is burned because of its aroma, as well as oak and pine. The chimney also acts as a permanent central-heating device. Its warmth heats oven, bedrooms, and even the hay loft, the smell from which mingles with the juniper smoke. The Swiss have similar buildings.

Production of Gruyère de Comté is dependent on *fruitières*. These are cooperatives formed by the milk producers of several villages. It takes 600 litres (132 UK, 159 US gallons) of milk to make one Comté cheese of 48 kg (106 lb), which necessitates communities working together. These cooperatives started in the high plateaux of Doubs in 1264, when they were called *froumaiges de fructeres*. Cheesemakers in other regions also use the cooperative principle and it is a pleasure, and amusing, to see the number of ways in which the milk arrives. Donkeys, pony carts, boys on bicycles with small trailers behind them, motorcycles with paniers, beaten-up old vans, all come down the mountain roads to the *fruitière* in the valley with their milk. Part of the timing of the craft involves leaving the milk for two days before starting to make the cheese; this is an essential point and it affects the taste. Copper cauldrons are used for the first part of the work. These vary in size from 800-2000 litres (176-440 UK, 211-528 US gallons). The milk is heated to 33°C and coagulated with rennet. The curd is then cut with long combs of thin wire and heated again to 56°C. The next process is the most extraordinary. A man holding an enormous cheesecloth between his teeth and outstretched hands literally dives forward across the cauldron and scoops up about 50kg (110lb) of curds, supporting himself in this Nijinsky-like effort by wedging his toes under a ledge. He then walks across, holding this dripping cheesecloth, to a wooden mould and deposits it there, folding the cloth in a way that has evolved over seven hundred years. It is put in a hydraulic press, and then in a cold cave or cellar for a few days, salted and brushed to accelerate the formation of a rind. The ripening process involves the following procedure. Over a period of four to six months, the cheese is kept at a controlled temperature of 16°C to 18°C for two months while the rind is rubbed with a salty cloth to develop the microbe flora which gives the cheese its taste of nuts. For the remaining period in the curing rooms it is turned daily. Guy Remier, the most knowledgeable and best of the *affineurs* in the Jura, gladly passed on much of his knowledge. 'The profane', he said, 'think that the more holes there are, the better it is. I do not hold with this. The finer the paste, the richer the flavour in my opinion. There are holes, but they have little to do with it.'

Brillat-Savarin, in *Physiologie du Goût*, insisted that Beaufort was the 'Prince of Gruyères'. It is certainly higher in fat content and therefore more buttery. There is also an attractive fruity aroma. The Swiss, however, who invented the original Gruyère and have been making it since Roman times, look very boot-faced about this French imitation. It is not possible, they say, to make a good fondue with it. Their Swiss fondue, one of the facts of Swiss life, when flavoured with garlic, pepper, white wine, lemon juice and Kirsch, has a nobility that this softer Beaufort cannot achieve. Beaufort is good to eat, nonetheless.

The regional cooking of the Jura and Franch-Comté is straightforward and simple; there is no sophisticated centre where a special gastronomy could be cultivated – or make it all too 'haute-cuisine'. Butter is the main cooking medium, and as cheesemaking is the important local industry a variety of dishes are based on it. Fondue is made with Comté or Beaufort, and Cancoillotte is made with Metton. There is a cream cheese flan, Tarte aux Fromage Frais, available everywhere and eaten daily.

The most important meat of the mountains is pork. The pig itself is given more thoughtful attention and solicitude than is normally associated with this animal. The death of the pig, which constitutes a family festival, starts with the 'pig's supper', which includes black pudding, chitterlings, cheese, and veal cutlets, and ends with a dance. (Ireland and England both had similar practices in the 18th and 19th centuries, not so elaborate, but solemn.) There are also *cochonailles*, such as brawn, black puddings and a greater variety of preserved sausages than anywhere else in France – they look gruesome but they have a memorable taste, and they last without refrigeration. Then there are the smoked hams of Luxeuil; the celebrated Morteau sausages, named Jésu de Morteau and Jambon Droz; and cured and smoked mountain ham, good with *langues fourrées*, stuffed tongues from Besançon. There is a Civet Savoyard, which is jugged hare seasoned, cooked in wine and served with cream, good after a day's climbing or shooting, and followed by *pogne* – pumpkin tart. If you have fished successfully there is also salmon trout cooked so that the skin retains its colours, and a court bouillon.

The streams of the Jura hold trout, pike, tench and barbel. Eels are available, and a fish called *omble chevalier* (like char), salmon trout and crayfish. *Pochouse* is a fish stew with white wine, usually a mixture of the fish mentioned above.

Wild fungi are everywhere in the landscape and used with every possible variation in the regional dishes: stuffed, *en croûte*, in omelets, in sauces or just cooked on their own. There are *chanterelles, oranges, cèpes,* and *lépiotes.* Morels, most fragrant of them all with their dark caps, appear in the woods in spring but they are collected, dried, and last all the year round, losing hardly any of their pervasive scent and flavour.

Frogs' legs appear as Grenouilles Comtoises which are grilled. There is a relative of the quiche lorraine called quiche comtoise – a flan filled with bacon, ham, eggs and cream. Four soups are memorable: Soupe aux Cerises, which is cherry soup poured over croûtons and then spiked with Kirsch; Soupe aux grenouilles (the frogs are barely noticeable); Potée Franche-Comtoise, a basic regional cabbage soup, plus potatoes and pork with a Morteau sausage for flavour; and lastly, suitable for Diane de Poitier, Potage aux Oranges et aux Noisettes, soup topped with cream in which orange-capped fungi vibrate. The ultimate pâté of the region, and there are all the usual ones, is *pain d'écrevisses,* crayfish pâté, getting more expensive annually but retaining its taste.

Festivals and other public events give indications of the interests in any province, and in this case they show a wide and healthy range: slalom kayak races down dangerous rivers; motor-cross by car and motorcycle; the cinema as an art form; and festivals concerned with the beauty of the countryside – fir trees, birds and gentians. Horses, wine and gastronomy, antiques and music are all represented. As this region is far from the ancient pilgrim routes, there are only two religious festivals: one at Champlitte to St Vincent, the patron saint of wine growers; and the other to Nôtre Dame de Mont-Roland at Dôle.

The Jura wine festival, called the Biou, is held on the first Sunday of September, when the Arbois wine growers make an enormous 100 kg (220 lb) bunch of the best grapes, which is carried on the shoulders of four men. These are preceded by violinists and are escorted by men in regional costume, carrying halberds decorated with vine leaves. The huge grape cluster is hung beside the altar as an offering to Saint Just. This wine festival is more solemn and less riotous than many others in France.

Two famous sons of Franche-Comté are Louis Pasteur (1822-95), scientist, biologist and inventor of pasteurization, and Jean Anthelme Brillat-Savarin (1755-1826), lawyer and author of *Physiologie du Goût.* He wrote this book towards the end of his life during many visits to Switzerland and America taken to avoid the Revolution; a lawyer-gourmet's *à la recherche du cuisine française* made more poignant by nostalgia.

Milk	Percentage fat	Weight	Type	Rind	Curing period	Form	Dimensions	Best season * = all year
BLEU DE GEX/BLEU DU HAUT JURA/BLEU DE SEPT-MONCEL								
C	45%	5-6 kg	slightly pressed blue-veined	natural brushed	2-3 months humid	disc	300 × 75 mm	2 3

Flavour: c to d

Wine: Côtes-du-Rhône

Milk	Percentage fat	Weight	Type	Rind	Curing period	Form	Dimensions	Best season * = all year
CHEVRET								
G	45%	200 g	soft	natural	4-5 weeks dry	various shapes; disc, loaf	90 × 30 mm	2 3

Flavour: c^2 with bouquet

Wine: Regional wines, especially rosé

Chevret is made in the Jura mountains, Doubs, Anjou and Ain, on farms. A goats' milk cheese with a blue rind, it is pink-spotted. Its shape varies depending on the farmer's wife who makes it – discs or little loaves. The taste is consistently good, due partly to the 5-week curing period, but mostly to the splendid Franche-Comté goats.

Milk	Percentage fat	Weight	Type	Rind	Curing period	Form	Dimensions	Best season * = all year

COMTÉ/GRUYÈRE DE COMTÉ

Milk	Percentage fat	Weight	Type	Rind	Curing period	Form	Dimensions	Best season * = all year
C	45%	30-35 kg	pressed and cooked	natural brushed	3-6 months humid	wheel	600 × 110 mm	2 3 4

Flavour: d^2 with bouquet

Wine: Regional wines of the Jura and Savoy, or Beaujolais-Villages.

EMMENTAL FRANÇAIS

Milk	Percentage fat	Weight	Type	Rind	Curing period	Form	Dimensions	Best season * = all year
C	45%	100 kg	pressed cooked	brushed oiled	6 months humid; 2 months warm		850 × 250 mm	*

Flavour: b to d and wholesome

Fresh, irradiated or pasteurized milk is used. The flavour varies from b to d (whereas Swiss Emmental is almost always c) and there is a decent smell, partly lactic and partly pasture. A pressed, cooked cheese with a brushed, oil rind, there are so many holes in the paste that the cheese does not weigh as much as might be expected. As it weighs 100 kg holes notwithstanding, this is a blessing.

METTON

Milk	Percentage fat	Weight	Type	Rind	Curing period	Form	Dimensions	Best season * = all year
C skimmed or whey	1%		hard	natural	2 months dry in warm cellars	lumps, hazelnut size		

Flavour: c. Not very pleasant, and with a strong smell – rather like cattlecake

Drink: Beer perhaps

Cancoillotte is a fruity concoction made from Metton. A cast-iron pot is used to warm up really ripe Metton in salt water (30% of its weight). Thirty per cent of the weight of cheese in butter is added and stirred in. When freshly made this is splendid, but it does go off, turning grey.

MORBIER

Milk	Percentage fat	Weight	Type	Rind	Curing period	Form	Dimensions	Best season * = all year
C	45%	6-8 kg	pressed uncooked	natural	2-3 months brushing		400 × 100 mm	1 2

Flavour: c lactic

Wine: Beaujolais or Côtes-du-Rhône

Morbier is the cheese with the thin black line running through it showing that it is made with morning and evening milk in two halves (the black line being the charcoal). The curds are pressed and heated to 40°C. Formed in a circular mould, the cheese is pressed gently, drained and placed between wooden discs. The other half is added and pressed again, after which it ripens in a cellar for two to three months.

VACHERIN MONT D'OR

Milk	Percentage fat	Weight	Type	Rind	Curing period	Form	Dimensions	Best season * = all year
C	45%	1-4 kg	soft	washed	2-4 months	cylinder, boxed and band of wood	200-300 × 25-50 mm	3 4

Flavour: b^2 with unique flavour of resin

Wine: Crépy, Roussette or Beaujolais

10. THE RHÔNE VALLEY, HAUTE-SAVOIE, ALPES AND THE LYONNAIS

Farmhouses vary from north to south of the Rhône valley but they are all solid, stone-built, and have seen a lot of work, change and history. In Forez and the Lyonnais regions they are built around a yard, and have wooden galleries upstairs. In the Dauphiné the walls have often been made of enormous boulders up to first-floor level, with smaller stones and woodwork above, and tiled roofs. In the Haut-Vivarais the roofs are usually thatched and very large. Windows throughout the region are small, and where the mistral blows, to the south, there are none at all on the side facing the wind. In general Rhône valley farmhouses have character and strength, and are an important feature of the region.

The regional cooking is outstandingly good in all areas, but particularly so in the Lyonnais area; Lyon itself is considered by many as better than Paris. Lyonnais farmhouse and *auberge* cooking is simple, real, and for everyday, compared with some areas of France where in the home there is a marked difference between weekend splendour followed by a black Monday of bread and soup. There is quality and integrity also in all the *bistros*, where there is a pride in cooking – together with what might be termed the abrasive vigilance for which their local customers are famed.

There are many Lyonnais specialities, including pike *quenelles, gratiné* in crayfish cream and butter; Lyon sausages; cold saveloy with nuts and truffles; stuffed trout, braised; fish cooked in Burgundy wine; birds cooked with strips of truffle between the skin and the flesh; chicken cooked in cream; *quenelles financières* which are stuffed with lamb sweetbreads, mushrooms and truffles. Artichoke hearts stuffed with *foie gras* accompany many dishes. Other regions nearby have their own specialities. The Bas-Dauphiné has Bœuf Braisé à la Grignairaise. The Vivarais cook thrushes with grapes in their case. Once you have overcome your inhibitions about eating this bird it is interesting to decide which of these recipes is the best: roasted between sage leaves, with myrtle berries, or with grapes. The walnut cakes of the Rhône are memorable, and Montélimar nougat studded with almonds and bright pistachios.

For those who would like to see the Rhône valley in complete comfort there is the Hostellerie La Cardinale at Baix 07210. Named after Cardinal Richelieu, who stayed there in the 17th century, it was the founding inn of the *Relais et Châteaux*, a list of castles, châteaux, country estates and old hotels all over France. (Particulars from 17 Place Vendôme, 75001 Paris.)

There are many festivals in the region, concerned with cattle, wine, fruit, farm produce, music and religion, but the most beautiful is the Passion procession, which began as a medieval mystery play, in the Ardèche village of Burzet (20 km/12½ miles north-west of Aubernas, D25 and D289 intersection). A Bishop in red robes leaves the church at 2 o'clock on Good Friday, followed by villagers in costume. First come Roman soldiers, then children carrying the instruments, the hammer and nails, lash, sponge, and Judas's purse with its thirty dinars. Then Veronica, Simon the Syrian, the Virgin, John, Mary Magdalene, and the two thieves, together with the daughters of Zion in black. Plaques depict the Stations of the Cross, and in the time of the pilgrimages, penitents gladly joined in, to be lashed in expiation of their sins by the Centurion. In the 13th century, real criminals were used for the thieves and actually crucified; or so the legends say.

The geological base of the whole area consists of clearly defined areas of volcanic, crystalline and limestone rock, but for two million years, glaciers and the Rhône itself transported huge quantities of one or the other of these rocks, tore thousands of tons from one mountain, hauled it elsewhere and mixed it. Finally by a stroke of luck or divine providence, variegated systems of beneficial alluvial terraces ran all down the valley from the source to the sea. Wherever there is a limestone base, it is suitable for vines, so we have the vines of Beaujolais on the Saône, and the Côtes-du-Rhône wines in two separate areas of the river, with different *crus* in each. All around the vineyards are fruit orchards – the people say that in spring the fields are laughing with the blossom of apples, pears, apricots, peaches and cherries. Chestnuts and walnut trees also provide crops that feature in the cuisine; these large trees provide shelter for the fruit trees and vineyards. Wine takes precedence in France over everything else, especially if it is good, and other things may be somewhat overlooked. In fact here the herbage is good, the cows are splendid, the milk is rich and the cheeses are exceptional, especially in the Haute-Savoie.

The mountains and valleys are one of the last outposts of Fauna, the nature goddess, fresh as the Thames in Shakespeare's time, when apprentices were given salmon from the river so often that they grumbled about it. The alpine herbs and flowers grow more vividly and bright than the pictures in botanical books. This is the main reason why the cheeses of Savoie are so numerous and so rich. Lying in this Eden with my Nikon focused on a cow's muzzle, I saw her munch through *ceillet des Alpes* (wild pink), *saussurée couchée* (gigantic clovers), *gentiane de Koch* (the largest gentians with the deepest blue), and a dozen *benoîtes des montagnes*, including a sleepy, exotic, *rosalie alpine*, one of the 'protected' beetles.

Exceptional milk and all manner of cheeses result from this daily feast of flora and fauna. Imagine how dull the cheeses would turn out if the cows were fed on seed catalogue grass. The hay when cut has a perfume that disturbs the spirit; and when dried for winter it keeps an aroma that pervades the whole farmhouse.

Tomme or *tome* is a dialect word for cheese, and there are many varieties. Tomme de Savoie, made daily and matured in cool *caves* cut out of the mountain beside the farmhouses, varies from farm to farm. It has a simple wholesome richness to it. Tomme de Fenouil is the same cheese with a fennel flavour. Tomme de Sixty has a rough crust and is very hard, being matured for several years. Tomme, or Vacherin, L'Abondance, made from the milk of Abondance cows, has become very rare. Tomme de Chèvre is an irresistible goats' milk cheese, eaten either fresh or matured.

The goats wander everywhere, friendly, gregarious and eating everything they can see. They are usually milked on the hoof by the farmers' daughters. Not so pedestrian as the cows, nor so hysterical as the squealing pigs, they seem to lead an idyllic life. However, we did see a huge billy being castrated. One of his horns was sawn off, symbolically, after the operation. The vet drove up

in his little *deux-chevaux*, drank the Cognac offered him and drew out his rather medieval instrument. The farmer bent the goat over backwards by the horns, his son grasped a foreleg as one might hold the hand of a friend in trouble, and the vet performed his diabolical act. The goat made a sound of unimaginable sadness, which seemed to echo down the mountains for ever.

Tomme aux Raisins is a cows' milk cheese ripened in grape pips, skins, stalks and *marc*, if you get it in the Haute-Savoie, with an eerie taste of some strength. There is another version about that is simply processed cheese ornamented with an artificial rind into which grape pips are stuck – which is about on a level with the dyed fish now sold as kippers.

The basic French cheese of the Haute-Savoie, after the *tommes*, is Reblochon. Made daily from cows' milk by the farmers' wives and daughters, it is sold in the weekly markets, where it is taken in long octagonal crates. A scalded, renneted, lightly pressed cheese, it is semi-hard and the paste has a subtle flavour. The name itself means the last milk of the day, and in the past it was always made with evening milk only.

One of the really rare cheeses is Vacherin de Beauges. This is the private cheese of the mountain farmers, kept specially for Christmas time. Neither sold nor commercialized, it is stored secretly in corners of cold cellars. The firm grey rind encloses a paste that is surprisingly soft and quite extraordinarily subtle.

There is a functional connection between cheesemaking and hams. When the curds have been turned into cheese, the whey is fed to the pigs. They are lucky, for it is full of protein, globulin, albumins, lactose and many soluble salts. The pigs are usually kept in close quarters and squeal continually, but eventually they become silent smoked hams (Janinges and Celliers are the special ones), salami sausages and rosettes.

Such strong tastes need fruit, and there is a profusion of berries. Wild strawberries for the picking, together with raspberries, mulberries, bilberries and cranberries, most of which go well with a soft cream cheese made from cows' and goats' milk mixed 50-50 and named Saint-Marcellin, which is good – but even better when also mixed with white of egg.

Cheese needs wine, and there is Beaujolais and Côtes-du-Rhône. Beaujolais, which is good even when young and fresh,has grand neighbours in the Côte d'Or such as Moulin à Vent, Morgon, Fleurie, Chénas and others; there is the Côte Rotie with a bouquet of violet for example, Condrieu and Château-Grillet. Hermitage wines are supposed to have a fragrance of raspberry, especially Saint-Joseph. Raspberry flavour or not, they are individual and memorable. Cornas was a favourite of Charlemagne, as well as the white wine Saint-Péray. Clairette-de-Die is *pétillante* and has a fascinating bouquet of its own. Finally, Châteauneuf-du-Pape, originally reserved for the Popes at Avignon, is dark, resonant and strong. There are the rosés of Lirac, Chusclan and Javel for hot afternoons and picnics; they are more potent, let me remind you, than their appearance might suggest.

The first fairs at Lyon were inaugurated by Charles VII in the 15th century, beginning an era in which the city became one of the most important commercial centres of Europe. A *change* was established for money changing, which later became the Crédit Lyonnais. At these same fairs Rabelais, between 1532 and '34, sold editions of his *Gargantua* and *Pantagruel*. In 1536 François I took possession of the Comté de Forez. Soon after this the religious wars between Protestants and Catholics broke out, bringing death and destruction on a large scale for a century.

In 1600 Olivier de Serres, called the father of French agriculture, published his *Théâtre d'Agriculture et Mésnage des Champs*. Henry IV was so impressed that he planted 20,000 mulberries in the Tuileries, with a silkworm-rearing house. This suggestion of *growing* French silk instead of buying it from the east at outrageous prices was part of the Serres doctrine. He also gave detailed instructions on tending vines, which were disregarded, as the wine growers knew it all and more. Rotation of crops, artificial meadows, maize culture, potatoes, hops, sugarbeet, however, were new and the advice was taken. Furthermore the writing was so admirable, the style so imaginative, the philosophy so sure, that Henry IV insisted that it should be counted among the great works of French literature, and Olivier was made to read it at a theatre every night for four months.

Even if your knowledge of the French language is more than adequate, you may still find some Lyonnais expressions mystifying. They are not to be found in dictionaries, so here are some translations. *Se bambanner*, to walk about with a suggestive swagger – males and females; *benazet*, stupid booby; *bugne*, beast; *se coquer*, to embrace; *fenotie*, wife; *fumerons*, exciting legs; *gongonner*, to grumble; *picarlat*, skinny girl; *toberlo*, idiot; *potouille*, mud, filth; *gone*, child; *catolle*, tough old lady; *ferais un baiser entre les cornes d'une chèvre*, to give a kiss between the horns of a goat. This phrase is used often, and in many ways, starting with the attitudes of skinny girls, encompassing dubious bets on horses, and going on, eventually, to Voltairean philosophy.

In 2000 BC, during the Bronze Age, the Rhône was used for the transport of amber and tin. Later it became a Roman trade route. Now it is part of a commercial waterway that starts in Normandy on the Seine at Rouen, glides through Paris to the Marne canal and on to the Burgundy canal, and then to the river Saône, which is a tributary of the Rhône. In earlier days there were portages between the rivers and goods were carried on donkeys and mules. The canal network has made this unnecessary, and helps to provide a complete circuit through France by water, with views that are not obtainable from the admittedly speedier motorways. It is good for the spirit to make the journey in your own (motor) boat from England, but easier to hire one at Rouen; in the latter case write to the Syndicat National des Loueurs des Bateaux de Plaisance, F.I.N. (Fédération des Industries Nautiques), Port de la Bourdonnais 75007, Paris. This organization will send you innumerable variations of boat, route, and cost. The voyage will teach you more about France than you ever expected, its landscape, language, art, wine, cheese, regional cooking and people.

OPPOSITE Cheese stall in a village market in the Rhône valley.

Milk	Percentage fat	Weight	Type	Rind	Curing period	Form	Dimensions	Best season * = all year

ABONDANCE/VACHERIN D'ABONDANCE

Milk	Percentage fat	Weight	Type	Rind	Curing period	Form	Dimensions	Best season
C	45%	1.5 kg	soft	washed	3 months humid	pancake	250 × 40 mm	3 4

Flavour: b[2]

Wine: Crépy, Gamay de Chautagne

Made in the Haute-Savoie in the Abondance region, and named after the local breed of cows, which are short, fat, liked by the farmers, but becoming rare. So, sadly, is the cheese.

ARECHES/GRATARON D'ARECHES

Milk	Percentage fat	Weight	Type	Rind	Curing period	Form	Dimensions	Best season
G	45%	200 g	pressed uncooked	washed	1 month dry	cylinder unwrapped	75 × 50 mm	2 3

Flavour: d[2] with bouquet and tang

Wine: Gamay, Crépy, Apremont, or the Hermitage it deserves

AROMES AU GÈNE DE MARC

Aromes au Gène de Marc, made in the Lyonnais area, are cheeses such as the Rigottes, Pelardons and Picodons, which are cured in vats in fermenting *marc*, and consequently are made during the two months following the grape pressing, when this is available. The length of curing varies, and the flavour with it, but the taste is usually e or f. The Tommes are also made into Aromes, for the winter, and they are stronger still.

AROMES DE LYON

These are the same as the Aromes de Marc except that white wine is used, with one month in wine followed by one month in a dry cellar. The taste is sharper than you might expect, about f[2].

BEAUFORT/GRUYÈRE DE BEAUFORT

Milk	Percentage fat	Weight	Type	Rind	Curing period	Form	Dimensions	Best season
C	50%	40-60 kg	pressed cooked hard	natural brushed	6 months humid	cylinder	600 × 130 mm	1 2 4

Flavour: d[2] bouquet and fruity

Wine: Chignin, Crépy, Gamay

BEAUMONT

Milk	Percentage fat	Weight	Type	Rind	Curing period	Form	Dimensions	Best season
C	50%	1.5 kg	pressed uncooked	washed	6 weeks humid	disc	200 × 40 mm	2 3

Flavour: c

Wine: Roussette, Crépy

OPPOSITE Pigs drink the whey and become the famous sausages of the region.

Milk	Percentage fat	Weight	Type	Rind	Curing period	Form	Dimensions	Best season * = all year
BESSAN/PETIT BESSAN								
G or CG	40-45%	60 g	soft	natural	3 weeks	truncated cone	40 × 40 mm	2 3

Flavour: d to e² bouquet and fruity

Wine: Tavel Rosé

Milk	Percentage fat	Weight	Type	Rind	Curing period	Form	Dimensions	Best season * = all year
BLEU DE BRESSE								
C	50%	various: 100 g, 300 g, 400 g, 2 kg	soft blue-veined	scraped	curing varies with sizes	loaf	varying sizes foil and box	*

Flavour: d

Wine: Côtes-du-Rhône

Started in 1950 by making smaller versions of Saint-Gorlon, which is a French imitation of Italian Gorgonzola (and nowhere near so good, for the latter is a classical cheese, difficult to copy).

Milk	Percentage fat	Weight	Type	Rind	Curing period	Form	Dimensions	Best season * = all year
BLEU DE SAINTE-FOY								
C	45%	2-3 kg	slightly pressed internal mould	natural	2-3 months humid	cylinder	180 × 90 mm	2 3

Flavour: d² bouquet and savoury taste

Wine: Crépy, Gamay

Milk	Percentage fat	Weight	Type	Rind	Curing period	Form	Dimensions	Best season * = all year
BLEU DE SASSENAGE								
C	45%	5-6 kg	slightly pressed blue-veined	natural	2-3 months humid	cylinder	300 × 90 mm	2 3

Flavour: d and sharp with it

Wine: Beaujolais or Côtes-du-Rhône-Villages

Known for at least 300 years and mentioned in Diderot's *Encyclopédie*, this blue has practically no smell and the taste is sharp.

Milk	Percentage fat	Weight	Type	Rind	Curing period	Form	Dimensions	Best season * = all year
BLEU DE TIGNES								
C	40-45%	3-4 kg	slightly pressed blue-veined	natural	3 months	cylinder	180 × 100 mm	2 3

Flavour: e² bouquet and savoury

Wine: Hermitage, Château Grillet

Milk	Percentage fat	Weight	Type	Rind	Curing period	Form	Dimensions	Best season * = all year
BRISE-GOUT/BRISEGO								
C skimmed	20%	5 kg	pressed and cooked	brushed	5 months	cylinder	230 × 190 mm	2 3 4

Flavour: e to f and sharp with it (the name is a dialect word meaning 'sharpish')

Wine: Savoie regional wines, Gamay and Crépy

Milk	Percentage fat	Weight	Type	Rind	Curing period	Form	Dimensions	Best season * = all year

CHAMBARAND/TRAPPISTE DE CHAMBARAND

Milk	Percentage fat	Weight	Type	Rind	Curing period	Form	Dimensions	Best season * = all year
C	45%	200 g	slightly pressed	washed	3-6 weeks	disc	80 × 25 mm	2 3 4

Flavour: b to c

Wine: Sancerre, Pouilly-sur-Loire, Pouilly-Fumé

CHANTEMERLE LES BLÉS/PICODON DE VALRÉAS

Milk	Percentage fat	Weight	Type	Rind	Curing period	Form	Dimensions	Best season * = all year
G	45%	100 g	soft, semi-fresh	thin	1 week dry	disc	70 × 25 mm	1 2 3

Flavour: b to c, slightly goaty

Wine: Rosés

CHEVRETTE DES BEAUGES

Milk	Percentage fat	Weight	Type	Rind	Curing period	Form	Dimensions	Best season * = all year
G	45%	1 kg	pressed uncooked	washed	2-3 months humid	disc	180 × 50 mm	2 3

Flavour: c

Wine: Roussette de Frangy, Crépy

CHEVRIN DE LENTA

Milk	Percentage fat	Weight	Type	Rind	Curing period	Form	Dimensions	Best season * = all year
G	45%	450 g	pressed uncooked	no rind	1 month	disc	100 × 90 mm	2

Flavour: d to e^2 bouquet but sharp flavour

Wine: Mondeuse, Chignin-Bergeron

CHEVROTIN DES ARAVIS

Milk	Percentage fat	Weight	Type	Rind	Curing period	Form	Dimensions	Best season * = all year
G	45%	450 g	pressed uncooked	natural	2 months humid	disc	130 × 50 mm	2 3

Flavour: d^2

Wine: Gamay de Chantagne, Roussette

CLAQUERET/CERVELLE DE CANUT*/CLAQUERET LYONNAIS

A home-made fresh cheese from cows' milk, flavoured with herbs.

Recipe: Beat curds with a spoon, adding salt, pepper, shallots, herbs and minced garlic. Allow to ferment for two days. Add a pony of vinegar, a glass of white wine and 2 tablespoons of oil. Serve chilled as an hors d'œuvre.

*This means 'silk weavers' brains': silk weaving is one of the industries of the Rhône valley.

Milk	Percentage fat	Weight	Type	Rind	Curing period	Form	Dimensions	Best season * = all year

COLOMBIÈRE

| C | 50% | 500 g | soft lightly pressed | washed | 6-8 weeks | disc | 180 × 40 mm thin board paper | 2 3 |

Flavour: c^2 bouquet

Wine: Roussette, Abymes, Crépy

A variety of Reblochon.

FONDU AU MARC/FONDU AUX RAISINS

| C | 45% | 2 kg | processed | artificial rind plus toasted grape pips | no curing | big disc | 200 × 50 mm | * |

Flavour: bland

Wine: Vins Mousseux

Made in commercial dairies. Not to be confused with Tomme au Marc.

FROMAGE FORT DU BEAUJOLAIS

Fromage Fort du Beaujolais has a flavour of f and is slightly more *haute-cuisine* than the Lyonnaise. Old dry grated Boutons de Culotte, and saponified Comté, oil, unsalted butter and really old *marc* are mixed together in a sealed crock and left for 2 weeks or more.

FROMAGE FORT À LA LYONNAISE

This is not a cheese but a recipe for making a cheese with flavour f^3. Dry, old, goats' cheeses are grated into an earthenware crock, macerated with hot leek water, then macerated with a pony of old Beaujolais, tarragon, thyme, bay leaf, salt and pepper. The crock is then sealed and left for 3 weeks. When it is opened, and stirred with a wooden spoon, there is a remarkable odour. Fromages Forts are made in Belgium, Lorraine, Dauphiné, Provence, and Vivarais. There should be a competition between them all to find the real 'devil' of the Fromage Forts.

GRATARON D'ARECHES/GRATARON DE HAUTELUCE/HAUTELUCE

| G | 45% | 200 g | pressed uncooked | washed | 1 month humid | cylinder | 75 × 60 mm | 2 3 |

Flavour: d^2 bouquet and real tang

Wine: Gamay de Chantagne, Abymes de Myans

LIVRON/TOMME DE LIVRON

| G | 45% | 280 g | soft | bloomy | 1 month | disc paper-wrapped | 75 × 60 mm | 2 3 |

Made in commercial dairies.

Milk	Percentage fat	Weight	Type	Rind	Curing period	Form	Dimensions	Best season * = all year
MONT D'OR								
G or CG	45%	200 g	soft	natural	2 weeks	disc	90 × 15 mm	*

Flavour: b^2 bouquet and savoury

Wine: Beaujolais-Villages

Milk	Percentage fat	Weight	Type	Rind	Curing period	Form	Dimensions	Best season * = all year
PERSILLÉ DES ARAVIS/PERSILLÉ DE THÔNES/GRAND-BORNAND								
G	45%	1 kg	pressed blue-veined	natural brushed	2 months humid	cylinder unwrapped	100 × 150 mm	2 3

Flavour: d^2 bouquet, savoury and sharp

Wine: Chinon, Mondeuse

Milk	Percentage fat	Weight	Type	Rind	Curing period	Form	Dimensions	Best season * = all year
PERSILLÉ DU MONT-CENIS								
C and G	45%	8 kg	pressed blue-veined	natural	3 months	cylinder	300 × 150 mm	2 3

Flavour: d

Wine: Côtes-du-Rhône-Villages

Milk	Percentage fat	Weight	Type	Rind	Curing period	Form	Dimensions	Best season * = all year
PICODON DE DIEULEFIT								
G	45%	100 g	soft	natural	1 month soaked in white wine	disc	70 × 25 mm	2 3

Flavour: d and taste of alcohol

Wine: Côtes-du-Rhône

Milk	Percentage fat	Weight	Type	Rind	Curing period	Form	Dimensions	Best season * = all year
RAMEQUIN DE LAGNIEU								
G or CG	30-50%	50 g	soft	natural	3 weeks		50 × 50 mm	1 2 3

Flavour: c^2 bouquet and nutty

Wine: Montagnieu

Milk	Percentage fat	Weight	Type	Rind	Curing period	Form	Dimensions	Best season * = all year
REBLOCHON/DEMI, PETIT, AND REBLOCHONNET								
C	50%	500 g	slightly pressed	washed	4-5 weeks humid	disc	120 × 30 mm	2 3

Flavour: c creamy and wholesome

Wine: Mondeuse, Gamay or Côtes-du-Rhône

Milk	Percentage fat	Weight	Type	Rind	Curing period	Form	Dimensions	Best season * = all year
RIGOTTE DE CONDRIEU								
G	50%	56 g	soft	coloured red with annatto	2 weeks dry	small cylinder	35 × 35 mm	*

Flavour: c lactic and no smell

Wine: Côtes-du-Rhône

Milk	Percentage fat	Weight	Type	Rind	Curing period	Form	Dimensions	Best season * = all year
SERAC								
C	30%	3 kg	pressed uncooked	natural	3 months humid	cylinder	400 × 50 mm	1 2 3 4

Flavour: c

Wine: Gamay, Crépy, or Côtes-du-Rhône

Milk	Percentage fat	Weight	Type	Rind	Curing period	Form	Dimensions	Best season * = all year
TAMIE/TRAPPISTE DE TAMIE								
C	40-45%	500 g	pressed uncooked	washed	2 months humid	disc	170 × 50 mm	2 3

Flavour: c and lactic

Wine: Abymes, Crépy, Mondeuse

Milk	Percentage fat	Weight	Type	Rind	Curing period	Form	Dimensions	Best season * = all year
TARARE								
C	75%	various	soft triple cream	bloomy			various wrapped	

Flavour: a to b

Wine: Vins mousseux

Tomme or *tome* is a name given to many cheeses in the Savoie, the Dauphiné, Provence and the Auvergne. There are similar names in Languedoc and Corsica. The *tommes* below are listed in the alphabetical order of the final element of their names.

Milk	Percentage fat	Weight	Type	Rind	Curing period	Form	Dimensions	Best season * = all year
TOMME DES ALLUES								
G	45%	3-4 kg	pressed uncooked	washed		disc	230 × 70 mm	2 3

Flavour: b with bouquet

Wine: Gamay de Chautagne and Roussette

Milk	Percentage fat	Weight	Type	Rind	Curing period	Form	Dimensions	Best season * = all year
TOMME DE BELLEVILLE								
C skimmed	30%	2-3 kg	pressed uncooked	brushed and washed	2 months	disc	200 × 50 mm	2 3

Flavour: c

Wine: All wines of the region

Milk	Percentage fat	Weight	Type	Rind	Curing period	Form	Dimensions	Best season * = all year
TOMME DE BELLEY								
G or CG	40-45%	100-200 g	soft	natural	4 weeks dry	disc or brick	70-100 × 25 mm	2 3

Flavour: c^2 with a splendid bouquet, whether G or CG milk

Wine: Mondeuse, Gamay or Beaujolais-Villages

Milk	Percentage fat	Weight	Type	Rind	Curing period	Form	Dimensions	Best season * = all year
TOMME BOUDANE								
C	30%	2-3 kg	pressed uncooked	natural	1 month humid	cylinder	200 × 80 mm	1 2 3

Flavour: c^2 with bouquet

Wine: Crépy

Tomme Boudane was actually the name given to household *tommes* in the Savoie – those not made for market. However, they are sometimes seen in the markets, and they are similar to the average Tommes de Savoie.

Milk	Percentage fat	Weight	Type	Rind	Curing period	Form	Dimensions	Best season * = all year
TOMME DE COMBOVIN								
G	45%	250 g	soft	natural	4 weeks dry	disc	200 × 25 mm	1 2 3

Flavour: c^3 with bouquet and savoury taste

Wine: Côtes-du-Rhône or Châteauneuf-du-Pape

Milk	Percentage fat	Weight	Type	Rind	Curing period	Form	Dimensions	Best season * = all year
TOMME DE CORPS								
G	45%	450 g	soft lightly pressed	natural	3-4 weeks dry	cylinder	100 × 75 mm	1 2 3

Flavour: c^3 with bouquet

Wine: Rosés are satisfactory, or Hermitage

Milk	Percentage fat	Weight	Type	Rind	Curing period	Form	Dimensions	Best season * = all year
TOMME DE COURCHEVEL								
G	45%	2 kg	pressed uncooked	washed	2 months humid	disc	220 × 50 mm	2 3

Flavour: c with bouquet and goaty tang

Wine: Regional wines of Savoie or Médoc

Milk	Percentage fat	Weight	Type	Rind	Curing period	Form	Dimensions	Best season * = all year
TOMME DE CREST								
G	45%	100 g	soft	natural	2 weeks dry	disc	80 × 25 mm	1 2 3

Flavour: c^3 bouquet and tang

Wine: Côte Rotie, Condrieu

TOMME AU FENOUIL

Exactly as Tomme de Savoie, but flavoured with fennel.

Milk	Percentage fat	Weight	Type	Rind	Curing period	Form	Dimensions	Best season * = all year
TOMME AU MARC								
C skimmed	30%	1.5-2 kg	pressed uncooked	brushed and coated with *marc*	2 months humid + 3-4 months cool + 1 month warm		200 × 60 mm	2

Flavour: f³ and sharp

Wine: Armagnac

Tomme au Marc, made in the Beaujolais and various mountain valleys, uses a partially skimmed cows' milk, is cured for 2 months with washings and brushings, and then macerated in vats with fermented grape *marc*, followed by 3 to 4 months in cool mountain caves and one month in a warm cellar. The resulting flavour is f³ with a positive edge to it – sharp! Rarely present in the marketplace, but invariably in the farms, for winter use when the snow is really deep. It has some similarities with Gènes de Marc, but it is a wilder taste, needing the winter and a good brandy to bring out its desirable qualities.

Milk	Percentage fat	Weight	Type	Rind	Curing period	Form	Dimensions	Best season * = all year
TOMME DU REVARD								
C	40%	1.5-2 kg	pressed uncooked	natural	1 month cool + 1 month warm		200 × 100 mm	1 2 3

Flavour: c

Wine: Mondeuse or Les Abymes

Milk	Percentage fat	Weight	Type	Rind	Curing period	Form	Dimensions	Best season * = all year
TOMME DE ROMANS								
C	50%	200 g	soft	natural	3 weeks dry		110 × 25 mm	2 3

Flavour: c lactic

Wine: Beaujolais

Milk	Percentage fat	Weight	Type	Rind	Curing period	Form	Dimensions	Best season * = all year
TOMME DE ST-MARCELLIN/ST-MARCELLIN								
C	50%	100 g	soft	natural	2 weeks humid 2 weeks dry		75 × 25 mm	*

Flavour: b (originally made from goats' milk)

Wine: Beaujolais-Villages

Tomme de St-Marcellin or St-Marcellin is made in the Isère Valley. There is a long story about the cheese and the future King Louis XI when he was still Dauphine. It does him no credit. Rescued from a bear by two woodcutters, he promised them knighthoods. He actually granted them coats of arms without the necessary finance – the gilt without the gingerbread. The story does date the cheese back at least to 1460.

Milk	Percentage fat	Weight	Type	Rind	Curing period	Form	Dimensions	Best season * = all year
TOMME DE SAVOIE								
C	40%	2-3 kg	pressed uncooked	natural	1 month humid 1 month warm	cylinder	200 × 80-120 mm	1 2 3

Flavour: c with wholesome flavour and some bouquet

Wine: Most of the wines of the Savoie go with it

Milk	Percentage fat	Weight	Type	Rind	Curing period	Form	Dimensions	Best season * = all year
TOMME DE VERCORS								
G	45%	100g	soft	natural	1 month dry	disc	90 × 25mm	1 2 3

Flavour: c

Wine: Côtes-du-Rhône

Milk	Percentage fat	Weight	Type	Rind	Curing period	Form	Dimensions	Best season * = all year
TOUPIN								
C	45%	6kg	pressed cooked	washed	4-8 months humid	cylinder	200 × 150mm	3 4

Flavour: c

Wine: Crépy or Gamay de Chautagne

Milk	Percentage fat	Weight	Type	Rind	Curing period	Form	Dimensions	Best season * = all year
VACHERIN DES AILLONS/VACHERIN DES BEAUGES								
C	45%	2kg	soft	washed	3 months cool	disc boxed and with strip of bark	250 × 25mm	3 4

Flavour: b

Wine: Roussette, Chautagne, Mondeuse

Milk	Percentage fat	Weight	Type	Rind	Curing period	Form	Dimensions	Best season * = all year
VALDEBLORE/TOMME DE VALDEBLORE/TOMME DE SOSPEL/VALBERG								
E	45%	10-12kg	pressed uncooked	natural and brushed	3-6 months depending on use		300 × 75mm	3 4 1

Flavour: f and sharp

Wine: Côtes-du-Rhône-Villages

11. THE AUVERGNE

Cantal, made in 50kg (110lb) cylinders, has been produced in the Auvergne continuously for thousands of years. Pliny, Caesar, Charlemagne and Napoleon, as well as millions of French people, have all eaten it with satisfaction. It is French and was not, like some cheeses, borrowed from the Swiss. It starts from the salts of the earth that pass into the flora; the ruminants turn this into milk; and for thousands of years the farmers' wives have, with infinite patience and the use of all manner of combs, vats, imprecations, cheesecloths, presses and *savoir-faire*, turned the milk into a dampish white fruit. Then Mother Earth takes over, with the help of the farmer's wife and the farmer, maturing it for 3 to 6 months in mountain caves until it is ripe. It exudes a bouquet like an echo chamber when eaten, a taste reminiscent of herbs, flowers, and the cow. Zola wrote, 'There, wrapped in pear leaves, arose a giant Cantal which looked as if it had been split open by an axe, to give out its richness.'

The best Cantals, made near Salers and Languiole, are called Cantal Haute-Montagne. There is also a 10kg (22lb) Cantalet or Cantalon, the baby farmhouse version, kept for special occasions and drooled over, even by big hairy farmers, in something approaching baby talk. As the wines of the region include so many classics, no one needs advice on what to drink with this cheese.

Altitude, geology and soil content have determined the agriculture of the Auvergne. On the high plateaux of the Dôme and the Dore, Gevaudan and Cantal, you find cattle and sheep. On the limestone hills and the valley slopes are the vines, and grain is grown in the rich black soil of the Limagnes plains.

In spring time the Salers cows, with their red and mahogany hides, fill the cowsheds with mooing and bellowing. They can sense the pollen silently exploding from the alpine flora, out already and being wasted, while they are cooped up in their musty sheds.

In May they will leave these byres and for five months live in the open air. Alpine pastures, once dangerous to cows who used to fall down ravines, now have walls, fences or electric wiring, so there is no longer need for cowherds to go and live in the *burons*, which are now used for keeping and maturing cheeses. One of the great pasture regions of France, this is where the classical mountain cheese Cantal has been made for thousands of years. The *Fourme* du Cantal is in fact the origin of the word *fromage*. The *forme* of wood that supports it gave *formage* and this became *fromage*. It takes the milk of 20 to 30 cows to make a Cantal of 40 kg (88 lb). The milk is put into a *gerle*, a narrow deep vat. Rennet is added and it is put aside to cool and drain for two to three days. This *tomme* is then salted and put into its *fourme* or mould. It is then pressed to remove the whey. The *fourme* is then placed in the *buron* and periodically turned, until it is convenient to put it in the cool mountain cave, where it will remain for three to six months, when it reaches full maturity. Alternatively it is taken to a *fruiterie* where an *affineur* will take over the business of maturing it.

At first the rind has golden spots, but as it matures these disappear and the rind turns dark, nearly black, then red, and finally pale grey. Curing time can be gauged from the colour of the rind.

There is a fresh herbal flavour to Cantal Fermier (farmhouse) which Cantal Laitier lacks, mainly because the milk used has been pasteurized, but also because the curing lasts only two months. The perfection of the Fermier cheese is protected, and only pastures with identical natural conditions to the Cantal mountains are allowed to make it. These places, apart from Cantal itself, are eight areas in Aveyron, twenty-five around Puy-de-Dôme and one in the Haute-Loire district.

The farmhouses in Auvergne, mainly made of volcanic stone, are dark grey and have stone roofs with rounded corners like fish scales. Agates, amethysts and blue chalcedony are found in this volcanic rock and, after polishing, are sold in the markets and fairs. There are spring and autumn fairs in all the agricultural areas, but those at Laguile, Nabinals and Châteauneuf-de-Randon probably represent the Auvergne at its best. Roads are blocked from dawn with cows, bulls, dogs, trucks, horses, carts, sheep, pigs and people. Auctions occupy the morning with shouting and mooing in discord, eating, drinking and discussing prices in the afternoon, and then a rest. There is country cuisine for the evening meal with better wines and a dance called the *borrée*; translated, the word means pummel, trounce, charge or ram. Bagpipes, a hurdy-gurdy and a violin keep up a mysterious musical incantation. Apparently they prefer it to modern pop music.

The *borrée* starts. Males charge and females avoid with more or less grace, many wearing clogs. Regional costumes, regrettably, have disappeared. The old invariably say that the girls are not graceful enough and the men cannot ram.

Black Boudin sausages and chestnuts, smoked mountain ham from Ussel, or potatoes whipped up with garlic and Aligot cheese on fried croûtons, are all available at the weekend markets and the fairs. There are stalls with handmade sweets, acacia flowers dipped in orange-flavoured batter and deep fried, stalls of cheeses including most of those on our list, and *sabot* (clog) stalls. Harness and new bells for cows are sold at stalls surrounded by strong grumbling farmers, swearing at them for their lack of quality. In the cafés around the markets they drink Vins de Pay from the Côtes d'Auvergne: Madargue, Boudes, Corent, Cantogne and Châteaugay, all good and not exported. In the restaurants they drink Saint-Pourçain-sur-Sioule, made since before Christ with a quality difficult to assess because of the mountain air and general excitement, but very good, especially with Friand Santlorin, followed by a cheese board with Cantal and Saint-Nectaire, and then a raspberry *clafoutis*. There are then strawberry and myrtle liqueurs from Bort. These same fruits can be eaten as you walk in the mountains if you prefer them fresh, which is no doubt what the pilgrims did, visiting Puy-de-Dôme after Vézelay, and heading for Toulouse and Compostela.

The First Crusade was preached by Pope Urban II in 1095 at Clermont, so the whole religious ferment that created subsequent crusades and also the pilgrimages, with thousands of pilgrims moving across France by various routes, actually began in the Auvergne. Religious conviction remains strong in this region. The festivals are predominantly religious processions; sixteen of them are for penitents, second only to Brittany's nineteen *Pardons*. There are also torchlight processions, the most spectacular being at Vichy, to Nôtre Dame des Malades. A religious procession connected with transhumance (the practice of taking the animals up to mountain pastures in summer) is that at Besse-en-Chandes, where there is a centuries-old custom of carrying a wooden statue of the Virgin up the mountain to a chapel on 2 July (Montée) and bringing it down again on the Sunday after St Matthew's day (Davalade). In August there is a Shepherds' Pilgrimage at La Font-Sainte, and a Feast to the Vierge Noire at Murat.

From the 6th to the 12th centuries the Counts of the Auvergne refused to accept the sovereignty of the King of France, and covered the mountains with castles and forts. There is not a pinnacle of basalt or a knoll without its fortress, many of them now romantic ruins, but with a few exceptions: Châteaugay, for example, with its keep, and the Bourbon-Archambault with its twenty more or less intact towers.

The famous Jean, Duc de Berry, noted for his court of artists and architects, and the beautiful book of hours *Les très riche heures du Duc de Berry*, married an Auvergne countess in 1360. This helped to bring the previously isolated Auvergne into the mainstream of French culture, but stopped the poor duke right in his tracks: he died in a state of unimaginable debt at the age of 76.

The mineral and thermal sources are internationally known features of the Auvergne, especially Vichy, queen of Spas, which fills 290 million bottles a year with its famous water.

Cheesemaking in the Auvergne, c. 1760.

At the centre of the Auvergne is the Puy-de-Dôme, the sacred mountain, which has always been concerned with mysterious matters: the Gallic deity Lug, the Roman deity Mercury, the Virgin Mary, and now the World Institute of Physics and a huge transmitter for French television. There have always been hot thermal springs in the area and the temperature at the top of the mountain is often +4°C when it is −16°C in winter elsewhere. All this has made the people of the area more than a little convinced that they have magical properties and that their special cheese Saint-Nectaire is much better than Brie, Camembert and Roquefort. The fact that the rind is sometimes violet helps this illusion, and the bouquet really is unusually subtle.

Milk	Percentage fat	Weight	Type	Rind	Curing period	Form	Dimensions	Best season * = all year
BLEU D'AUVERGNE								
C	45%	2.5 kg	soft blue-veined	natural	3 months dry	cylinder foil with label	200 × 100 mm	2 3

Flavour: e³ with bouquet and slightly buttery

Wine: The best available – Hermitage, Margaux, Pauillac

Bleu d'Auvergne comes from an area near Thiézac and the Puy-de-Dôme, where pasture is scarce and the farms have no more than 15 cows. The curd is innoculated with *Penicillium glaucum* after it has been transferred to the moulds. The time and temperature of salting is critical. Bleu d'Auvergne is rubbed with dry salt at 10°C, and Bleu de Thiézac at a warmer temperature; this fact alters the taste markedly. When the blue veins appear, the metal foil is added and the cheeses are stored for three weeks at 2°C. Such variations account for the differing characteristics of the *bleus*.

Milk	Percentage fat	Weight	Type	Rind	Curing period	Form	Dimensions	Best season * = all year
BLEU DE COSTAROS/BLEU DE LOUDES/BLEU DU VELAY/AUVERGNE/COSTAROS AND FOURME DU MEZENC								
C	35%	1 kg	soft blue-veined	natural		cylinder	125 × 150 mm unwrapped – no foil	2 3

Flavour: d

Wine: Cornas, Cahors, Châteuneuf-du-Pape

Milk	Percentage fat	Weight	Type	Rind	Curing period	Form	Dimensions	Best season * = all year
BLEU DE LAQUEVILLE								
C	45%		soft blue-veined	natural	3 months dry	cylinder foil with label	220 × 100 mm	2 3

Flavour: d² with bouquet and pleasant smell

Wine: The best available red – Hermitage, Châteauneuf-du-Pape

In 1850 Antoine Roussel modified Fourme de Rochefort by sprinkling the curds with the blue moulds growing on rye bread to create this cheese. It has a less accentuated flavour than Bleu d'Auvergne, and the paste is less greasy.

Milk	Percentage fat	Weight	Type	Rind	Curing period	Form	Dimensions	Best season * = all year
BLEU DE THIÉZAC								
C	45%	3 kg	soft blue-veined	natural		cylinder	200 × 90 mm foil wrapped	2

Flavour: e² bouquet and savoury taste; strong smell

Wine: Cahors

Milk	Percentage fat	Weight	Type	Rind	Curing period	Form	Dimensions	Best season * = all year

BRIQUE DU FOREZ/CHEVRETON D'AMBERT/CHEVRETON DE VIVEROLS/CABION DU FOREZ

Milk	Percentage fat	Weight	Type	Rind	Curing period	Form	Dimensions	Best season * = all year
G or CG	40-45%	350 g	soft	natural	2 months on rye hay	brick unwrapped	50 × 25 mm	2 3

Flavour: c to d for CG, d^2 for goats' milk, when the rind is blue

Wine: Regional reds and rosés of Auvergne

CANTAL/FOURME DU CANTAL/SALERS/FOURME DE SALERS

Milk	Percentage fat	Weight	Type	Rind	Curing period	Form	Dimensions	Best season * = all year
C	45%	35-45 kg	pressed uncooked	natural brushed		cylinder	350 × 380 mm	2 3 commercial plants *

Flavour: c^2

Wine: Côtes d'Auvergne, Beaujolais

See also page 23

CANTALON

Cantalon is a small Cantal.

Making Cantal cheese.

Milk	Percentage fat	Weight	Type	Rind	Curing period	Form	Dimensions	Best season * = all year
CHAMBÉRAT								
C	40%	1 kg	pressed uncooked	washed	2 months humid	disc	175 × 40 mm	2 3

Flavour: e with the washed-rind tang

Wine: Côtes Roannaises

Milk	Percentage fat	Weight	Type	Rind	Curing period	Form	Dimensions	Best season * = all year
FOURME D'AMBERT/FOURME DE MONTBRISON/FOURME DE PIERRE-SUR-HAUTE								
C	45%	1.5 kg	soft lightly pressed internal veining	natural	3 months dry	cylinder unwrapped	110 × 230 mm	2 3

Flavour: d to e slightly bitter

Wine: Coteaux d'Auvergne, Côtes Roannaises

Milk	Percentage fat	Weight	Type	Rind	Curing period	Form	Dimensions	Best season * = all year
FOURME DE ROCHEFORT								
C	45%	5-10 kg	pressed cooked	natural		cylinder	200 × 200 mm unwrapped	2 3

Flavour: c, lactic but with a tang

Wine: Côtes d'Auvergne

Linked to the history of Cantal, but smaller, from upland farms.

Milk	Percentage fat	Weight	Type	Rind	Curing period	Form	Dimensions	Best season * = all year
GALETTE DE LA CHAISE-DIEU								
G or CG	45%	250 g	soft	natural	3 weeks humid	disc or brick	80 × 25 mm	1 3

Flavour: d^2

Wine: Coteaux d'Auvergne

Galette means a biscuit or cake (or money). It is very popular: the taste is nutty, and ideal with the Coteaux d'Auvergne.

Milk	Percentage fat	Weight	Type	Rind	Curing period	Form	Dimensions	Best season * = all year
GAPRON or GAPERON								
C skimmed or buttermilk	450 g		pressed uncooked garlic-flavoured	natural	2 months dry	ball	90 × 70 mm	2 3

Flavour: d but the garlic predominates

Wine: Côtes-du-Rhône

Kept in rye straw or hanging in the kitchen. *Gap* or *Gape* means 'buttermilk' in Auvergne dialect.

Milk	Percentage fat	Weight	Type	Rind	Curing period	Form	Dimensions	Best season * = all year
MUROL								
C	45%	450 g	pressed uncooked	washed	6 weeks humid	disc with hole	125 × 40 mm	2 3

Flavour: b to c, used in pastry baking as a flavouring

Wine: Coteaux d'Auvergne

Invented by Jules Bérioux; it has a pink rind.

| **PAVIN** | | | | | | | | |

Pavin, made in the Auvergne from cows' milk, is similar to Murol, with a mild flavour – b – cured for 6 weeks.

| **RIGOTTE DE PELUSSIN** | | | | | | | | |
| G or CG | 45% | 100 g | soft | natural | 2 weeks dry | cylinder or cone | 50 × 25 mm | 1 2 3 |

Flavour: c

Wine: Côtes Roannaises

| **ST-NECTAIRE (Appellation d'origine)** | | | | | | | | |
| C | 45% | 1.5 kg | pressed uncooked | natural | 8 weeks on rye straw | disc | 200 × 40 mm | 2 3 |

Flavour: c^2 with remarkable bouquet; the rind is violet

Wine: The light wines of Auvergne are suitable, but it deserves something special like Pouilly-Fumé or Montrachet.

An old cheese much venerated by the people of the Auvergne.

| **SAVARON** | | | | | | | | |
| C | 45% | 1.5 kg | pressed uncooked | washed | 3 months humid | disc | 200 × 50 mm unwrapped but labelled | * |

Flavour: c

Wine: Côtes d'Auvergne

Imitation St-Nectaire made from pasteurized milk in commercial dairies.

| **VACHARD** | | | | | | | | |
| C | 45% | 1.5 kg | pressed uncooked | natural | 2 months humid | disc | 200 × 40 mm | 2 3 |

Flavour: d^2 with bouquet and strong smell

Wine: Côtes d'Auvergne or Beaujolais

An old cheese and possibly an ancestor of St-Nectaire, made on farms in the Dore mountains.

12. POITOU, CHARENTES AND LIMOUSIN

There are more than thirty goats' milk cheeses produced in this area, and very few from cows' milk, yet everywhere there are cows grazing and mooing. The reason is simple. The butter of Poitou and Charentes is known all over Europe for its quality and fine texture, and that is where the cows' milk goes. The milk is also used for industrialized dairy products, especially long-life milk, widely used in France. This milk, one stage beyond pasteurized, has been developed and is now produced by the enormous Association Centrale des Laiteries Co-opératives Charentes-Poitou, which began with a small cooperative at Surgères, in 1888.

Poitou is a limestone plain, criss-crossed by deep valleys and almost devoid of trees. It presents, in fact, what appears to be an infinity of meadows without variation. There are, however, a few nuances. Towards Châtellerault there are moors where sheep graze. To the west there are fields of asparagus. To the east, towards Mont Morillon, on reclaimed moors, goats roam and Chabichou is made. The twenty goats' milk cheeses in the Poitou-Charente area are all made on very small farms. The Gatine de Parthenay has golden-coloured Spanish broom, prairie grass, boulders and sunken roads, but there are unusual plants besides – difficult to find in botany books; easily found and voraciously eaten by the goats. Thatched farmhouses are dotted about in this happy wilderness where the custodians of the goats live.

Charentes has the same variegated terrain as Poitou, but is a little more colourful, and this applies to the people as well as the landscape. The Charentais call each other *Cagouillards*, the name for those fat blue vine snails. They also have a saying: 'Les Charentais boiront du lait quand les vaches mangeront les raisins.' They also define themselves as *Gueux, Glorieux, Gourmand* (*gueux* means a rascally tramp). The women used to wear the neatest, tallest, thinnest of *quichenottes* with a patois word for 'Kiss me not'.

The Bordelais region grows the vines and produces some of the best wines in the world; and the grape harvesters eat goats' milk cheese. The vineyards that produce the white wine to be distilled into Cognac take up a large area in the Charente, with the Grande Champagne centring around Segonzac. Unlike Champagne, most of which is consumed in France, 80% of Cognac is exported. (Strange, in view of the number of Cognacs you see swallowed daily.) The fact that there are at any one time the equivalent of nine million bottles of Cognac being matured in their oak casks made from Limousin trees may be the answer.

The Limousin consists of two plateaux, the high and the low, separated by a desolate mountain range that has been levelled by erosion. This region, like the Jura, is noted for its rainfall. It is in fact almost as green as Ireland, and it is a huge cattle-rearing area. Specially sown pastures, with grass of a continuously identical shade of green, have been added to an already enormous indigenous meadowland, and 800,000 head of cattle, about a quarter of the French total, continuously graze there. It is an important breeding centre; superb and expensive bulls of the Limousin breed are exported to South America, Canada and Russia. White veal, increasingly sought after in the restaurants of Paris, Lyon, Turin, Milan, Florence and Rome, is produced from the young calves. The horses for Napoleon's cavalry were once bred there.

Dax, 60 km (37 miles) north-east of Biarritz, is the second busiest spa in France and in ancient times popular with both Greeks and Romans. There are handy take-away packs of radioactive mud, which restores beauty. An old spring in a valley outside the town, with stones well worn by pilgrims' feet, has a historically interesting pile of crutches, discarded by grateful ex-cripples. Presumably the curative powers are more than skin-deep, and still working.

Pilgrims going to the tomb at Santiago de Compostela beat three tracks through western France, and two of them converged at Parthenay. The third was the sea route from Britain, which landed at Soulac on the estuary of the Gironde. There were tens of thousands of these pilgrims, medieval tourists in search of holy relics to assist them in the afterlife, going south because that was the direction of the holy places. Current tourists in search of the sun, bathing, sailing, crustaceans and

OPPOSITE A small farmer carrying his milk to a cooperative.

the Mediterranean have the *Guide Michelin*. The pilgrims had a guide written by a Poitevin named Alméri Picaud which describes the customs and climate of the countries to be traversed, together with advice on food, drink, general health, and moral welfare. Parthenay, a fortified town, provided them with all the amenities: two churches for prayer, inns, taverns, shops and hospitals for the sick. One of the best-preserved medieval towns in Europe, it shows how comprehensively those early tourists were taken care of. Towards the end of the Middle Ages, however, there were as many thieves and brigands as pilgrims. These false pilgrims, called Coquillards, turned the pilgrimages into something different altogether from the simple and religiously credulous journeys of the first believers. The 15th-century François Villon was one of these Coquillards, finding materials for his vivid poems on the journeys and among the motley crowds.

Pilgrims who had met at Poitiers, at Notre Dâme de le Grande with its oriental domes, met again at Parthenay, and then at Toulouse. The pilgrimages sound altogether better than the package holidays of today. There was a definite profit motive for the French. The goats' cheeses of this particular area did not have time to go off, and vast quantities of regional wines must have been sold to keep up the spirits of the footsore. Those who could afford it would also widen their horizons by eating the regional dishes, which may well have been more inspiring than their home cooking.

There was La Mouclade, mussels in cream with white wine and shallots; Chaudrée, conger eel with sole and whiting, cooked in white wine; Lamproie à la Bordelaix, lamprey in thin slices with a red wine sauce; Entrecôte à la Bordelaise, beef with marrowbone jelly and red wine sauce; Cèpes à la Bordelaise, mushrooms or other fungi sautéed in oil and garlic with chopped shallots; Clafoutis, the archetypal *pâtisserie* of south-west France with cherries. And, of course, truffles used in every conceivable way. Curnonsky (M.E. Sailland), the great 19th-century writer on cuisine, described the cooking of this area of France as 'simple, honest, straightforward and rather countrified'. He lived in Paris, of course.

Milk	Percentage fat	Weight	Type	Rind	Curing period	Form	Dimensions	Best season * = all year
BOUGON								
G	46%	250 g	soft	bloomy	2-3 weeks dry	cylinder boxed	110 × 25 mm	1 2 3

Flavour: c

Wine: Beaujolais or regional wines of Poitou

Made in commercial dairies.

BÛCHE DU POITOU

Bûche du Poitou is a mild goats' milk cheese (flavour c^2) made in small dairies in Poitou: a long cylinder 350 mm × 75 mm, packaged in a wooden box.

Wine: Vouvray

BÛCHETTE D'ANJON

Bûchette d'Anjon, a small goat's cheese made in Anjon, is cured for 3 to 6 weeks and has a flavour c^2.

OPPOSITE The milk from Limousin cows is used for the manufacture of long-life milk, not cheese.

Milk	Percentage fat	Weight	Type	Rind	Curing period	Form	Dimensions	Best season * = all year

CAILLEBOTTE

Milk	Percentage fat	Weight	Type	Rind	Curing period	Form	Dimensions	Best season * = all year
C								

Flavour: a or b

Wine: None

A fresh unsalted cheese made on farms and ideal with fruit.

CAILLEBOTTE D'AUNIS

Milk	Percentage fat	Weight	Type	Rind	Curing period	Form	Dimensions	Best season * = all year
E								

A sheep's milk fresh cheese, unsalted and packaged in rush baskets, with flavour b, and interesting because of the subtle sheep's milk flavour.

Caille means curdled milk; the shelves on which the milk drains are called *caillebotis*.

CHABICHOU/CIVRAY/CHAUNAY

Milk	Percentage fat	Weight	Type	Rind	Curing period	Form	Dimensions	Best season * = all year
G	45%	100 g	soft	natural	3 weeks dry	truncated cone	60 × 60 × 60 mm	1 2 3

Flavour: e^2 with bouquet

The rind should be blue-grey. If it is dark grey it will be sharp and salty.

CHÈVRE LONG/ST-MAURE

Milk	Percentage fat	Weight	Type	Rind	Curing period	Form	Dimensions	Best season * = all year
G	45%	280 g	soft	bloomy	1 month dry	cylinder paper-wrapped	150 × 40 mm	1 2 3

Flavour: c^2 with bouquet and goat taste and strong smell

Wine: Marigny-Brizay

COUHÉ-VÉRAC

Milk	Percentage fat	Weight	Type	Rind	Curing period	Form	Dimensions	Best season * = all year
G	45%	250 g	soft	natural	1 month dry	square chestnut leaves	90 × 90 × 25 mm	1 2 3

Flavour: c^2, nutty and goaty

Wine: Côtes de Blaye, Barbe

GUÉRET/CREUSOIS

Milk	Percentage fat	Weight	Type	Rind	Curing period	Form	Dimensions	Best season * = all year
C skimmed	10%	400 g	soft	natural	6 months in sealed crocks		120 × 150 × 25-50 mm	2 3 4

Flavour: d + strong smell

Wine: Bergerac

Milk	Percentage fat	Weight	Type	Rind	Curing period	Form	Dimensions	Best season * = all year
JONCHÉE NIORTAISE/PARTHENAY								
G	45%		fresh					

Flavour: a or b

A fresh, unsalted cheese, on rush mats. The *jonchées* were much used in the châteaux of the Loire, at the end of banquets and served with fruit.

Milk	Percentage fat	Weight	Type	Rind	Curing period	Form	Dimensions	Best season * = all year
LA CHAPELLE								
C	45%	480 g	soft	bloomy	1 month dry	disc	125 × 25 mm	1 2 3 4

Flavour: c² and savoury

Wine: Regional wines

Milk	Percentage fat	Weight	Type	Rind	Curing period	Form	Dimensions	Best season * = all year
LUSIGNAN								
G	45%	250 g	fresh		1 to 2 weeks	disc	90 × 25 mm	1 2 3

Flavour: b and velvety texture

Wine: None necessary

Milk	Percentage fat	Weight	Type	Rind	Curing period	Form	Dimensions	Best season * = all year
MOTHAIS/CHÈVRE À LA FEUILLE/LA MOTHE-ST-HÉRAYE/ST-HÉRAYE								
G	45%	250 g	soft	bloomy	2 weeks dry	disc boxed	100 × 25 mm	1 2 3

Flavour: c²

Wine: Côtes de Canon-Fronsac, or Poitou regional reds

It is sold in all shapes, logs, pyramids, batons, etc.

Milk	Percentage fat	Weight	Type	Rind	Curing period	Form	Dimensions	Best season * = all year
OLÉRON/JONCHÉE D'OLÉRON/BREBIS D'OLÉRON								
E								

Flavour: a or b

Wine: Light, white wines

A fresh sheep's milk cheese that originated on the Île d'Oléron.

Milk	Percentage fat	Weight	Type	Rind	Curing period	Form	Dimensions	Best season * = all year
PIGOUILLE								
C G or E	45%	250 g	soft	natural	no curing draining only	disc unwrapped on straw	110 × 25 mm	*

Flavour: b to c

Wine: Light wines, Muscadet for example

The name is a dialect word of uncertain meaning. There is a velvety white rind, and a flavour stronger than most fresh cheeses.

Milk	Percentage fat	Weight	Type	Rind	Curing period	Form	Dimensions	Best season * = all year

RUFFEC

Milk	Percentage fat	Weight	Type	Rind	Curing period	Form	Dimensions	Best season * = all year
G	45%	250 g	soft	natural	1 month dry	disc	100 × 50 mm	1 2 3

Flavour: c^2 with bouquet; the rind should be a delicate blue

Wine: Chinon, Bourgueil

SABLEAU/TROIS CORNES

Milk	Percentage fat	Weight	Type	Rind	Curing period	Form	Dimensions	Best season * = all year
G	45%	250 g	fresh	no rind	drained 1 week	triangle	110 × 110 × 25 mm	1 2 3

Flavour: b. Similar to the Caillebottes

Wine: Muscadet

ST-CYR

A factory in the Vienne area produces goats' milk cheeses under this brand name with a certain uniformity of flavour, texture, etc.

ST-GELAIS/ST-MAIXENT

Milk	Percentage fat	Weight	Type	Rind	Curing period	Form	Dimensions	Best season * = all year
G	45%	280 g	soft	natural	6 weeks dry	square	100 × 100 × 25 mm	1 2 3

Flavour: d^2 with bouquet; the bluish-grey rind has red spots

Wine: Champigny, Bourgueil

ST-SAVIOL/ST-VARENT/SAUZE-VAUSSAIS

Trade marks of goats' milk cheeses produced by commercial dairies in most shapes, but mainly with a flavour c and no bouquet.

VALENÇAY/PYRAMIDE

Milk	Percentage fat	Weight	Type	Rind	Curing period	Form	Dimensions	Best season * = all year
G	45%	280 g	soft	natural + charcoal	5 weeks dry	truncated cone unwrapped	75 × 75 × 75 mm	1 2 3

Flavour: c^2 and nutty

Wine: Wines of Berry and Tours

Valençay is the Fermier (farmhouse) version, Pyramide the Laitier (dairy). Pyramide is made all the year round with frozen goats' milk curds and powdered goats' milk. The flavour is c and remarkably goaty.

13. THE PYRENEES, AQUITAINE, ROUERGUE, LANGUEDOC AND ROUSSILLON

The Michelin *Green Guide* begins by saying that the Pyrenees are the sunniest mountains in France. True, but you should read on and also visit them. You will discover that they are actually more of a dark shadow on the map between France and Spain. They are full of mysteries, partly due to the difficulty of transport, a result of their fragmented nature. The Pyrenees had an unstable time, 200 million years ago, compared with the Massif Central, the Jura, the Vosges and French Alps. Earth upheavals dislocated its granite spine completely, producing axial satellites of schist and crystalline rock, together with limestone ridges. Geological chaos, in fact. This produced pockets of land that are difficult of access without a helicopter or a mule; Rip Van Winkle areas, which had to make complete worlds of their own in order to survive.

The Landes, for instance, south-west of Bordeaux was a huge desolate swamp in the 19th century, but through modern technology it is now profitable, and also contains an interesting Regional Park and Nature Reserve. The profit comes from the forests of pine and oak masterminded by Chambrelent. The pines produce wood for paper and cellulose as well as resin.

On other upland areas, less tortured by earth movements, there are often neat chains of mountains, and long tranquil valleys that can be linked together by tunnels or mountain passes for transport purposes. The Pyrenees never had the advantage of this; the chaotic earth's crust forces the roads into impossible gradients and repeated hairpin bends, more difficult than anywhere else in Europe. Cloistered by winter snow as well, this has produced areas like Pays Toy, Quatres Vallées, Lavedan and Couséans, which still wear regional costumes as a matter of course; they have never been put away, out of embarrassed comparison with new fashions brought in by tourists. There are no tourists in the really awkward areas. We once stayed in Lavedan in a farm that had vertical cliffs of rock above and below. A village was to be seen above, but the road started miles below the farm, which meant driving down a narrow medieval track past springs, lakes and fountains, all complete with lizards, snakes, toads, but above all wild boars, which go through the forest like driverless tanks. Fortunately, you can hear them coming. There is one notable constant: the sheep. Everywhere there are sheep looking remarkably like those in medieval manuscript pictures, with small bodies, skinny legs, and neat bone-box muzzles sorting out the herbs and grasses of the region which will eventually effect the taste of the sheeps' milk cheese.

The history of the Pyrenees and the adjacent regions follows different courses from the rest of France because of this geological structure that splits it into disparate areas. The Pays Basque to the Côte Vermeille, the Coteaux Gascogne, Béarn, the Pays de Foix, Andorra, the mountains of Corbière and the valleys of Roussillon all have their different characteristics and histories, but the regional cuisine and the cheeses have a lot in common superficially. There is a preponderance of sheep in all areas, producing succulent mutton and a diversity of sheeps' milk cheeses.

The prehistory of this diverse region is remarkable for the amount of evidence of early man. The Pyrenees have more museums of prehistory than anywhere else in the world: Arudy, Lourdes, Foix, Aurignac, Mas d'Azil, Montmaurin, Saint-Gaudens, Tautavel and Eine all have museums, and there are also the caves and grottos themselves, with the wonderful paintings and objects found there. It all suggests a centre of early human activity. Later, in neolithic times, the routes by which new influences spread north along the European seaboard to Shetland and beyond, leaving evidence in the shape of standing stones and dolmens, start from the Pyrenees. One route starts from La Tenareze and reaches Bordeaux 'without using a bridge or a boat', so they say. The dolmen and megalith builders kept sheep and goats and practised transhumance; they also made cheese. Advanced cheese pots with holes in the base were found at Lake Neuchatel dating from 3000 BC, and more rustic pots in the Pyrenees dating from even earlier.

To spring from prehistoric man to the present, a National Park was created right in the centre of the

101

Pyrenees in 1967 between the Aspe valley and the Massif de Néouvielle: no dogs, camping, picking flowers, fires, or hunting. The park stretches for more than 95 km (60 miles) along the frontier between France and Spain, and contains more than 4000 wild goats and many brown bears, eagles, vultures, grouse and blackcock, as well as wild boar and various types of lizard.

There are more underground lakes in the Pyrenees than anywhere else in Europe. Since 1907, when E. A. Martez began his research in hydrogeology, underground lakes and rivers from one end of the Pyrenees to the other have been discovered, some of them hundreds of miles long. Mountaineering now has a spectacular rival, especially as the systems are so formidable, the lakes so phenomenally deep. Speleology is already concerning itself with the problems of underworld pollution, with how the insecticides and the artificial fertilizers may well eventually penetrate the underground lakes, rise up in the thermal springs and give spa patients something worse than the arthritis they are attempting to cure.

The annual festivals include seven religious processions and there are three concerned with the theatre and music, two with dancing, three with cars, and four with bulls (two at Bayonne and one each at Vic-Fezensac and Pomarez). The dance of the Pyrenees is the sardane, which is performed in both France and Spain. It is danced in its ritual circle at Vallespir, Céret, Prats de Mollo and at villages in Roussillon, and is accompanied by nine to fourteen musicians playing woodwind instruments, many of them antique and rarely seen elsewhere. There is a real sobriety of movement, but with occasional high vertical jumps. It bears a close relationship to the ancient classical dances with their strophe and antistrophe. In Spain, Franco tried to suppress it, but the Catalans continued to dance their sardana as a symbol of their striving for independence. Casals, himself a Catalan, wrote music for the sardana.

Catalan cuisine uses its olive oil in two basic forms: with garlic (ail y oli), and oil with anchovies (el pa y ail). One of the specialities of the Languedoc is cassoulet, originally from Toulouse but with variations in many areas, the other is brandade de morue, Cassoulet is an aromatic amalgamation of haricot beans, sausage, pork, mutton and preserved goose, cooked at great lengths in an earthenware pot with garlic and herbs. It has a golden crust. Brandade is from Nîmes and consists of dried salt cod pounded with garlic and olive oil to a creamy paste, and usually served on a fried crouton. The Languedoc soups are ouillade and aigo bouillado; the first is bean and cabbage with salt pork, the second is the same with garlic and egg. Meat in the Languedoc is often grilled over vine stocks; sausages are fried in goose fat with tomato sauce; and the lobsters have a sauce made with spiced tomato and brandy.

Basque cuisine is characterized by red pepper seasoning. The bouillabaise of the region is called ttoro and has a base of conger eel, turbot, and red gurnet. Chipirones are cuttlefish either stuffed or casseroled. Piperade is a green pepper and tomato seasoning that can be added to almost anything, but usually to omelets. Gascony and the Béarnais both use goose fat for frying; this is a characteristic regional taste, as butter is for Normandy and olive oil for Provence. (Goose fat starts to break down or burn at 250°C, whereas for pork fat it is 200°C and butter 130°C.) The livers of ducks and geese are sold in the marketplaces of the Landes in November at the St Catherine's fair and also in Gers. This is the province of the farmers' wives and daughters, both the work and the profit thereof. Preserving birds and pork, another feminine department, used to be an important matter, but with the progress of refrigeration it is dying out.

The Gascon cuisine is very ancien régime. There is no trimming down of the full menus of soup and hors d'œuvre, entrée and roast, cheese and dessert; and achieving an art form with it. Some of the great chefs have always been there and their assistants are now great chefs, making a continuous tradition.

The Causses and Cévennes add truffles to their cooking and the game of that area acquires its particular flavour from eating thyme and other herbs and juniper berries. There are trout in the streams, and they are cooked many ways. A characteristic local dish is trenels, mutton tripe, stuffed with ham, garlic, eggs and parsley.

Aligot is made throughout the Pyrenees in the following way. A pan rubbed with garlic is put on a hot stove with a mixture of butter and cream, and 400 g (14 oz) of grated Laguiole added little by little, together with 600 g (22 oz) of puréed potatoes. With a long-handled wooden spoon, this mixture is turned continuously and always at the same speed, in order to keep the mixture smooth, and not to break the thread of the cheese. It can take three quarters of an hour, but the resultant taste is worth it. If La Guiole, the ancient cheese of the Gauls, is unobtainable, Cantal can be used instead.

Other dishes and delicacies include tunny fish, which tastes completely different here, partly because it is cooked in sea water and many herbs, but also because it is fresh and not tinned. Then there are *estofinado*, fish stock with eggs, nut oil, milk and potatoes; *flaunes*, a strange pâté of sheep's milk cheese mixed with pounded cabbage; *melsat*, white pudding made with sausagemeat, eggs, and bread soaked in milk; *oreillettes*, cakes flavoured with orange and fried in olive oil; *petits pâtés de pézanas*, minced mutton covered in caramel in rolls; *soleil*, circular yellow cakes, orange-flavoured, with dried almonds. It is very satisfying to see students hitch-hiking and eating *t'elles*, which are tomato turn-overs with pieces of squid and cuttlefish: very sustaining. I ate them years ago as a student, when we called them *chaussons de calmar* – squid slippers.

So far as cheese is concerned the Causses are

Entrance to the caves at Roquefort, c. 1870.

renowned for producing Roquefort, the most expensive, and arguably the best cheese in the world. Pliny the Elder knew it, and it was also Charlemagne's favourite cheese. In 1411 Charles VI signed the first charter to protect its monopoly, which was signed by every subsequent king of France until 1925, when a French Law continued the right. The Stresa Convention of 1951 has protected the name Roquefort at an international level ever since.

Sixteen thousand tons of Roquefort are made annually, of which 10% is exported. The ewes' milk comes from a wide area, including Corsica. The milk is renneted and the drained curd goes into moulds in alternate layers with breadcrumbs on which *Penicillium glaucum* (var. *roqueforti*) has been grown.

Then, after salting and lightly pressing, the cheese goes into the caves to mature, where the temperature stays at 70°C, for three months. After this, it is wrapped in foil to prevent dehydration and stored at the correct temperature. These mountain caves provide in effect a gigantic controlled temperature area, and this is the really unique feature in the making of Roquefort. Cambalou, which is the home of the Roquefort *cabanes*, is a mountain that has been subject to water erosion and there are gigantic *fleuves* or chimneys which allow the air to penetrate to the caves from above. Similar shafts strike downwards from the caves to an underground lake, and the currents of damp air retain a constant temperature and humidity.

Roquefort cheese *à point* should have a consistent texture throughout, with the blue mould and a white untouched by any traces of grey.

Casanova avowed on several occasions that Roquefort had the properties of an aphrodisiac, when accompanied by Chambertin or Champagne, and thin slices of Italian ham. Curnonsky, in his *Lettres de Noblesse*, wrote that he preferred it with Clos de Vougeot or Château Latour, but he was a gourmet *in excelsis*.

The Pyrenees represent an enormous area of southern France. These few pages, together with the thirty or so cheeses listed represent a very small part of it all. However hard you try, the Pyrenees have areas that remain undiscovered and unexplored, and it is to be hoped that they remain so.

Milk	Percentage fat	Weight	Type	Rind	Curing period	Form	Dimensions	Best season * = all year
AMOU								
E	45%	5 kg	pressed uncooked	brushed washed and oiled	2-6 months humid	wheel	350 × 75 mm	1 2 3

Flavour: d and sharp

Wine: Rosés

Milk	Percentage fat	Weight	Type	Rind	Curing period	Form	Dimensions	Best season * = all year
ARDI-GASNA								
E	45%	4 kg	pressed uncooked	natural	3 months or 6 months	wheel unwrapped	320 × 70 mm	1 2 3

Flavour: c or d depending on curing period

Wine: Beaujolais

Made on mountain farms. Ardi-Gasna is Basque for 'local cheese'.

Milk	Percentage fat	Weight	Type	Rind	Curing period	Form	Dimensions	Best season * = all year
ARNÉGUI								
E	45%	variable	pressed uncooked	natural			variable	1 2 3

Flavour: c

Wine: Light red or dry white wines of the region

Milk	Percentage fat	Weight	Type	Rind	Curing period	Form	Dimensions	Best season * = all year
AULUS/BETHMALE/OUSTET/SAINT-LIZIER/ERCE/CASTILLON/CIER DE LUCHON								
C	45%	5-7 kg	hard pressed cooked	natural brushed	3-4 months	wheel	450 × 75 mm	1 2 4

Flavour: Varies from c to e, wholesome

Wine: Corbières, Roussillon, Madiran

Used for cooking.

BELLE DES CHAMPS

Belle des Champs is made by Chaumes in the Pyrénées-Atlantiques *département* from pasteurized milk. Cured for one month, this is a very mild bloomy rind cheese.

Flavour: b

Wine: Rosé

Milk	Percentage fat	Weight	Type	Rind	Curing period	Form	Dimensions	Best season * = all year
BLEU DES CAUSSES								
C	45%	2-3 kg	soft blue	natural	3 months in caves like Cambalou	cylinder	200 × 100 mm	2 3

Flavour: e^2 and bouquet; an excellent cheese

Wine: Châteauneuf-du-Pape, Hermitage, Chambertin

Milk	Percentage fat	Weight	Type	Rind	Curing period	Form	Dimensions	Best season * = all year

BOSSONS MACÉRÉS

Milk	Percentage fat	Weight	Type	Rind	Curing period	Form	Dimensions	Best season
G	45%		soft	natural	4 weeks			3 4

Flavour: g or h

Wine: Costières du Gard or Roussillon are suitable, but Armagnac preferable

An ordinary Tomme de Chèvre is macerated in crocks with a mixture of olive oil, wine and *marc*. The crocks are sealed in cool cellars for 3 months.

CABECOU DE GRAMAT

A small goats' cheese made in the Causses, it has a flavour c^2 with bouquet.

CABECOU D'ENTRAYGUES

Milk	Percentage fat	Weight	Type	Rind	Curing period	Form	Dimensions	Best season
EGC or mixed	45%	30g	soft	natural	1 month dry	disc	40 × 10mm	

Flavour: b to d depending on milk, sometimes with a bouquet

Wine: Roussillon or Châteauneuf-du-Pape

CAJASSOU

Milk	Percentage fat	Weight	Type	Rind	Curing period	Form	Dimensions	Best season
E	45%		soft	natural				

Flavour: c

Wine: All regional wines of the area

CHAUMES

Chaumes, made from pasteurized milk by the commercial dairy of this name in Pyrénées-Atlantique, this pressed uncooked cheese, with washed rind, appears as discs 175 × 30mm. The flavour is bland and mild.

CHIBERTA

Milk	Percentage fat	Weight	Type	Rind	Curing period	Form	Dimensions	Best season
C	45%	480g	soft	bloomy	5 weeks dry	disc	120 × 25mm	1 3 4

Flavour: c^2 and rare

Wine: Roussillon or Châteauneuf-du-Pape

ÉCHOURGNAC/TRAPPISTE D'ÉCHOURGNAC

Milk	Percentage fat	Weight	Type	Rind	Curing period	Form	Dimensions	Best season
C	45%	300g	pressed uncooked	washed	3 weeks humid	disc	100 × 25mm	*

Flavour: c^2 with bouquet and delicate texture

Wine: Madiran, St-Chinian

Milk	Percentage fat	Weight	Type	Rind	Curing period	Form	Dimensions	Best season * = all year

ESBAREICH/TARDETS

Milk	Percentage fat	Weight	Type	Rind	Curing period	Form	Dimensions	Best season
E	45%	4 kg	pressed	natural	3-6 months humid	loaf	250 × 75 mm	1 2 3

Flavour: c^2 with bouquet or e^2 if cured for 6 months

Wine: Regional wines of the Béarn or Madiran

FOUDJOU

This is a Languedoc cheese recipe, with a flavour f^3 to g or z. Tommes de Chèvre are used, half of old hard ones, and half of fresh; just drained, and kneaded together with crushed garlic, brandy and pepper. There is another even stronger variety made entirely with old cheeses grated and left to macerate in a 50/50 mix of brandy and olive oil. Made in the autumn, this *fromage fort* is ready in February, by which time it has made a red skin. The crock, ideally, should never be emptied, as the residue helps to 'feed' the new mixture when it is added.

Wine: Armagnac is the perfect drink with this strong taste.

IRATY

Milk	Percentage fat	Weight	Type	Rind	Curing period	Form	Dimensions	Best season
C & E mixed	45%	4 kg	pressed uncooked	natural	3 months humid	loaf unwrapped	300 × 80 mm	1 2 3

Flavour: d to e and very positive

Wine: Strong enough for the local Spanish wines

Iraty is made near Roncevaux (the Pass of Roncevalles, where Roland fell) and the Spanish border.

LA GUIOLE-AUBRAC/FOURME DE LA GUIOLE (Appellation d'origine: Aubrac Mountains)

Milk	Percentage fat	Weight	Type	Rind	Curing period	Form	Dimensions	Best season
C	45%	30-40 kg	pressed uncooked	natural brushed	3 months humid		400 × 400 mm with hoops	

Flavour: d with a tang and bouquet

Wine: Costièrs du Gard or Châteauneuf-du-Pape

One of the most ancient cheeses of Gaul.

LARUNS

Milk	Percentage fat	Weight	Type	Rind	Curing period	Form	Dimensions	Best season
E	45%	5 kg	pressed heated twice	natural	2 months or 6 months for cooking cheese	loaf unwrapped	300 × 70 mm	1 2 3

Flavour: b or c normal; f for hard cooking variety

Wine: Madiran

LES ORRYS

Milk	Percentage fat	Weight	Type	Rind	Curing period	Form	Dimensions	Best season
C	45%	10 kg	pressed uncooked	natural	3 months	wheel	400 × 90 mm	2 3 4

Flavour: d^2 with bouquet and a pleasant smell

Wine: Corbières or Roussillon

This is an outstanding cheese, similar and almost as good as the classical Italian Fontina made in the Val d'Aosta.

Milk	Percentage fat	Weight	Type	Rind	Curing period	Form	Dimensions	Best season * = all year

LOUBRESSAC

Milk	Percentage fat	Weight	Type	Rind	Curing period	Form	Dimensions	Best season
C	50%	200 g	soft	natural	2 weeks	disc	80 × 25 mm	*

Flavour: c

A cows' milk cheese made in the Quercy area and similar to Saint-Marcellin.

MONSÉGUR

Milk	Percentage fat	Weight	Type	Rind	Curing period	Form	Dimensions	Best season
C	45%	3 kg	pressed uncooked	washed and coloured	1 month humid	disc unwrapped	230 × 75 mm	*

Flavour: b to c and lactic

Wine: Any of the regional wines, or Beaujolais

PASSÉ L'AN

Milk	Percentage fat	Weight	Type	Rind	Curing period	Form	Dimensions	Best season
C	30%	35 kg	hard pressed cooked		2 years dry	cylinder coated in oil and umber	400 × 350 mm	*

Flavour: d

Wine: Strong red wines like Corbières

Mainly used in cooking, it can also be eaten but is very brittle. An imitation of Italian Grana.

PELARDON DES CEVENNES/PELARDON D'ANDUZE/PELARDON D'ALTIER

Milk	Percentage fat	Weight	Type	Rind	Curing period	Form	Dimensions	Best season
G	45%	100 g	soft	natural	2-3 weeks	disc	75 × 25 mm	2 3

Flavour: c^2

Wine: Côtes-du-Rhône or Roussillon

There are many more Pelardons, this being the generic name for this type of cheese, made with goats' milk, cured for a short time, and with a very thin skin.

PICADOU/CABECOU

Milk	Percentage fat	Weight	Type	Rind	Curing period	Form	Dimensions	Best season
E or G	45%	28 g	soft	natural	1 week	disc	50 × 10 mm	*

Wine: Armagnac

Picadou is Rocamadour cheese wrapped in leaves, and placed in a crock and sprinkled with wine or brandy, and left there till the flavour is just right – f^2.

PICODON DE ST-AGRÈVE

Milk	Percentage fat	Weight	Type	Rind	Curing period	Form	Dimensions	Best season
G	45%	140 g	soft	natural	2-3 weeks dry	disc	90 × 25 mm	2 3

Flavour: d^2 with a strong bouquet

Wine: Châteauneuf-du-Pâpe

The name means piquant: the cheese is flavoured and used in *fromage fort* when it has become too hard.

Milk	Percentage fat	Weight	Type	Rind	Curing period	Form	Dimensions	Best season * = all year

POUSTAGNACQ

A sheep's milk cheese, flavoured and fermented in sealed crocks.

Flavour: f

Wine: Armagnac

PYRÉNÉES BREBIS

C

Flavour: b²

Wine: Côtes-du-Rhône

PYRÉNÉES VACHE

Milk	Percentage fat	Weight	Type	Rind	Curing period	Form	Dimensions	Best season
C	45%		pressed uncooked	paraffined	2 months	cylinder	300 × 75 mm	1 2 3 4

Flavour: b

Wine: Roussillon, Corbières

Made by cooperatives from pasteurized milk.

ROCAMADOUR/CABECOU DE ROCAMADOUR/LIVERNON/CABECOU DE LIVERNON/CAHORS

Milk	Percentage fat	Weight	Type	Rind	Curing period	Form	Dimensions	Best season
E or G	45%	28 g	soft	natural	1 week dry	disc	35 × 10 mm	1 2 3

Flavour: varies with milk; c² sheep's milk, d² goats' milk

Wine: Cahors or Roussillon

Cabecou means 'little goat' in the patois.

ROGERET DES CEVENNES

Milk	Percentage fat	Weight	Type	Rind	Curing period	Form	Dimensions	Best season
G	45%	100 g	soft	natural	4 weeks humid	disc	65 × 25 mm	1 2 3

Flavour: c and nutty

Wine: Côtes-du-Rhône or Roussillon

ROQUEFORT (Appellation d'origine)

Milk	Percentage fat	Weight	Type	Rind	Curing period	Form	Dimensions	Best season
E	45%	2 kg	soft	natural	3 months	cylinder foil-wrapped	180 × 100 mm	*

Flavour: d² or e² with subtle bouquet

Wine: It deserves a Grand Cru, château-bottled Bordeaux wine, or Champagne

As the curing is constant, differences in flavour must be due to different grades of sheep's milk. All Roquefort is cured in the humid natural caves of Cambalou. One of the very best cheeses in the world, the flavour is extraordinarily subtle with a distinct bouquet. The taste is a fine balance, neither too dry nor too buttery. The blue mould *should* be marbled right to the rind, but this does not always happen. One of the ancient cheeses of the Gauls and mentioned by Pliny, it was enjoyed by Charlemagne. Charles VI granted a charter (1411) to the people of Roquefort establishing their monopoly, and subsequent kings all confirmed it. Roquefort is now protected internationally under the Stresa Convention (1951).

Milk	Percentage fat	Weight	Type	Rind	Curing period	Form	Dimensions	Best season * = all year
SARRASSON/SARRASSOU								
C buttermilk or whey								

Hot water is poured into the churns after the butter has been made, and the buttermilk is used as a sauce for potatoes.

Milk	Percentage fat	Weight	Type	Rind	Curing period	Form	Dimensions	Best season * = all year
TOMME DE VILLEFRANCHE								
C	45%	200 g	soft	natural	1 month	disc	120 × 25 mm unwrapped	1 2 3

Flavour: c^2 with bouquet

Wine: Clairette du Languedoc or Collioure

14. PROVENCE, ALPES AND THE CÔTE D'AZUR

Provençal landscapes vary from the marshes of the steaming Camargue, through the high plateau of Vaucluse, to the perpetually white summit of Mont Ventoux – winter snow, or summer's glistening crystal. Alluvial plains lie in the Rhône valley and the Comtat Venaissin. Below Nîmes is the wine-growing area, continuing into Languedoc. There are fertile areas to the east in the Petite and the Grande Crau, and westwards in the Camargues as the marshes are drained. There are underground rivers and lakes in many parts of Provence where the water has seeped down through the calcareous rock. Pressure creates the springs that delighted the Greeks, Romans and Moors and are such a feature of Provence today.

There are two flowering periods: the spring, followed by a summer of such heat that everything dries up – rivers, flowers and leaves, roots even – followed by autumn rains that bring renewed flowering. The extent of this rain has to be seen. A single downpour often exceeds the total annual rainfall of Paris, and the tributaries of the Rhône rise anything from 7 to 20 metres (23 to 66 ft). The Ouvèze and the Durance, on the east bank of the Rhône, are also flooded annually by the melting alpine snow while the western tributaries are still dried up.

Farming has followed different patterns down the centuries with the Romans, medieval monks, peasant farmers, and now cooperatives with an eye on technology and labour saving. The espalier method of growing fruit trees is being introduced in Provence. Old olive trees, gnarled veterans, are being uprooted and replaced by little walking sticks that will be easier to cope with. I found a farmer in the summer of 1982 smouldering under his best old olive tree, discussing it with his Greek and Moorish forebears over a bottle of Armagnac and giving them his solemn oath that the tree would never be uprooted. I agreed with him. They must have been watching from the farmhouse because a girl came out with green figs, *pèbre d'ail*, black olives and *caladons* (almond biscuits).

The annual festivals reveal something of the regional character. In Provence there are forty-three festivals of which ten are religious; eight are concerned with bullfighting; four with the sea, fish, and boats; the remainder with flowers, dancing, wine, music, olives, drama, gypsies, folklore and fertility. There are two that are processions of decorated carts, similar to the famous Sicilian ones, but the horses are also caparisoned with antique or reproduction Saracen harness and silver bells. The carts contain all sorts of things, including cheese, fruit, girls and sweetmeats.

The Gypsy Pilgrimage at Les Saintes Maries de la Mer on 24 and 25 May is one of the most astonishing festivals of France. This is the harbour where

Christianity first came to France in May, AD 40. A boat without sails or oars, bearing Mary Magdalene, Mary, mother of St John, Mary Salome, sister to the Virgin, and a servant girl named Sara (who was a gypsy) together with Lazarus, Martha and Bishop Maximinus, floated into the bay. The Gypsy Festival centres round the fact that Sara was a gypsy. A chest of relics is let down with ropes from the upper part of the church, while the gypsies sing. Two days are spent in horse racing, feasting, flamenco dancing and fortune telling. Above all they tell stories around the fires, for this is the gypsies' great annual meeting. Many are Spanish, but there are other nationalities who have come a very long way to trade horses, and swop gossip and objects of all kinds. It is wild, unimaginable and you would be quite unacceptable unless you are a gypsy or amazingly rich. The skull of Mary Magdalene, smooth, brown and hypnotic, can be seen in its sarcophagus at the church of Saint-Maximin, if you can persuade the old lady with the big key to open the chapel. This means finding her first, and your Provençal patois, full of old Latin words as it is, may not be up to it.

With the Mediterranean coast annually eating more fast foods, and meals that are easy to forget, those who recognize cuisine as an art may like to visit the birthplace of Escoffier in the village of Villeneuve-Loubet, near Cagnes-sur-mer, where the Fondation August Escoffier has been set up, including a small museum.

Escoffier founded the Society of Gourmets, whose annual dinner is held in London on 13 December. (This is the birthday of St Fortunatus, c. 530-610, patron saint of chefs, and also Bishop of Poitiers, author of some of the best early writing on food and wine.) Escoffier was known to say that good cheese such as Roquefort had the advantage of being a ready made course, and that all you have to do is to serve it properly: nature, sheep's milk, tradition, the *affineurs* and the caves of Cambalou will have done the rest.

The cheeses of Provence, almost all made from ewes' or goats' milk, include several that are outstanding. Banon is the archetypal Provençal cheese, as Camembert is for Normandy and Brie for the Île de France. It is made from goats', ewes', or cows' milk in that order or preference. It is available in spring and summer from goats' or sheep's milk,

and in the winter from cows' milk. One way or another they manage to eat variations on Banon all the year round. A small disc, 75 mm × 25 mm, wrapped in chestnut leaves and raffia-tied, it has a tacky rind under those leaves, and a surprisingly mild but subtle flavour. Cured both on farms or by *affineurs*, it takes two weeks for fresh Banon, and two months for the fully cured one. It is named after the town of Banon where there is a small fountain much used by children and animals in the market-place. The town itself is on a hill surrounded by fields of lavender and rosemary. Banon is excellent for picnics or at the end of dinners, and the local rosé of Mont Ventoux is ideal with it. In the unlikely event of it being forgotten in the cool part of the larder for too long, Banon can be used in a *fromage fort*. Bad Banons are rare but easily recognized. They sweat and have a terrible smell.

Tomme de Camargue (or Tomme Arlésienne) is the other basic cheese of Provence and it gets five stars from me. A sheep's milk cheese and therefore available in winter and spring, it is semi-fresh (drained for a week) and flavoured with thyme. It is made in little squares with a bayleaf attached, and the taste is creamy with a bouquet. When it gets older its aromtic charm is stronger, so you change the wine from Listel from the Camargue to Châteauneuf-du-Pâpe, together with black olives.

A lot of different people have enjoyed Provence: Greeks, Romans, Vandals, Franks, Alamans, Visigoths, and the Moors. It is for these reasons that Provençal man differs physically and mentally from the people of all other French provinces. Small, dark, ebullient, mercurial and violent, he has a liking for bullfighting. He is capable of Muslim fanaticism, Arab fatalism, and Greek cunning. The goat cheeses of Provence show positive Saracen influence, if you compare them with Syrian Akavi and Ilfravi, or Gibne.

Brousse du Rove and Cachat are basically fresh Greek cheeses, made the same way, and in baskets identical to those of the Greeks. The Romans initiated Poivre d'Ane − a similar cheese is mentioned by Columella in *De Re Rustica*. The Greeks also brought the olive and the vine, the fig and the chestnut, serenity and sun worship. The Romans built arenas at Nîmes and Arles, theatres at Orange and Vienne, the aqueduct at Pont du Gard, law, and a road system. There is an old Provençal saying: 'Provence was in Europe before France existed'; and it certainly was. It is still a part of older civilizations, making the rest of France seem simple and innocent; compare Banon or the other Provençal cheeses with Camembert of Normandy, for example, or Île de France Brie.

Milk	Percentage fat	Weight	Type	Rind	Curing period	Form	Dimensions	Best season * = all year
ANNOT/TOMME D'ANNOT								
E or G	45%	750 g	pressed uncooked	natural brushed	2 months humid	disc	210 × 50 mm	2 3

Flavour: c

Wine: Villars-sur-Var

Milk	Percentage fat	Weight	Type	Rind	Curing period	Form	Dimensions	Best season * = all year
BANON/BANON À LA SARIETTE								
E, G or G	45%	150 g	soft	natural	2 weeks to 2 months dry	disc + chestnut leaves and raffia	75 × 25 mm	*

Flavour: Whatever the milk, the flavour remains within the range b to c but with subtle nuances

Wine: Mont Ventoux Rosés

Milk	Percentage fat
BROUSSE DE LA VESUBIE	
E or G	45%

Flavour: b with bouquet

Wine: Lirac Rosé

The fresh cheese of Provence, obtainable in the mountains north of Nice and the Vesubie valley.

Milk	Percentage fat
BROUSSE DU ROVE	
E	45%

Flavour: a or b

Wine: Rosé Coteaux d'Aix

A fresh unsalted cheese usually beaten and served with fresh fruit. *Brousser* means 'beat' in Provençal dialect.

BÛCHETTE À LA SARIETTE

Bûchette à la Sarietta, a small goats' cheese from Provence, is cured for 3 to 6 weeks and has a flavour c^2, with bouquet.

Milk	Percentage fat
CACHAT/TOMME DU MONT VENTOUX	
E	45%

Flavour: b and creamy

Wine: Mont Ventoux Rosé

A fresh, salted cheese, drained in a cheesecloth and sold in bulk.

Milk	Percentage fat	Weight	Type	Rind	Curing period	Form	Dimensions	Best season * = all year

FONTAL

| C | 45% | 10-13 kg | pressed uncooked | brushed | 3-4 months humid | wheel | 400 × 90 mm | * |

Flavour: c without bouquet (Fontina has one)

Wine: Côtes de Provence

French imitation of Fontina, the fabulous and classical Italian cheese.

FROMAGE FORT DU MONT VENTOUX

| E or G | 45% | | | | | | | |

Flavour: f^2 and very sharp

Cachat cheese (see above) is kneaded, and placed in a *toupin* (crock). Pepper and salt are added and the cream which rises to the surface is stirred back. The longer it is kept and stirred the stronger it becomes; finally add a pony of *marc* brandy. Eaten with slices of onion and Châteauneuf-du-Pape.

PICODON DE VALRÉAS

| G | 45% | 100-150 g | semi-fresh | thin | 1 week | disc | 75 × 25 mm | 1 2 3 |

Flavour: b* bouquet and nutty

Wine: Châtillon-en-Diois Rosé

Sold in the Avignon market.

POIVRE D'ÂNE/PÈBRE D'AIL/BANON AU PÈBRE D'AIL

| E or G | 45% | 100-105 g | soft | natural with herb covering | 1 month | disc | 75 × 25 mm | * |

Flavour: Aromatic c

Wine: Châteaneuf-du-Pâpe or Provençal Rosé

Sold in baskets full of the savoury herbs that grow around Banon.

POIVRE D'ÂNE/PÈBRE D'AIL

| C G E or mixed | 45% | 100 g | soft | natural + sprigs savory | 1 month | disc | 75 × 25 mm | * |

Flavour: b or c with aromatic taste and perfume

Wine: Gigondas Rosé

TOMME DE CAMARGUE/TOME ARLÉSIENNE

| E | 45% | | fresh | | | | | |

Flavour: b creamy

Wine: Camargue Listel

Fresh, drained, and flavoured with thyme or bay. Sold in small squares, 60 × 60 × 15 mm, with a bayleaf attached.

OPPOSITE A stall in a weekend market in Provence.

Milk	Percentage fat	Weight	Type	Rind	Curing period	Form	Dimensions	Best season * = all year
VALBERG/TOMME DE VALBERG/VALDEBLORE/TOMME DE SOSPEL								
E	45%	10-12 kg	pressed uncooked	natural brushed	3-6 months	wheel	300 × 75 mm	1 3 4

Flavour: e to f and sharp

Wine: Cornas, Lirac, or Côte Rotie

Also used for cooking when cured for the full 6 months.

15. CORSICA

Goats and sheep have many exotic tastes to assist them in producing milk with potential for the Corsican cheeses. The wild uncultivated areas of the islands are called *maquis*. The dictionary translation of this word is 'scrub', which hardly conveys the nature of these expanses where the vegetation is a combination of beautiful flowers and shrubs. Many are admired and cultivated for their beauty in Asia Minor, Spain, and North Africa, but seventy-eight varieties are unique to Corsica. It is in the *maquis* that the sheep and goats, with their specialist understanding of flora, find the ingredients for their milk and our cheeses. The full-blast bouquet from a really peak-flowering *maquis* in midsummer is quite an experience. Similarly, the taste bouquet from Fleur du Maquis, the goats' milk cheese, is something beyond most people's experience unless they have lived on the island.

Corsica has a basically Mediterranean climate, with variations due to the heights and the sea winds. The rivers are irregular: thin and shallow from June to October, voluminous and impetuous from October to April. To the tourists, most of whom visit in the spring or summer, the bridges appear to be ridiculously high over trickles of water – but they should come back in the winter.

Two types of cooking exist on the island, one for hotels, restaurants and tourists, imitating Spanish, Italian and Provençal dishes, and the other for Corsicans, which is rich and varied. The Corsican variant of bouillabaisse, called *aziminu*, uses the wide variety of fish caught around the coast. There is another soup, a bouillon, which includes Broccio, the fresh sheep's milk cheese. The best of Corsican gastronomy centres round wild pig, its

OPPOSITE A corner in a Corsican farm cellar.

flavour enriched by the chestnuts, wild herbs and fruits they have eaten. The little pigs are often smoked over fires of chestnut. Wood-smoked ham is usually served with fresh figs, and there are splendid smoked sausages called *figatelli*.

There are roasts of wild boar with chestnut purée and sauces with deep indefinable qualities. The Corsican dialect does not help, but it is worth the effort to ask the cooks, or watch them to see what they use.

Blackbird pâté, or a lighter variety made with thrushes, is perfumed with the junipers, arbutus and myrtle that they have eaten, and which are used again in cooking them. *Piverunata* is stewed kid with peppers. There are other dishes such as lamb and goat cutlets cooked in the herbs from the *maquis*. Tripe and onions, based on goats and sheep, are served with little chitterling sausages which are enjoyable, but *piverunata* is *the* unique Corsican dish. Lobsters are found all round the coast and there are blue trout in the mountain streams. The simplest dessert is Broccio, or Brocciu, the fresh cheese, mixed with wild honey, or a brioche called *faculelle*, also made with fresh Broccio cheese. Letizia, Napoleon's mother, raised him on Broccio sheep's milk cheese, beaten up with warm pure goats' milk in the winter. He was also fond of *torta castagnina*, which are made with pine seeds, almonds and hazelnuts, and *canistrelli* cakes made with ground almonds and anis served with wild honey.

Traditional Corsican farmhouses are stone-built, solid and austere. The stone huts in the mountains used by the shepherds during transhumance are made without cement or mortar, as are the drystone wall enclosures, square for sheep and circular for goats.

Corsican festivals include a folklore festival with dancing and singing; a commemoration of the birth of Napoleon; a procession for fishermen; and an automobile race. The remaining ten festivals are exclusively religious. Singing is part of the Corsican way of life. Like the Welsh and the Italians, they sing with tremendous gusto. Tino Rossi is Corsican.

There was a Greek colony in Corsica from 555 to 81 BC, which accounts for the figs, the chestnuts and the fresh Broccio cheese. The Romans lived there for six hundred years, which explains Sarteno cheese, so similar to Italian Provolone. The early Phoenicians had an influence on the shape and decoration of the fishing boats. The tourists of today are having much less real influence on Corsica than the ancient Greeks, Phoenicians and Romans – which is a blessing, considering the damage done to some places around the Mediterranean.

Milk	Percentage fat	Weight	Type	Rind	Curing period	Form	Dimensions	Best season * = all year
BLEU DE CORSE								
E	45%	3 kg	soft	natural	3 months humid	cylinder	200 × 100 mm	1 2 3

Flavour: e² with sparkling bouquet

Wine: Patrimonio, Sciaccarello

Made on farms on the high plateau of northern Corsica

Milk	Percentage fat	Weight	Type	Rind	Curing period	Form	Dimensions	Best season * = all year
BROCCIO/BROCCIU								
E	45%		Fresh		unsalted	made in a basket heated and churned		fresh 3 4 stored *

Flavour: normally b; sometimes salted and stored in crocks for 6 months, when the flavour becomes f and sharp

Wine: When fresh: a rosé; when salted: Patrimonio

Made on farms in central Corsica, this fresh sheep's cheese starts from milk that is heated and churned. Letizia, Napoleon's mother, used to beat it with warm goat's milk as well.

Milk	Percentage fat	Weight	Type	Rind	Curing period	Form	Dimensions	Best season * = all year
CALENZANA/CALENSA								
E or C	40%	200 g	soft	natural	1 month humid	disc	125 × 25 mm	2

Flavour: varies E=c with bouquet; C=c

Wine: Patrimonio or Rosés of Provence

Milk	Percentage fat	Weight	Type	Rind	Curing period	Form	Dimensions	Best season * = all year
FLEUR DU MAQUIS/BRINDAMOUR								
G	45%	750 g	soft	natural	3 months on herbs	square with herbs	130 × 130 × 50 mm	2

Flavour: c³ with bouquet and aromatic smell

Wine: This cheese deserves Chambertin, but Châteauneuf-du-Pape or Patrimonio would be suitable.

This is an exceptional cheese with an outstanding bouquet.

Milk	Percentage fat	Weight	Type	Rind	Curing period	Form	Dimensions	Best season * = all year
GOLO								
E	45%	140 g	soft	natural	3 months humid	square	120 × 120 × 50 mm	1 3 4

Flavour: c and rich

Wine: Regional wines

Milk	Percentage fat	Weight	Type	Rind	Curing period	Form	Dimensions	Best season * = all year
NIOLO/NIOLIN/ASCO								
E	45%	170 g	soft	natural	3-4 months humid soaked in brine	square unwrapped	140 × 140 × 50 mm	2 3

Flavour: f^2 or g^2 with bouquet

Wine: The best obtainable

Made on farms in the Niolo plateau, this cheese at its best has a remarkable, unquenchable bouquet, reminiscent of the myrtles, asphodels, juniper, flax and honeysuckle eaten by the sheep. It deserves a château-bottled Premier Cru Bordeaux, but the local Patrimonio goes with it. This cheese is sometimes made and eaten fresh, when it shows none of its fabulous bouquet whatsoever – a rather nondescript mild cream taste.

Milk	Percentage fat	Weight	Type	Rind	Curing period	Form	Dimensions	Best season * = all year
SARTENO								
G or E or both		1 kg	pressed uncooked	natural	3 months dry	ball	125 × 100 mm	1 2 3

Flavour: f

Wine: Cahors, Corbières, or Roussillon

Made in Sartène and the plateau to the south-west. The rind has a natural glossy texture and is yellow. Related to Italian Provolone, and probably Roman in origin.

Milk	Percentage fat	Weight	Type	Rind	Curing period	Form	Dimensions	Best season * = all year
VENACO								
G or E	45%	450 g	soft	scraped	3-4 months humid	square	125 × 125 × 50 mm	1 2

Flavour: d and sharp, with smell

Wine: Patrimonio

GLOSSARY

A

Abbaye Abbey: cheese made or started at a monastery

Acidity One of the factors in the coagulation of milk, together with temperatures and rennet enzymes.

Acid-curd aerobe A micro-organism that can live only in the presence of oxygen: e.g. penicillium, album, *Penicillium candidum, Penicillium glaucum.*

Acid curd milk Milk coagulated by lactic acid rather than by rennet.

Aerobe A micro-organism that does *not* require oxygen for maintaining itself.

Affinage Treatment for bringing cheese to maturity

Affiné Cured or ripened.

Affineur Skilled person who carries out ripening and storing of cheese.

Albumin cheese Cheese made not from the casein protein in the milk alone, but from the albumin protein, or both albumin and casein proteins, which flocculate when heated.

Ammoniacal When a cheese has passed maturity there is a smell of ammonia.

Annatto Colouring matter for some cheeses includes this, the orange-coloured pulp around the seeds of the annatto tree (Livarot and Munster). Marigold and carrot are also used for colouring cheeses.

Appellation d'Origine Legal description, regulating all aspects of cheese:
1. breed of cows, goats or sheep
2. geographical area
3. methods of production
4. chemical composition
5. physical characteristics
6. specific attributes
The Institut National des Appellations d'Origine supervises the above in the same way that it controls wines.

Aromatized To change flavour and smell by the addition of aromatic chemicals.

Aromes Cheeses steeped in *marc.*

B

Babeurre Milk remaining after cream is removed.

Beestings Another name for colostrum. The first milk after delivery of calf.

Becs Small fissures beneath the rind of Gruyère-type cheeses.

Body The interior of the cheese.

Birou Needle used to aerate Roquefort.

Bleu Generic name for cheese with internal moulds; or cheese with natural blue rind (Olivet Bleu).

Bloom 1. A cheese that releases the scent of flowers
2. Growth of *Penicillium candidum.*

Bondard Cheese shaped like the bung of a barrel.

Bondon Cheese shaped like the large bung of a tun or cask.

Boucané Smoked or dried in the open air

Boulette Moulded by hand into a ball shape.

Bouquet Used of the agreeable smell of certain cheeses.

Boutons de culotte Trouser buttons. Small cheeses.

Breaking up curd Machine or hand breaking of the curd into small particles e.g. Comté and Saint-Paulin. Soft and washed-rind cheeses have the curd broken into coarse particles.

Brine A solution of salt in water used to impregnate cheeses with salt.

Brique, briquette Like a brick.

Broussé Provençal *brousser* means to stir and relates to cheeses made from milk that is stirred during the heating process.

Brushed *Brossé.* During ripening, some cheeses are brushed by hand or machine.

Buron Mountain hut used as a creamery (Auvergne and Jura).

Buttermilk A by-product of churning milk to make butter.

C

Cabane Stone hut where some cheeses are salted (Causses).

Cabecou From *cabrecou*, Languedoc patois for goat; it means a very small goat cheese.

Caillage First action in making cheese.

Cancoillotte Generic name for cooked-whey cheese.

Caprin Odour showing character of cheese.

Casein The crux of the matter: the part of the milk that solidifies. During ripening, the casein of soft cheese becomes soluble, pressed cheese becomes soft, and cooked cheese becomes hard.

Caseic ferment Red mould.

Caserette From *cagerette*, Normandy patois for a rush or straw basket and also the cheese drained in these baskets.

Cellar Room or cave for curing or storing cheese with regulated temperature and humidity.

Cayolar Stone hut (Béarn).

Cendré Cheese ripened in wood ashes.

Chabichou Name for goats' milk cheeses; *chabi* is the diminutive in Poitou.

Charbonné Dusted with powdered charcoal to encourage blue mould.

Charpenté Rich in tannin or alcohol (borrowed from the wine-tasting vocabulary).

Chaumes High pastures in the Vosges.

Cheddaring Stacking and turning large pieces of curd to make them form a thick fibrous mass.

Chevreton The generic name for the goats' milk cheeses of Burgundy and the Massif Central.

Chevrotin The same, but of Savoie.

Cooked curd Cheeses when the curd is heated after curing.

Colostrum The first milk (beestings) produced by a mammal after giving birth.

Crémet Generic name for the cream

cheeses of Anjou, Brittany and Maine.
Crottin The goats' milk cheeses of Berry.
Croûte French word for rind.
Cru As in wine tasting: cheeses which have a characteristic taste of the region.
Cuite Enormous hole in a Comté-de-Gruyère – an accident.
Curdling The first step in cheesemaking; usually involves the use of rennet.
Curing The ripening treatment: of infinite variety.
Cuyala Shepherd's hut in the Pays Basque.

D

Demi-étuvé Term relating to Dutch cheeses, defining state of hardness.
Desiccation Excessive dryness of rind and paste.
Double crème Cheese with 60-75% fat content.
Draining Soft cheeses are drained naturally. Hard and cooked cheeses are pressed to drain.
Drying An operation before curing.
Dur Quantity of a cheese with a firm paste which has aged.

E

Echauffé Said of cheese that has gone putrid.
Enriched milk Milk with cream added.
Ensemencé Cheese in which the paste has been injected with a penicillium.
Extra gras Fat content 45-60%.
Eye Hole in Gruyère or other cheeses.

F

Faisselle Cheese drainer.
Fermier Farm-produced cheese.
Feuille Generic name for cheese wrapped in tree leaves.
Feuilleté Flaky: a cheese that breaks up into layers.
Fleurines Currents of air in caves, helping curing (Roquefort).
Foin Hay: ripened in.
Fondu Cheese melted down and blended with other dairy products.
Form The shape of the cheese. Ultimate origin of word *fromage*.
Fourme Generic name for the Auvergne and Languedoc cheeses.
Frais, fraîche Unripened.

Fromage fort Generic name for cheese that has been kneaded, beaten and fermented in crocks.
Fromage tartiné Processed cheese with maximum moisture content of 56%.
Fruitières Cooperative dairies.

G

Gapron Cheese made from buttermilk, from Auvergne dialect *gap*.
Gazimelle Generic name for goats' milk cheese in the Cevennes.
Gène Generic term for dry *marc* left after grape pressing, used to flavour some cheeses (Lyonnaise).
Gouleyant A term borrowed from the wine-tasting vocabulary meaning light and fresh.
Grana Generic name for grating cheese, like Parmesan.
Gras Cheese made from full-fat, unskimmed milk.
Grataron Goats' milk cheese from Beaufort.
Guilde des Maîtres Fromagers A French professional association concerned with the promotion of cheese and the maintenance of the highest standards in its production.

H

Haloir Cheese drying room.
Haut-montagne Mountain cheese.
Hard Cooked cheese, e.g. Emmental.
High With a flavour like game (Faisande).

J

Jasserie Shepherd's hut in the Livradois mountains of Auvergne.
Jonchée Cheese taking its name from the rush basket in which it is contained.

L

Label All French cheeses by law must carry a label stating origin, name and maker.
Lacaune Breed of sheep.
Lactation Period during which animals produce milk. Cows have no fixed period. Sheep lactation is from autumn to spring. Goats from spring to autumn.
Laitier Factory-made from pasteurized milk.
Lénures Small fissures in Beaufort and Comté (connoisseurs like this).
Lissé Very smooth; fresh cheese processed in a *lissoir*. Like Petit-Suisse.

M

Macerated Cheese immersed in a liquid, which transforms the fermentation and taste, depending on the liquid and the time immersed.
Mache Borrowed from the wine tasters, meaning an aftertaste.
Maigre Low fat; less than 20%.
Maturation Ripening
Mélange Mixture of cows' and goats' milk.
Metton, mattons Dialect words, from Comté and Lorraine, meaning whey cheeses.
Mille trous A Gruyère type with too many holes.
Molle Cheeses with a crust that has been neither pressed nor cooked.
Mou Excessively runny or too tender cheese.
Mould The container that moulds or shapes the cheese.
Moulds The microflora that grow on the surface of cheeses.
Mousse The moment when a cheese starts growing its mould, and is taken to the cellars.

N

Natural A rind neither washed nor seeded with mould.
Nerveux Wine taster's term borrowed – meaning slight acidity or other dubious qualities.
Nutty In French *noisette*, the flavour of fresh hazelnuts.

O

Oiled The rind of hard cheese is sometimes rubbed with oil to prevent desiccation.
Ouvert Gruyère with holes that are too big
Ovine Smell and taste of sheep's milk cheese.

P

Paraffined Waxed, e.g. Edam.
Passé Over-cured or over-aged.
Paste The interior of the cheese.
Pasteurized Sterilized. A process named after Louis Pasteur: heat treating to destroy pathogenic micro-organisms, without damaging the nutritional properties of the milk.
Pâté The paste as opposed to the rind.
Pavé Square cheese, literally 'paving stone' (Normandy).
Pelardon Goats' milk cheese (Cevennes).
Persillé With parsley.
Petit lait Whey.
Picodon Generic name for goats' milk cheese (Rhône).
Plastic curd Cheese where the curd has been heated in hot whey and kneaded, which facilitates shaping and moulding.
Pleurer 'To weep'. The sign of a fine cheese: a Beaufort or Comté in which the holes are damp.
Pressed Cheese that has been subjected to hand or mechanical presses.
Processed cheese Made from natural cheese in which the natural development has been stopped by processing, rendering it more uniform.
Propionic fermentation The action that releases carbon dioxide and produces the holes in cheese.
Puant Stinking. Especially used of some of the cheeses of northern France.

R

Ramquin Dialect word for goats' milk cheese (Bugey).
Rance Said of triple cream cheeses that have gone dry.
Recuire Reheating the whey from Gruyère, making Brise-Gout, a whey cheese.
Rennet Substance that coagulates milk, obtained from the fourth stomach of ruminants.
Ressuage Action immediately following salting, in a ventilated drying room.
Rigotte The family of Lyon cheeses.
Rindless cheese Natural cheese foil-wrapped to stop rind forming.
Rind flora Moulds of bacteria growing on the rind of a cheese.
Rogeret Goats' milk cheese (reddish) from the Cevennes.

S

Saltage Salting – either hand-sprinkling or immersion in brine depending on the cheese. The more frequent the salting, the thicker the rind.
Saponified Rancid.
Sec Cheese in an advanced stage of desiccation.
Serum Whey.
Soudure Period when a change of pasture or feed causes a change in the taste of milk and therefore the cheese.
Standard milk French legal standard is 34 g of butterfat for each kilogram of milk.
Starter Culture of milk acid bacteria added to milk to increase its acidity.
Sterilized milk Milk subject to prolonged heat treatment to eliminate micro-organisms. Sterilized milk is unsuitable for cheese making.
Stresa Convention An international agreement by Austria, Denmark, France, Italy, the Netherlands, Norway, Sweden and Switzerland protecting cheese names.
Suraffiné, surfermenté Overcooked.

T

Tannic Astringent taste: in wine, due usually to the tannin in the oak barrels; in cheese due to various reasons.
Tastefromage Confrérie de Chevaliers du Tastefromage de France, founded 1954. A cheese fraternity now associated with the Wine Society.
Tomme, tome Savoyard for cheese.
Toupin Savoyard for pot or crock but in the Jura mountains it means the big bell worn by the queen cow of the herd.
Triple crème Minimum fat content 75%.

V

Vache Cow.
Vachard, vacherin, vacherol Cows' milk cheese.
Vermiculée Badly cured cheese (Peau de Crapaud).

Y

Yeux The holes in cheese.

RECOMMENDED CHEESE SHOPS

RECOMMENDED CHEESE SHOPS

The Guilde des Fromages and the Compagnons de Saint-Ugozon are associations concerned with all aspects of French cheese, its quality, its production and marketing. They have between then 1830 members, from 22 regions and 79 *départements*. They offer the 280 names and addresses of cheese shops listed below as representing the highest professional standards.

PARIS

1st Arrondissement
Jean-Claude Benoît, 38, rue de Richelieu

2nd Arrondissement
Michel Azemard, Au Petit Fermier, 8, rue des Petits-Carreaux
Michel Le Quen, La Ferme Montorgueil, 86, rue Montorgueil

4th Arrondissement
Anne-Marie Alfonso, 38, rue Saint-Louise-en-l'Ile
Claude Anthes, 9, rue Geoffroy-l'Angevin
Raymond Lecomte, 76, rue Saint-Louise-en-l'Ile

5th Arrondissement
Jacques Barrilliet, 131, rue Mouffetard
Marcel Charbonnel, Crèmerie des Carmes, 47 ter, boulevard Saint-Germain
Claude Limousin, Crèmerie des Carmes, 47 ter, boulevard Saint-Germain

7th Arrondissement
Roland Barthélémy, 51, rue de Grenelle

8th Arrondissement
Pierre Androuët, Androuët S.A., 41, rue d'Amsterdam
Pierre Lagoidet, Produits du Terroir, 25, rue Royale
Claude Rayot, 7, rue de Castellane
Henry Voy, Ferme Saint-Hubert, 21, rue Vignon

9th Arrondissement
Michel Marquis, Fromagerie des Martyrs, 5, rue des Martyrs
Jean Molard, 48, rue des Martyrs

10th Arrondissement
Roger Alléosse, 160, rue du faubourg Saint-Denis

11th Arrondissement
François Franceschi, Les Provinces du Fromage, 205, boulevard Voltaire
Raymond Lefebvre, 112, rue de la Roquette
Jean Perdrigeon, 36, rue du faubourg du Temple

12th Arrondissement
André Chalopin, 144, rue du faubourg Saint-Antoine
José Lima, 1, rue Marsoulan

13th Arrondissement
Maurice Corbeau, 53-55, rue du Moulin de la Pointe
Patricia Duplant-Lasnier, La Fromagerie, 204, rue du Château-des-Rentiers
Claudine Gente, Crèmerie Saint-Hyacinthe, 198, rue Saint-Jacques
Thierry Lasnier, La Fromagerie, 51, rue de Tolbiac

14th Arrondissement
Jacques Vernier, Fromagerie Boursault, 71, avenue du Général-Leclerc

15th Arrondissement
Jean Bouttier, La Ferme du Hameau, 223, rue de la Croix-Nivert
Christian Cantin, 2, rue de Lourmel

Pierre-Louis Mijs, Ferme du Champ de Mars, 1, rue Desaix
Pierre Serraz, 110, rue Saint-Charles

16th Arrondissement
Guy Genève, S.A. Genève et Fils, 16, rue Dufrenoy
Galerie Saint-Didier, 10, rue Belles-Feuilles
Jean Lesieur, 2, rue de Passy
Jacques et Josette Minard, Ferme de Passy, 39, rue de l'Annonciation
Dominique Sellier, Fromagerie de Courcelles, 11, avenue de la Grande-Armée

17th Arrondissement
Patrick Carmes, 24, rue Lévis
Alain Dubois, 80, rue de Tocqueville
Guy Genève, 11, rue Lebon
Philippe Sellier, Fromagerie de Courcelles, 79, rue de Courcelles
Jean Travet, Ferme Valérie, 14, avenue Stéphane-Mallarmé

18th Arrondissement
Denise Barile, 71, rue Marx-Dormoy
Alain Barthélémy, Marché Riquet, 36, rue Riquet
Roger Bobbi, Crèmerie du Château Rouge, 48, boulevard Barbès
Jack Chaput, Ferme Poitevine, 64, rue Lamarck
Edith Delbey, 110, rue Marcadet
Claude Gervais, La Fromagerie, 92, avenue Saint-Ouen
Maurice Grousset, La Fromagerie, 9, rue du Poteau
Joël Guet, Le Pot au Lait, 65, rue des Abbesses
Jacques Maubert, 20, rue Lepic
Odile Naussac, La Fromagerie, 92, avenue de Saint-Ouen
Roland Ruffier, Fromagerie Damrémont, 54, rue Damrémont

THE DÉPARTEMENTS AND THE PARIS REGION

Ain
Robert Maublanc, La Grotte aux Fromages, 01540 Vonnas
Michael Rupani, Chez Mireille, 6, rue de Lyon, 01170 Gex

Aisne
Willy Pierrard, Comestibles, 8, rue Théodore-Blot, 02170 Le Nouvion-en-Thierac

Alpes-Maritimes
Edouard Cénéri, La Ferme Savoyarde, 22, rue Meynadier, 06400 Cannes
Ange Paperon, A la Petite Bressanne, 13, rue Assalit, 06100 Nice

Ardèche
Robert Bourgeat, 59, Grande-Rue, 07300 Tournon

Ardennes
Jacques Baudin, 3, chemin des Romains, 08200 Sedan

Aube
André Julien, 19, route de Villenauxe, 10400 Nogent-sur-Seine

Aude
René Bousquet, A la Bonne Cave, 51, rue Aimé-Ramon, 11000 Carcassonne

Aveyron
Jean Cadilhac, Lou Pastrou, 1397, avenue de l'Aigoual, 12100 Millau
Jacques Chalvet, Crémafix S.A., passage du Mazel, 12000 Rodez

Bouches-du-Rhône
Gérard Paul, 35, boulevard Clémenceau, 13300 Salon-de-Provence et 9, rue des Marseillais, 13100 Aix-en-Provence

Cantal
Henri Grillet, Crèmerie du Gravier, 22, cours Monthyon, 15000 Aurillac
Alain Muzac, 2, rue des Frères-Charmez, 15000 Aurillac

Charente-Maritime
Patrice Galamez, La Fromagerie, 19, avenue La Fayette, 17300 Rochefort
Gilles Pouilloux, Le Petit Marchand, rue Charles-Hervé, 17750 Etaules

Côte-d'Or
Françoise Cauvard, Centre Commercial, Fontaine d'Ouche, 21000 Dijon

Jacques Delin, Crèmerie de la Vouge, Gilly-les-Citeaux, 21640 Citeaux
Michel Guillermier, Adipal, 5, rue de l'Est, 21000 Dijon
Gérard et Philippe Leboda, Sodiprolait, La Baratte, 70, avenue de Stalingrad, 21100 Dijon
Henry Maronat, Fromagerie des Settons, 4, place de la République, 21210 Saulieu
Jean-Pierre Mille, La Fine Fourchette, 3, avenue Eiffel, 21000 Dijon
Jean-Claude Overney, 6, rue des Fours, 21210 Saulieu
Robert Perrot, 28, rue Musette, 21000 Dijon
Simone Porcheret, 14, 18, rue Bannelier, 21000 Dijon

Eure
Robert Jollit, 7, rue Gambetta, 27500 Pont-Audemer

Eure-et-Loir
Philippe Plot, Ferme Sainte-Suzanne, 7, rue de la Pie, 28000 Chartres

Haute-Garonne
Xavier Bourgon, Fromagerie Xavier, 6, place Victor-Hugo, 31000 Toulouse
Yves Segur, route de Toulouse, 31460 Caraman

Gironde
Serge Penault, Beaupied, 33750 Saint—Germain-du-Puch
Pierre Viaut, Au Palais du Fromage, 57, place des Capucins, 33000 Bordeaux

Hérault
Francis Espinasse, Produits Saint-Michel, 34540 Balaruc-les-Bains
Jean-Pierre Gimenez, La Vacherie, Centre Commercial, 34500 Béziers
André Minoves, 19, boulevard Alexandre-Dumas, 34500 Béziers
Aimé Teissier, Le Buron, le Polygone, avenue des Etats du Languedoc, 34000 Montpellier

Indre-et-Loire
Gérard Goby, Le Calendos, 11, rue Colbert, 36000 Tours

Isère
Georges Blanc-Gonnet, 17, rue Bayard, 38000 Grenoble
Maurice Gauthier, La Fromagerie, 2, rue de Bonne, 38000 Grenoble
Simone Henry, 37, avenue de la Chartreuse, 38240 Meylan
Léa Journel, 38850 Charavines
Roger Maravigna, 29, avenue du Ml Randon, 38000 Grenoble

Jean Micheli, Le Fontanil, 38120 Saint-Egrève

Loire
Francis David, rue A. Guitton, 42000 Saint-Etienne

Loire-Atlantique
Georges Parola, Ferme de Retz, 1, rue du Lt Jacques-Blanchard, 44210 Pornic
Gérard Penau, Au Val d'Or, 5, rue Contrescarpe, 44000 Nantes

Loiret
Bruno Galichet, La Bergerie, rue du Châtelet, 45000 Orléans
Maurice Lavarenne, Les Halles Châtelet, 45000 Orléans

Marne
Alain Charlet, La Cave aux Fromages, 12, place du Forum, 51100 Reims
Pierre Lacour, 24, rue de Guignicourt, 51100 Reims
Pierre Le Reculley, Les Délices de la Ferme, 19, rue Saint-Thibault, 51200 Epernay

Meurthe-et-Moselle
Pierre Jacquot, Crèmerie Centrale, 22, rue de la République, 54200 Toul
Michel Marchand, Marché de Nancy, 14, rue de Saurupt, 54000 Nancy

Morbihan
Michel Stintzy, 52, rue du Maréchal-Foch, 56100 Lorient

Moselle
Christian Lévêque, Les Trois Vallées, 18, rue de Castelnau, 57100 Nivelange
Lucie Steinmetz, 11, rue Sainte-Croix, 57200 Sarreguemines

Nord
Jean Baclet, Produits des Flandres, 33, rue du Sec Arembault, 59000 Lille
Roger Boucaut, 6, avenue Jean-Jaurès, 59243 Quarouble
Etienne Gourlin, Au Maître Fromager, 112, rue de Paris, 59500 Douai
Jean-Pierre Haquette, Au Pré Fleuri, 143, rue Nationale, 59800 Lille
Paul Hazebroucq-Moreau, Ets Homo, 16, rue des Chasseurs à Pied, 59570 La Longueville
Jacques Hennart, 68, rue Maison-Blanche, 59320 Sequedin
Louis Loridan, Aux Frais Pâturages, 73, rue de Dunkerque, 59280 Armentières
Schouteeten, Le Relais du Fromage, 212, rue Gambetta, 59000 Lille

Jean-Pierre Wambre, Le Relais du Fromage, rue Guérin, Ennevelin, 59710 Pont-à-Marcq

Pas-de-Calais
George De Paepe, 39, rue Laloy, 62300 Lens
Jacques Guislain, Maison du Fromage, 1, rue André-Gerschel, 62100 Calais
Christian Leclercq, Aux Fromages, place Courbet, 62000 Arras
Jean-Clause Leclercq, Le Fromager des Arcades, 39, place des Héros, 62000 Arras
Philippe Olivier, 45, rue Thiers, 62200 Boulogne

Puy-de-Dôme
Albert Paquet, 56 ter, avenue Charras, 63000 Clermont-Ferrand
Michel et Jacqueline Quinty, Fromagerie des Halles, Marché Saint-Pierre, 63000 Clermont-Ferrand

Basses-Pyrénées
Jean Dufourg, Mille et un Fromages, 8, avenue Victor-Hugo, 64200 Biarritz
Claude Dupin, 41, rue Gambetta, 64500 Saint-Jean-de-Luz

Bas-Rhin
Marcel Fritz, 20, rue de Bischwiller 67240 Gries
Catherine Gross, Epicerie Antoine, 4, rue des Bouchers, 67000 Strasbourg
Georges Kern, 8, avenue de l'Europe, 67000 Strasbourg
Raymond Scherrer, La Ronde des Fromages, 14, rue du Rosenberg, 67590 Schweighouse
Jean-François Vilpoux, Au Bec Fin, 8, rue des Orfèvres, 67000 Strasbourg

Haut-Rhin
Claude Bronner, Calas, 18, rue des Vallons, 68200 Brunstatt-Mulhouse
Rachid Chikhi, Mini Halles, 6, rue de Belfort, 68200 Mulhouse
Santa de Nivolas, Les Petites Halles, 22, rue du Sauvage, 68100 Mulhouse
Roger Greising, 38, rue du 1st Mars, Bourgfelden, 68300 Saint-Louis
Jean-Paul Kipfer, Comestibles, 18, rue du Maréchal de Lattre-de-Tassigny, 68360 Soultz
Gilbert Ladouce, 10 bis, passage de l'Hôtel-de-Ville, 68100 Mulhouse
Pierre Michel, 75, Route de Neufbrisach, 68000 Colmar
André Wilhelm, 68, A. rue de Bâle, 68300 Saint-Louis

Rhône
Irène Beninca, La Vacherie, 9, rue C.-J. Bonnet, 69004 Lyon
Gilbert Blanc, Marché de Belleville, 69220 Belleville-sur-Saône
Emile Bounay, la Maison du Fromage, 122, boulevard de la Croix Rousse, 69001 Lyon
Lucien Broc, Marché de Gros, 69002 Lyon
Josette Cabecas, La Jasserie, 9, Quai des Célestins, 69002 Lyon
André Choron, Choron et Delphin, Centre Commercial de la Part Dieu, 69003 Lyon
Lucien Colombet, chemin de la Chapelle, 69140 Rilleux-la-Pape
Joseph Garambois, 15, rue Viala, 69003 Lyon
André Gentelet, La Fromagerie, 18, rue de Marseille, 69007 Lyon
Jean-Luc Gibaud, 6, rue de la Poste, 69220 Belleville-sur-Saone.
Jean-Paul Loos, 2, rue de la Combe, Vourles, 69330 Vernaison
Elénore Maréchal, Halles de la Part Dieu, cours La Fayette, 69006 Lyon
Paul Pechoux, 4818, route de Strasbourg, Vancia, 69140 Rilleux-la-Pape
Henri Pichois, 258, rue Paul-Bert, 69003 Lyon
Renée Richard, Halles de la Part-Dieu, 102, cours La Fayette, 69003 Lyon
René Roul, 39, rue de la Charité, 69002 Lyon
Serge Sarda, 154, avenue Paul-Kruger, 69100 Villeurbanne

Haute-Saône
Paul Figard, 3, rue du Breuil, 70000 Vesoul
Paul Figard, 70300 Luxeuil-les-Bains
Daniel Lalot, 2, Grande-Rue, 70250 Ronchamp
Robert Michel, 30, place de la République, 70200 Lure
Robert Morf, 19, rue du Coteau Fleuri, 70100 Gray-la-Ville
Bernard Petit, 10, rue Paul-Morel, 70000 Vesoul

Saône-et-Loire
Alain Frieddrich, 13, rue Guérin, 71400 Autun
Gilles Guyon, 4, Grande-Rue, 71500 Louhans
Christiane Polo, Au bon fromage, 215, rue Carnot, 71000 Mâcon

Savoie
Jean Duc-Goninaz, La Glivrehaz, 73270 Beaufort-sur-Doron

Armand Perrière, La Crèmerie, 26, rue de la République, 73200 Albertville
Denis Provent, Laiterie des Halles, 2, place de Genève, 73000 Chambéry

Haute-Savoie
Janine Bouchardy, Laiterie Chablaisienne, 1, place Jules-Mercier, 74200 Thonon-les-Bains
Ferdinand Boujon, La Fromagerie, 7, rue Saint-Sébastien, 74200 Thonon-les-Bains
Robert Buchs, Fromagerie de Megevette, 74490 Saint-Jeoire-en-Faucigny

Seine-Maritime
Philippe Jollit, Halles Centrales, place du Vieux Marché, 76000 Rouen
Robert Lhernault, Au Faisan Doré, 1, place du Vieux Marché, 76000 Rouen
Claude Olivier, Ets Olivier Père et Fils, 16, rue Saint-Jacques, 76200 Dieppe

Seine-et-Marne
Jean Braure, 18, rue de la Cordonnerie, 77160 Provins
Pierre Chassagne, 92, rue Grande, 77300 Fontainebleau
Claude et Nicole Lauxerrois, Ferme Jehan-de-Brie, 15, place du Marché, 77120 Coulommiers
Jean-Claude Loiseau, 39, rue du Closeau Meun, 77116 Ury
Claude Plier, 17, route de la Libération, 77340 Pontault-Combault

Yvelines
Viviane Azzopardi, Ferme du Val de Saane, 75, rue du Gl-de-Gaulle, 78120 Rambouillet
Philippe Colombo, Centre Commercial des Grandes Terres, 78160 Marly-le-Roi
Serge Huot, Au terroir, 10, rue Marcel-Sembat, 78800 Houilles
Raymond Noë, Supérette, 2, place de l'Eglise, 78670 Villennes-sur-Seine
Marcel et Liliane Olivry, Ferme Sainte-Suzanne, 37, rue au Pain, 78100 Saint-Germain-en-Laye
Lucien Peytevin, 24, rue de la Forêt, 78140 Vélizy

Deux-Sèvres
Jacques Guérin, La Maison du Fromage, 19, rue Saint-Jean, 79000 Niort
Robert Lepage, Sté Lepage et Fils, 22, avenue Blaise-Pascal, 79000 Niort
Jacqueline Seigneuret, Marché de Saumur, 4, rue Javelle, 79600 Airvault

Somme
V. et Gérard Quentin, Marchés, 10, avenue du Maréchal-Foch, 80600 Doullens

Tarn

Roland Coste, 2, rue de Verdusse, 81000 Albi

Mony Garet, Crèmerie Fromette, 54, rue de la Résistance, 82000 Montauban

Vosges

Albert Courroy, Affineur, 4, rue de la Libération, 88360 Rupt-sur-Moselle

Jean-Claude Rouillon, 24, rue de la Courtine, 88200 Remiremont

Jean-Claude Rouillon, 44, faubourg Ambrail, 88000 Epinal

Hubert Lahaye, 77, rue Charles-de-Gaulle, 88400 Gérardmer

Territoire-de-Belfort

Bernard Maillot, A la Renommée du Bon Fromage, 70, fg de Montbéliard, 90000 Belfort

Marie-Madeleine Meyer, Crèmerie Valiton-Meyer, 1, rue de l'Eglise, 90100 Delle

Jacques Poirel, 1, rue Michelet, 90000 Belfort

Essonne

Victor Bardau, 4, rue Félix-Faure, 91170 Viry-Chatillon

Jacques Bouillet, Fromagerie Corbeilloise, 48, boulevard Jean-Jaurès, 91100 Corbeil

Bernard Constancien, 187, boulevard J.-F. Kennedy, 91100 Corbeil

Michel Dubois, 6, place de France, 91300 Massy

Jean Fanjat, La Charrette aux Fromages, 1, rue de la Chapelle, 91310 Montlhéry

Paul Houdard, 40, avenue de l'Abbaye, 91330 Yerres

Jacques Martinot, 96, Grande-Rue, 91290 Arpajon

Claude Neuilly, 1, avenue de Jussieu, 91600 Savigny-sur-Orge

Jean-Pierre Simonard, Aux Halles de Soisy, 20, rue des Francs-Bourgeois, 91450 Soisy-sur-Seine

Michel Tellier, Les Fromages de France, 8, rue Boursier, 91400 Orsay

Hauts-de-Seine

Albert Allamargot, Ferme Sainte-Cécile, 21, rue Voltaire, 92250 La Garenne-Colombes

Gilbert Angot, La Pierrette, 6, rue du Pinsard, 92230 Gennevilliers

Jean-Jacques Carmes, Promenade de la Tour, rue d'Alsace, 92300 Levallois-Perret

Pierre Faia, Le Petit Fromager, 108, avenue du Général-de-Gaulle, 92200 Neuilly-sur-Seine

André Guinepain, 12, rue de Chateaubriand, 92290 Chatenay-Malabry

Bernard Laudrin, La Fromagerie, 33, rue Saint-Denis, 92700 Colombes

Jean Meret, 1, avenue Joseph-Froment, 92250 La Gerenne-Colombes

Raymond Mineau, 66, rue de Neuilly, 92110 Clichy

Jacques Maronat, Au Château de Mareil, 32, rue Henri-Barbusse, 92000 Nanterre

Priet, Station du Fromage, 4, rue de la Station, 92600 Asnières

Auguste Royer, Libert S.A., 17, rue Henri-Barbusse, 92300 Levallois-Perret

Catherine et Daniel Salmon, La Maison du Fromage, 37, rue Carnot, 92300 Levallois-Perret

Seine-Saint-Denis

Robert Braquart, Beurrerie Nogentaise, 1, rue de l'Ecluse, 93330 Neuilly-sur-Marne

Maurice Delarue, Affineur, 16 rue de la Nouvelle-France, 93300 Aubervilliers

Yves Guillaumel, 34, avenue Outrebon, 93250 Villemomble

André Le Jolu, Fromagerie de Montreuil, 5, avenue de la Résistance, 93100 Montreuil-sous-Bois

Etienne Magnon, Ferme d'Evreux, 70, rue de Paris, 93260 Les Lilas

Guy Rannou, 52, rue Rouget-de-Lisle, 93500 Pantin

Christian Scheltienne, Fromagerie de la Chaumière, 12, avenue Henri-Barbusse, 93150 Le Blanc-Mesnil

Alain Vaurillon, Ferme Sainte-Suzanne, 14, place du Général-de-Gaulle, 93340 Le Raincy

Jacques Vezzani, Crèmerie Centrale, 5, avenue Charles-Infroit, 93220 Gagny

Val-de-Marne

Jean Bordier, J.B.S.A. 23 bis, avenue des Lacs, 94100 Saint-Maur

Patrick Brisset, Multi Cash, 5, rue des Alouettes, 94320 Thiais

Philippe Dorsemaine, Les Tentations, 106 bis, avenue du Général-de-Gaulle, 94170 Le Perreux-sur-Marne

Jacques Moreau, P.D.G. de Ferme d'Orly, Galerie Marchande S et O, 94396 Orly Aérogares

Robert Launay, 19, rue du Midi, 94300 Vincennes

Daniel Lohier, 26, avenue Galliéni, 94340 Joinville-le-Pont

André Martin, Ferme de Villiers, 52, rue du Général-de-Gaulle, 94350 Villiers-sur-Marne

Jean Maudry, Marchés de Nogent et du Perreux-sur-Marne, 13, rue Kléber, 94130 Nogent-sur-Marne

André et Simone Rebeix, Marchés, 18, 20, rue Paul-Doumer, 94350 Perigny-sur-Yerres

Claude Volle, 14, rue Albert 1er, 94240 L'Hay-les-Roses

Alain et Isidore Charbonnel, 1, rue des Alouettes, 94230 Thiais

Robert Letul, Fromagerie Sainte-Cécile, 14, avenue Charles-de-Gaulle, 94100 Saint-Maur

Val-d'Oise

Michel Bois, 28, rue du Général-de-Gaulle, 95880 Enghien

Claude Le Bihan, 77, rue de Taverny, 95550 Bessancourt

BELGIUM

Henri Bruwier, Crèmerie Fay-Falize, 10, rue du Pont, 5000 Namur

Jean-Marie Cheval, Cheval-Berger et Fils, chaussée du Châtelet 100, 6060 Gilly

Clémy Delorie, Fromagerie des Ardennes, Clérue 7, 6980 La Roche-en-Ardenne

René Duysens, Fromagerie Dana, 40, rue de Herve, 4651 Battice Herve

Jean Eggerickx, 3, avenue des Hêtres, Rhode Saint-Genève

André François, Fromagerie Au Coq, 730, chaussée de Wavre, 1040 Brussels

Camille Gaspard, 28, rue Longue Vie, 1050 Brussels

Claude Hoeylaerts, 12, chaussée de Bruxelles, 1190 Brussels

Paul Jadot, Aux fromages de France, 28, rue Saint-Paul, 4000 Liège

Sylvain Lambeau, Au Coq, 730, chaussée de Wavre, 1040 Brussels Etterbeek

Pierre Leperre, 19, rue Fransman, 1012 Brussels

Rudiger Loiseaux-Stalpaert, Rijselsestraat 60, 8200 Sint Michiels Bruges

Nelly Mastelinck D'Hertoge, Kaas Hoeve, Gentpoortstraat 38, 98000 Deinze

Michel Peeters, Kaashandel Peeters, Hornstraat 7-9, 9000 Ghent

Georges Raeymacters, Produits St-Michel, chaussée de Bruxelles 244, 1410 Waterloo

Frank Rastelli, Langhendries, 41, rue de la Fourche, 1000 Brussels

Marie Rogge Van Zeveren, Maison Rogge Grotaert, Groetenmarkt 15, 9000 Ghent

Harry Schockaert, 28 Yserenleen, 2800 Malines

Jean-Claude Servais, 7, rue Bâtonnier Braffort, 1040 Brussels

Alphonse et Renée Thyssens, Crèmerie Suzanne, 79, avenue Houba de Strooper, 1020 Brussels

Antoine Top, Ooststraat 32, 8800 Roeselare.

Charles Uyttendaele, A la Petite Vache, 69, Chaussée de Louvain, Saint-Josse Ten Node, 1030 Brussels

René Van de Mergel, La Baratte, 55, rue de Tervaete, 1040 Brussels

José Van Alderweireldt, Fromagerie Saint-Pierre, 9, rue Poissonnière, 7500 Tournai

Rosane Vandevelde, Roeselaerestraat 118, 8160 Esen Diksmuide

José Vanderwalde, 133, Sint Michielsstraat, 8330 Tielt

Frans Vandoorne, 98, rue des Canadiens, 7000 Mons

Guido Vandoorne, 40, route d'Eugies, 7000 Mons

Patrick Van Hee, 33, Grote Markt, 8600 Menin

Michel Van Tuykom, 674, chaussée d'Alsemberg, 1050 Brussels

Pierre Viroux, 14, rue du Pot-d'Or, 4000 Liège

André Willekens, rue de Namur 15, 1400 Nivelles

GREAT BRITAIN

John Cavaciutti, Delicatessen Shop, 23 South End Road, Hampstead, London NW

SWITZERLAND

Willy Bill, rue du Trésor, 2000 Neuchatel

Jean-Pierre Dufaux, 4, rue Centrale, 1110 Morges

Alfred Fragnière, Laiterie Centrale, rue Centrale, 1350 Orbe

Philippe Olivier's shop, 45, rue Thiers, Boulogne.

BIBLIOGRAPHY

GENERAL

La Cuisine Francaise: Classique et nouvelle R. J.
Courtine *Marbout*
La Cuisine due monde entier R. J. Courtine *Marabout*
Mon Bouquet de Recettes R. Coutine *Marabout*
Dictionary of Gastronomy Andre L. Simon & Robin
Howe *Nelson*
An Outline of European Architecture N. Pevsner *Penguin*
Everyman's France Maxine Feifer *J. M. Dent, London*
Romanesque France Violet Markham
A Medieval Garner G. C. Coulton *O.U.P.*
Chronicles Froissart *Dent Everyman/London*

ILE DE FRANCE

La Region de l'Ile de France J. Beaujeu-Garnier
Flamma-Sion
L'Ile de France B. Champigneulle *Arthaud*
Paris John Russell *Thames & Hudson*

BURGUNDY

Toute la Bourgogne P. Poupon *Presseo Universitaire
Paris*
Guide Bleu 'Bourgogne' *Hachette*
Habitat et vie Paysanne en Bresse J. Freal *Editions Garnier*
La Bourgogne insolile et Gourmande F. Benoit & H.
Clos-Jouve *Solarama, Paris*

NORMANDY

Brittany & Normandy Mary Elsy *Johnson*
Madam Bovary Gustave Flaubert *Penguin Classics*
Merveilles des Cha Teaux de Normandie C. Fregnac
Hachette

BRITTANY

Brittany Rene Jacques *Panorama Books*
The Valley of the Loire & Brittany Georges Phille Ment
Johnson
The Celtic Realms Dillon & Chadwick *Weidenfeld &
Nicolson*
The Celts Tde. Powell *Thames & Hudson*
Pecheur d'Islande Pierre Loti *Cladman-Levy, Paris*
Guide de Bretagne Mysteriuse Le Scouezec *Tcaou*
Prestiges du Finistere Yann Brekiuen *France Empire*
Prominades en Bretagn Henri Queffellec *Calman-Levy*

NORTH FRANCE/PAS DE CALAIS
PICARDY

Histoire du Nord, Flandre, Artois, Hainaut, Picardie
P. Bierrard *Hachette*
La France due Nord *P.U.F./Paris*
Histoire de la Champagne Crubilier et Juillard
P.U.F./Paris
Dictionnaire des Eglises de France. Vol. 8 *Laffont, Paris*
*L'Habitation rurale en Champagne Comite due Folklore
Champenois*
Petite Histoire du Champagne – Comite P. Anrieu
La Journee Vinierle
Histoire de la Flandre et de l'Artoise S. Lestocquoy
P.U.F./Paris
Histoire de la Picardie S. Lestocquoy *P.U.F./Paris*
Les Cahiers Ardennais Ecrivains Ardennais *Mezieres*

LORRAINE, ALSACE & THE VOSGES

Histoire de L'Alsace F. L'Huillier *P.U.F./Paris*
L'Alsace H. Muller *Sun. Paris*
Histoire de la Lorraine M. Parisse *Touloux, Privai*
Guides Bleus 'Alsace' *Hachette*

Guides Bleus 'En Lorraine' *Hachette*
Richesses de France *Delmas, Paris*
Les Ardennes *Delmas, Paris*
La Meurthe-et-Moselle *Delmas, Paris*
Terres Lorraines E. Moselly

FRANCHE/COMTE & JURA

Jura-Franche-Comte-Belfort M. Piquard *Artaud*
Histoire de la Franche-Comte J. Vartier *Hachette*
La France a Table: Dours, Jura, Haute Saunt et
   Belfort/Paris

RHONE VALLEY/SAVOIE/ALPS
LYONNAIS

Le Lyonnaise *Horizons de France*
Au Fil du Rhone *Horizons de France*
Visages du Dauphine *Horizons de France*
L'Hommes et le Rhone D. Faucher *Gallimard*
La Region Lyonnaise J. Labasse *P.U.F./Paris*
Chateaux de l'Ardeche L. Bourbon *N.E.L./Paris*
La Folklore de Maut Vivarais P. Charrie *Guene*
   Guad/Paris
La France a Table (Rhone, Ardeche, Isere, Locre, Haut
   Loire, Drome)
Savoie J. Lovie *Arthaud/Grenoble*
Le Dauphine L. Lachat *Sun/Paris*
La Savoie M. Aldebert *Sun/Paris*
Au Coeur de l'Europe: Les Alps P. Dreyfos *P.U.F.*
Flore et Faune des Alps Schauer Et Caspari *Nathan/Paris*

AUVERGNE

L'Auvergne G. Conchon *Arthaud/Paris*
L'Auvergne A. Vialatie *Sun/Paris*
Les Pays d'Auvergne A. Coulaudon *Delmas/Paris*
Volans d'Auvergne A. Rudel *Ed. Volcans*
Guide Blue, 'Auvergne' *Hachette/Paris*
Histoire de L'Auvergne J. Anglade *Hachette/Paris*
Chateaux en Auvergne H. Pourrat *Delmas/Paris*
Le Vie Quotidienne en Auvergne J. Anglade
   Hachette/Paris

POITOU CHARENTES/LIMOUSIN

The Hungry Archeologist in France Glyn Daniel *Faber*
   & Faber
Recettes Gastronomiques Charentaises J. Progneaux
   Rupella
Visages du Poitou *Horizon/Paris*
Visages de L'Aunis *Horizon/Paris*
Les Hauts Ponts J. De Lacretelle *Fontenay*
Oeuvre Romanesque F. Mauriac
Le Region de Sud-Ouest Barrere, Helsot Lerat *P.U.F.*
Le Roman d'un Enfant Pierre Loti *Paris*

PYRENEES
+Aquitaine/Basque/Rouergue/Causses
Roussillon/Languedoc/Cevennes

Three Rivers of France Freda White *Faber & Faber*
The Caves of France A. & G. Sieverking *David & Charles*
Customs & Cookery in the Perigord & Quercy Anne
   Penton *David & Charles*
The Lascaux Cave Paintings F. Windels *Faber & Faber*
Ways of Aquitaine Freda White *Faber & Faber*
Lascaux A. Laming *Penguin*
Montagnes Pyrenees Peres & Ugiergo *Arthaud*
Pyrenees Francaises J. J. Cazaurang *Arthaud*
Visages du Languedoc (Folklore) *Horizons/Paris*
Flore & Faune des Pyrenees *Saed*
Histoire du Languedoc *Univers de la France*
Itineraires Romans en Roussillon Andre Duprey
La Croisade Albigeuse M. Zerner-Chardavoine
   Gallimard/Paris
Causses et Cevennes Girou & Burucoa *Arthaud*
Quercy P. Grimal *Arthaud/Paris*
Guide-Blue Cevennes-Bas-Languedoc *Hachette/Paris*
Rovergue Jean Gazave *Horizons/Paris*
Histoire du Languedoc E. Le Roy Ladurie *P.U.F./Paris*
Rovergue et Languedoc Roman *Zodiaque*
L'Architecture Militaire au Moyen Age R. Ritter
   Fayard/Paris
La Speleologie F. Trombe *P.U.F./Paris*
Travels with a Donkey in the Cevennes R. L. Stevenson
   Penguin

PROVENCE/ALPS COTE D'AZURE

Discovering Provence P. Turnbull *Basford*
Provence *Sun. Vilo*
The Golden Riviera C. Roderick *Weidenfeld & Nicholson*
Lure of the Riviera F. H. Gostling *G. Gordon Press*
The French Riviera *Sun. Vilo*
The South of France A. Lyall *Collins/London*
Visit Arlaten Museum in Arles *Provençal Life & Customs*

CORSICA

Colomba Prosper Merimee *Loire De Poche/Paris*
Les Agriates P. Benoit *Albin Michel/Paris*
Histoire de la Corse P. Arrighi *P.U.F./Paris*
La Corse Avant l'Histoire R. Grosjean *Klincksieck/Paris*
La Gastronomie Corse Simon Costanti *Klincksieck/Paris*
Grandes Heures du Tourism en Corse Xavier Versini *Klincksieck/Paris*
Corse Etinne Leca *Arthaud/Paris*
Corse Romane Genevieve Moracchini-Mazel *Zodiaque/Paris*

INDEX